CULTURAL CYCLES

This book is one to treasure. Reveal[...]
core of human wisdom and culture[...]
throughout the story of man and civilisation. In his review of these cycles,
Paul Palmarozza, shows that the focus on this subject, is of great necessity
in our time, raising consciousness to the challenges we are currently facing
and highlighting the direction that human culture and wisdom should be
moving towards in the future. *Prof Brikha Nasoraia, Professor of Arabic, Semitics
and History of Religions, University of Sydney*

Our hope through this period of crisis lies in recovering wisdom which is
timeless and universal. But it needs contemporary transmitters. It is simple
and unitive, but it needs diverse authentic expressions. Paul Palmarozza has
creatively responded to this need by distilling first-hand knowledge of
wisdom into a work that is historically stimulating and yet rooted in the
immense needs and challenges of the present. No one who reads this book
with an open mind and heart could fail to be moved, in their own unique
way, along their own pathway into wisdom and its great fruit, compassion.
*Father Laurence Freeman - Director of World Community of Christian Meditation,
Author of several books on Contemplation, Meditation and Silence*

The twenty first century is fateful in two respects. First, it is likely the
make or break century for the future of mankind. Second, working out
this future sustainably, creatively and universally will need to embrace the
entire human community. Our shared destiny demands that the resources
of wisdom, knowledge and capability of all contribute to the success of
this striving. Works like this are essential software to help us towards this
joined awareness. From the extensive reading and deep learning of the
author the work, presented as 'cycles', is a compact, insightful and essential
education on our collective heritage. *Kamalesh Sharma, former Secretary General
of the Commonwealth*

A wonderful and compelling story that communicates the subtlest of
spiritual messages. *John Adago, Author of 'East Meets West', 'Ancient Wisdom' and 'The
Story Teller'*

This book shows the strong need to think in terms of cultural cycles instead of promoting an ever up going line of development. It uniquely emphasises the influence of the cyclic format of time on mankind, and the explicit need to apply consciousness to support the natural flow of events as indicated by the planets and the stars. *Jan Willem van Doorn - MHS (Master of Hindu Studies), Vedic Astrologer*

Paul Palmarozza's grand review of the historic cultural cycles of East and West shows us that we all are in deep trouble, unless we can learn from the past and turn away from our self-absorbed materialism to rediscover our essential human values, particularly those of love and service to others... *Charles Fowler - Chairman of the Human Values Foundation, Co-ordinator of World Values Day, Steering Group of UK Values Alliance*

This book provides a clear insight into what all of us need to do in order to bring the desired lift of consciousness in Western culture; to bring about a true 21st Century Renaissance. If we follow this excellent advice, there will be greater social cohesion and, yes, true wealth for all, notwithstanding a certain economic and ecologic decline. This book by Paul is an absolute must read and then we need work together to improve the existing conditions. *Hans Leewens, Founder and Chairman of Resourcement BV, businessman, author and lecturer on a '21st Century Renaissance'*

Crises mostly present themselves to us as accidental; Paul's clear-minded and articulate book is a wonderful reminder to look beyond the distracting surface of things. Behind all the spasms of human culture there are rhythms and themes that should guide our thinking and actions. Thank you Paul, for the timely and very engaging guide you have written for us. *Matthew Pye - Philosophy teacher, member of the Club of Rome, Founder of the Climate Academy & author of 'Plato Tackles Climate Change'.*

by Paul Palmarozza

In Praise of Silence
If I can... Timeless Values for Today
Ethical Entrepreneur (E-book)

co-authored with Chris Rees:
From Principles to Profit – The Art of Moral Management;

Contributing author:
Managing by the Bhagavad Gita,
Timeless Lessons for Today's Managers
The Return of Ethics and Spirituality in Global Development

CULTURAL CYCLES & CLIMATE CHANGE

A Nine Step Action Plan

from

MORE QUIET TIME

to

A GOOD LIFE

PAUL PALMAROZZA

ISBN 978-18-383222-3-6
Published in 2021 by White Oak
an imprint of Fitzrovia Press
Glastonbury BA6 8HF, UK

printed by 4edge Ltd
Essex SS5 4AD
typeset in Centaur 12 point on 15
printed on Novel Bookwove 70gsm

WHITE OAK

DEDICATION

To the Palmarozza family, which includes my dear wife Judica, our two lovely daughters, Jessica and Olivia, and my sister Linda. In the Indian tradition, women represent shakti, 'power' and, I certainly have benefited from their powerful support. Judica is an excellent example of the benefits of quiet time. With her it is there all the time; deep within. As a result, our home is a haven of peace and beauty.

CONTENTS

FOREWORD

Cultural Cycles & Climate Change is a wake-up call for people of all ages and cultures, asking that we look more honestly and objectively at the dominant conditions in our society today so that we are better able to decide on the way forward. The conditions existing today have been put in a clearer perspective by the assessment presented of historical cycles showing that the current values, attitudes and behaviour were evident in the past. What was also learned from historical research were the best ways in which such negative conditions were addressed. Another discovery is that the cyclical pattern we discovered applies not only in Western culture, but also to the Chinese, Indian and Arab cultures which became part of our study. It is important that we learn lessons from the past. If not, then we are bound to repeat our past errors again and again. From a historical perspective, we can learn about the key ideas that have shaped our current culture, both the positive values as well as the mistakes and errors in judgement. The aim in better understanding the major influences within our society is that we can more intelligently deal with the inevitable challenges and in doing so be in better position to be of true service to ourselves, to our family, community, nation and to all of humanity. A vital example of an issue that needs to be addressed today, one which has not been present in the historical analysis of the any culture over past 2500 years, is the impending disaster due to the negative influences of Climate Change. All cultures need to work together to change the habitual behaviours that have resulted in a dramatic change in the quality of our environment, the condition of the oceans, the state of wildlife and our woodlands. Lessons learned from our historical analysis help us to have a better perspective as to the way forward.

The cyclical view of time, which is rarely used in the study of history, is based on an assumption that time can be viewed in terms of cycles and that over a period of time there is a general repetition of existing conditions. There are still many people who have difficulty in accepting the inevitability of cycles in life. This was very evident in the response of the business community during the dot - com boom of 20 years ago and at the time before the financial crisis of 2008 when the common view was that the cycle of boom and bust had been eliminated.

The message that is continually being promoted is that for Western culture this is a time of great wealth, prosperity and technological progress. It is getting better every day. There are some more perceptive people who say that a great disease has manifest, not Corona Virus, but Affluenza, the disease of excess. This is the essential cause for the Climate Change disaster. It does seem clear from our analysis that the common factor in the move from Affluence to Decadence is a strong sense of pride.

If one is not careful, continued success can confuse our powers of discrimination which then inevitably leads to unabated egotistic demands for More—More for Me which results in a life of excess, which in turn inevitably leads to decadence and decline.

The historical analysis, when compared to the vast amount of available historical data, is simply a sketch that focuses on the major positive and negative events of each period. What is revealed is an unmistakable pattern which follows the stages of the inevitable cycle of life; birth, growth, maturity, decline and then death. The close correlation of current human behaviour when compared with similar periods in previous cycles is another important lesson. The assessment reveals the significant problems in the attitudes, values and actions that exist in the final stage of a cycle. This is especially relevant in the Western culture today which is experiencing challenging conditions very similar to those that prevailed at the end of the Roman Empire. The revelations about the current state of Western culture might seem quite depressing for some people, which is why an important focus of this book is placed on a call to action with emphasis on the need for more quiet time. The underlying principle being that we can all make a difference. We do not need to be subject to the negative conditions. The assessment shows that there are also positive factors operating now that we need to take on board. The recommended Nine Step Action Plan to address the current issues, is divided into three stages:

I-3 The acknowledgement of the existing conditions including the mistakes being made and the resulting problems. It is here that the threatening Climate Change conditions need to be fully acknowledged. Many people have seen the need, especially young people from around the world, but there is not yet sufficient support coming from those in power in both politics and business.

4-6 The application of practices designed to quiet the ever-moving mind so that more conscious, good decisions can be made. These include mindfulness, contemplation, meditation and silence

7-9 The final stage involves living the natural values and principles revealed in quiet reflection which will then help widen individual attitudes and concerns for the needs of others. This will allow how we think, how we relate to others and how we act in life to be properly guided. When the values are lived, then there will be a natural inclination to serve the common good. Some guidance will then be offered on the various ways we as individuals can support positive Climate Change initiatives. Contributing to the global efforts to address this issue, however small, is truly serving the common good.

The 21st century is bringing not only the continual expansion of science and technology, but also a renaissance of philosophic and spiritual thought. The aim of this book is to provide a perspective that unites these two paths of human wisdom, the scientific and the spiritual.

1

INTRODUCTION; HISTORY, TIME

There is a continual stream of negative daily news and numerous books and articles stating that all is not well in our Western culture. However, the assumption by many people is that we are on a linear path of increasing progress based on the continual advances in technology, scientific knowledge and prosperity. This book attempts to look more objectively at that claim.

Using a multi-cultural view of history over a long period of 2500 years gives a fresh perspective. It shows for example the conditions existing today in the West actually reflect a way of thinking and acting that is causing damage economically, environmentally and morally. When you look with a more impartial eye, you see that Western culture is being driven by the mistaken belief that the acquisition of wealth, power, fame and pleasure will make us truly happy. The intense pressure to achieve these values has created a highly competitive atmosphere, leading to incessant activity with little time for rest, especially for the mind.

What has become clear is that there is a real need for people of all cultures to acknowledge the actual state of their society and then to make a firm resolution to act in such a way as to eliminate the obstacles blocking the way towards living a truly happy, peaceful and productive life. Clear direction is presented about how a more positive life can be achieved when our intention and attention focus more on serving the needs of others, as well as our own. Our concern would then be more often about We, instead of only about Me. One relevant example of the negative impact of excessive concern for material gains is the issue of Climate Change which we will deal with in more detail as we proceed.

The historical assessment shows that the West, like all other cultures, has been there before in this state of excessive focus on the materialistic aspects of life. The lessons learned from the historical analysis have not only confirmed the repetition of these conditions but have offered some useful suggestions on a good path to follow to meet the challenges. What is first needed is a more open and honest assessment of the current state of play. Then, and only then, will we be able to discover the best way forward with greater clarity so that we may understand fully and respond effectively to the following critical issues:

- The real meaning of freedom, a fundamental aspect of our democratic society. We need to acknowledge that freedom does not mean freedom to do anything I want, nor is it only a concern for my individual rights. The needs of others and my duties also need to be considered.
- The limitations of the scientific approach as the means for

2

explaining all aspects of life, for example, the rejection by many scientists of the spiritual dimension of our being, one which is beyond the mind.

- The negative aspects of becoming embroiled in a highly competitive lifestyle, which results in excessive focus on how I am doing compared to others and thus does not allow for enough empathy or compassion.

- The importance of avoiding a life of incessant physical and mental activity which inevitably causes tension, stress and unhappiness. Greater attention should be given to the spiritual realm of our life which has been sorely neglected.

- The natural human values that can best guide our life, as opposed to the current materialistic oriented values, in how we think, how we relate to others and how we act.

The depth of the historical evidence gathered is most complete for the Western culture, where much data is available and where we have first-hand experience of the three key elements of a culture; language, law and religion. Considerable research was carried out regarding the other three cultures based on numerous books and online material. Further insights were provided by knowledgeable individuals from all four cultures, as well as historians and Astrology experts who reviewed and commented on the draft versions. Many people in the West are uninformed about the rich cultural history of China, India and the diverse Arab/Islamic community located in several areas of the world. In their peak periods, they all have made important contributions to human civilisation. A more objective view of their impressive historical achievements will help build a greater sense of mutual respect and a willingness to work together in guiding society on a path towards greater peace and happiness.

To help explain in more detail the cyclical pattern and prepare the way for the historical analysis, we will briefly cover the basic elements of these subjects:

HISTORY AND TIME
CYCLES, ASTRONOMY AND ASTROLOGY

We will then proceed to look at the historical events in each of four cultures covering the period from the 5th century BCE until the present day. Our cyclical approach to time is rarely considered in academic presentations of history. The same holds true for the correlation of the historical periods of the four cultures we are considering. The way forward is presented in terms of a Nine Step Action Plan in three sections:

- Acknowledging the problems and the needs
- More quiet time - using mindfulness, meditation and silence to enhance our ability to respond to the needs
- Living natural human values in how we think, relate to others and act in our daily lives which will manifest naturally in service for the common good

History, science and spirituality have been combined in the diagnosis of the existing conditions and in the formulation of the recommended approach. It is hoped that you will find some useful insights from the assessment of the different ages and cultures that can act as inspiring guides for the next phase of your own journey.

HISTORY

What can we learn from history?

This question has been asked by people from all cultures down through the ages. It is surely important that we learn lessons from the past in order to avoid repeating our mistakes, and then we will be better able to make right and good decisions in the present. This principle also applies to the way we work to refine our individual lives. By better understanding the major influences within our society, as well as our own personal tendencies, we can more intelligently respond to the existing conditions with increased clarity and confidence. If we can correct mistaken views, shed light on overly optimistic projections and deluded thinking and at the same time avoid excessive negativity, we will be in a better position to make the right decisions and act accordingly. Such a refined action is more likely to be of true service to ourselves, to our family, community, nation and to all of humanity. Mohamed El Bachini in his book *A Jihad for Love* expresses it this way, *"The future... it starts with history."*

The headline of a Times newspaper article which appeared in January 2019 was, *'Whitehall historical adviser will help us learn from mistakes.'* The article went on to explain how the United Kingdom government is considering appointing someone to fill the role of an historical adviser, which would be similar to the existing Chief Scientific Adviser. This issue had become more pressing because of the Brexit situation. It is important in attempting to learn from the past, that we consider the history of the other major cultures as well as our own. Individuals, nations and cultures tend to have certain ideas about the way of the world, which if not questioned, can create a very thick cover over the light of true knowledge. At a certain stage in the history of a culture a limited set of ideas and tendencies that govern the thoughts, words and actions of people, become fixed and rigid. If this 'norm' is not reviewed and assessed, it can act as a major obstacle in dealing effectively with the conditions existing here and now. Learning from the past does not mean simply copying or repeating the past. It means studying carefully the past conditions, including the values that were the basis for the decisions made at that time, so that we can address the situation of today with more insight and confidence. In order to avoid the subtle working of the mind that tends to justify conclusions that comply with the rigidly accepted current standards, you need to fearlessly examine the situation with an open mind and heart. You need to be present, to reflect carefully on what is presented before making the decision that is right for today.

Understanding History

For the definition of the English word 'history', one source is the comprehensive Sanskrit language, the foundation of many Indo-European languages including Greek, Latin, English, and German. History is defined as *itihas*; *iti* meaning 'thus' and *as* meaning 'it was'. Thus it was.

The offering from the Oxford English Dictionary is that 'history' has evolved from an ancient Greek noun, *historia*, meaning 'a learning or knowing by inquiry, an account of one's enquiries, narrative, history.' It means both the inquiry, the act of seeking knowledge, as well as the knowledge that results from inquiry. This corresponds to the account given by Skeat where the root of the word history is the Sanskrit word *vid* meaning knowledge. So, history is not concerned with theories or assessments, but with how things truly were. The Greeks held history in high regard, with a presiding divinity named Clio, one of the nine Muses. She was always depicted with a pen and a laurel wreath. The pen indicates the recording of events; the laurel signifies greatness and success. This view relates closely to a definition of history from the Indian culture as presented by the wise Indian sage of the 20th century, Sri Shantananda Saraswati, who was asked:

To what end is history?

"The modern approach to history has almost become a glorification of individuals or societies, rather than charting out the journey of consciousness in search of the glorious aspects of life of those who contributed to the making of history. The good approach needs unbiased accounts of lives and events for a general uplift of moral values so that it may inspire others to face the challenges of evil & ugly forces with courage and confidence."

This last statement about the purpose of history being to inspire others to *'face the challenges'* is actually one of the main aims of this book. When one looks closely at the current state of our Western society, the increasing degree of stress and tension being experienced by people of all ages and the excessive focus on the material realm which is causing great damage to nature and the environment, can and should cause some concern. On the other hand, the mind, being a very subtle and convincing instrument, can paint a glorious picture of the state of our culture today; 'We are living in the most technically advanced and materially prosperous culture in history, so all is well'. When the basis for the decision is material prosperity, this view becomes credible. Should wealth be the basis for assessing the state of our culture?

While this positive perspective is commonly accepted in our Western culture today, there are indications that many people, especially the younger generations, do not share this view. This book confirms that all is not well, but there are steps that can be taken to improve the current position and help us prepare for the inevitable challenges that the future will bring.

The initial direction is to gain a more objective view of the state of our society by exploring the historical patterns of our culture and that of three other major world cultures during the same timeframe. It is only by looking beyond our world, beyond our culture, that we can come to better appreciate the universal laws governing humanity. In the periods of a flowering culture, there is an extensive manifestation of spiritual, intellectual and physical brilliance and beauty which are easily accessible to the people of that time and place. For other people of that time from a different culture, the conditions might not be so favourable.

While the universal forces are readily available at any time, when the negative cultural conditions exist, all too often they are ignored - people live in a state of ignorance. In our exercise of cultural self-examination, we also need to be truthful about the *evil & ugly forces* that inevitably manifest in all cultures. Acknowledging their existence is the first important step in attempting to remove them.

Sir John Glubb, a prolific 20th century author on historical subjects wrote *The Fate of Empires and The Search for Survival,* which charted the rise and fall of 11 empires going back as far as 859 BC. His premise was that a cycle in power lasts about 250 years. Among his astute observations in examining periods of history is his statement that, *The teaching of history should include the history of the human race and not just 'our culture'.*

Another very perceptive view comes from Philip Parker, the author of a magisterial work. *World History,* whose response to the question *What is History?* is most revealing. He starts off with a simple statement: *History is not the same as the past, it is our attempt to reconstruct the past from the evidence that remains.*

J H Plumb wrote, in a work published by The History Book Club entitled *The Death of the Past,* that the aim of history is to help understand people both as individuals and in their social relationships in time. Social embraces all human activities; economic, religious, political, artistic, legal, military, scientific, and everything that affects the life of mankind. It is not a static study, but a study of movement and change. To be an effective historian, you need to avoid any preconceived notions about the past and investigate historical conditions with detachment, which has been one of our guiding principles.

In order to truly be able to learn from an historical analysis, important questions are asked by highly qualified historians which include the following:

- What happened?
- Why did it happen?
- How did it happen?
- What were the consequences?

They use the answers to put together a continuous narrative which provides important lessons for those people who, like us, are anxious to understand where we are and what is the best path forward on our journey.

In our assessment of the historical patterns of the four cultures, we highlight the positive values as espoused by their respective spiritual traditions, their accomplishments in art, in science, in economic development, as well as the influential individuals and most significant events during each period. We also point out some of the mistakes and errors in judgement that created negative conditions that have existed in these cultures at certain times. An important aspect of our historical analysis is the cyclical view of time, which reveals interesting insights into the patterns of historical events for each of the four cultures.

The introductory statement to the book, *The Cycle of Time*, by Simone Boger describes the current view about this approach. *"The cyclical view of history is a complete and integrated model of reality that was the basis of ancient philosophical thought for millennia before it was relegated to oblivion."*

The unique aspect of this study of cycles is the discovery of a particular planetary configuration, which repeats every 854 years in the way that correlates with the human activities happening during those periods. What has been discovered is how this planetary cycle sets out a pattern, which each of the cultures followed. Recognition that the qualities prevailing in our society vary according to a measurable cycle is a big step in being able to look afresh at patterns of history.

TIME

The nature of time

Time is a important aspect of life in today's world. It is seen as a commodity to be saved and spent wisely—which isn't always the case. All too often we waste time in useless activities.

> *"I wasted time and now doth time waste me."*
> Shakespeare, Richard II

Performing an activity using time well means getting the right measure, finding the right moment to start as well as knowing how long to stay with it. What guidance from the wise is there about the nature of time?

> *"The Creator resolved to have a moving image of the eternal. But moving according to number, while eternity rests in unity; and this image we call Time. The past and the future are created species of time, which we unconsciously, but wrongly transfer to the eternal essence."*
> Plato

> *"There are three periods of time:*
> *the present of things past,*
> *the present of things present;*
> *the present of things future.*
> *The present of things past is memory; the present of things future is expectation. the present of things present is immediate vision."*
> St Augustine

11

These two views acknowledge the three periods of time, but also put special emphasis on the present moment as the essence of time. When a person is fully present, he or she is not subject to the power of the vast store of past experiences, nor is the mind weighing up all the options which might happen in the future. This represents a victory of the conscious over the mechanical, of reason over desire. There is true freedom to respond to the need of that present moment. As we proceed, we shall look further at the positive influence of the present moment, of being here, now.

In Sanskrit the word for time is 'kaala' from the root word *kal* meaning to count, enumerate, push on, drive forward. The essential meaning being - *in moving and counting*, which corresponds nicely with **Plato's** view *"...a moving image of the eternal, but moving according to number."*

There are several different ways to understand time.

- Proper time; appropriate time for an action.
- Measure of time; seconds, minutes, hours.
- Point of time; a specific moment.
- Musical time; the relationship between sound and silence.
- Quality of time; good times and hard times.
- Destiny, fate; our time has come and death.
- Regulation; a recommended amount of time.

The desire to measure or count time involves not only the quantitative aspect, for example 6:30am, but also a qualitative difference between moments of time. Depending on the nature of a particular moment certain actions are more appropriate. Here are two well-known quotes about the right time to act.

"There is a tide (time) in the affairs of men which taken at the flood, leads to fortune; Omitted, all the voyage of their life is bound in the shallow and in miseries."
Shakespeare, Julius Caesar

"There is a time for everything, and a season for every activity under the heavens:
a time to be born and a time to die,
a time to plant and a time to uproot,
a time to kill and a time to heal,
a time to tear down and a time to build,
a time to weep and a time to laugh,
a time to mourn and a time to dance,
a time to scatter stones and a time to gather them,
a time to embrace and a time to refrain from embracing,
a time to search and a time to give up,
a time to keep and a time to throw away,
a time to tear and a time to mend,
a time to be silent and a time to speak,
a time to love and a time to hate,
a time for war and a time for peace."
Ecclesiastes 3.1

By understanding the qualities of the moment, we are better able to decide when to act or not to act, and also how best to act.

The dominant idea about time in today's world is that it is linear, ordered into past, present and future. Our days are organised by the progression of the clock, in the short and medium time by calendars and diaries and by timelines stretching back over millennia. In our current culture there seems to be a constant impulse to move forward, to overcome former achievements and move on to the next discovery. The main ideas are 'progress and production.' This view of life has been amplified by science where the idea about linear time is fixed. This misconception blocks one from seeing a much larger view offered by seeing the cyclical nature of time, one which is necessary if we are to look at history from the right perspective.

Author Julian Baggini in *How the World Thinks: A Global History of Philosophy,* describes how various cultures view time. His observation is that the linear view of time is the default view of the largely Christian Western culture which reached its peak in the Enlightenment Period when rapid progress in all aspects of life seemed to be the case. This idea of progress fostered the view that the human race was moving forward to a happier future. The misguided conclusion drawn was that of the inevitable superiority of the present age over supposedly less advanced times. While this was true in some technical fields, it certainly is not a valid assumption about all aspects of humanity.

A Special Time—The Axial Age

The phrase Axial Age originated with the German psychiatrist and philosopher Karl Jaspers, who noted that at this time there was a shift or a turn, as if on an axis, away from more predominantly localised concerns towards transcendence. What does transcendence mean? The term connotes *going beyond*. In the case of the Axial Age it was a *revolution* in human thought about the world. During this pivotal period, estimated to be between the 700 BCE and 500 CE, several very influential teachers were born in different cultures around the world. A modern author, Karen Armstrong, has written extensively about this period. In her book *The Great Transformation* she describes in some detail the major advances in the world's political, philosophical, and religious systems which were prompted by the teachings of inspiring leaders of various cultures. The date 610 BCE is referred to as a low point in human society, a time when a new impulse was required. In several spiritual traditions it is said that when the conditions in a society reach a low point, an avatar, a teacher, is born to help humanity recover. The great teachers born during this period seem to confirm that it was a very difficult period for the world. These teachers set in motion powerful impulses for positive development in several cultures which manifested in different ways in the succeeding period. Here are the estimated birth years of some of the more prominent sages from various philosophic and spiritual traditions:

Thales	624	Pre-Platonic – Greece
Anaximander	610	Pre-Platonic – Greece
Lao Tzu	604	Taoism – China
Mahavira	600	Jainism – India
Zoroaster (II)	588	Zoroastrian – Persia
Pythagoras	580	Pre-Platonic – Greece
Buddha	563	Buddhism – India
Confucius	551	Confucianism – China
Socrates	470	Teacher of Plato
Plato	428	Platonic Tradition

The Universality of the Golden Rule
Here is how it was expressed by the various traditions.

GOLDEN RULE ACROSS THE WORLD'S RELIGIONS

Bahá'í Faith
Lay not on any soul a load that you would not wish to be laid upon you,
and desire not for anyone the things you would not desire for yourself.
Bahá'u'lláh, **Gleanings**

Buddhism
Treat not others in ways that you yourself would find hurtful.
The Buddha, **Udana-Varga 5.18**

Christianity
In everything, do to others as you would have them do to you; for this is
the law and the prophets.
Jesus, **Matthew 7:12**

Confucianism
One word which sums up the basis of all good conduct loving-kindness.
Do not do to others what you do not want done to yourself.
Confucius, **Analects 15.23**

Hinduism
This is the sum of duty: do not do to others
what would cause pain if done to you.
Mahabharata 5:1517

Islam
Not one of you truly believes until you wish
for others what you wish for yourself.
The Prophet Muhammad, **Hadith**

Jainism
One should treat all creatures in the world
as one would like to be treated.
Mahavira, **Sutrakritanga 1.11.33**

Judaism

What is hateful to you, do not do to your neighbour.
This is the whole Torah; all the rest is commentary. Go and learn it.
Hillel, **Talmud, Shabbath 31a**

Native American Indian Spirituality

We are as much alive as we keep the earth alive.
Chief Dan George

Sikhism

I am a stranger to no one; and no one is a
stranger to me. Indeed, I am a friend to all.
Guru Granth Sahib, p.1299

Taoism

Regard your neighbour's gain as your own gain and
your neighbour's loss as your own loss.
Lao Tzu, **T'ai Shang Kan Ying P'ien, 213-218**

Unitarianism

We affirm and promote respect for the interdependent web
of all existence of which we are a part.
Unitarian principle

Zoroastrianism

Do not do unto others whatever is injurious to yourself.
Shayast-na-Shayast 13.29

Source: Scarboro Missions, http://www.scarboromissions.ca/Golden_rule/

17

2

CYCLES; ASTRONOMY / ASTROLOGY

CYCLES

What is a cycle?

If you put your hand on your heart or your fingers on the veins of your wrist, you can feel a rhythmic cycle, something that repeats itself at a more or less uniform time interval. Our world contains hundreds of similar repetitive patterns. Another example is breathing; a natural rhythmic breathing in and then breathing out. A cycle has recurrent periods of a definite duration, which are repeating and measurable. The Oxford Universal Dictionary states a cycle is:

> *'A circle or orbit in the heavens. A recurrent period in a definite period of years. A period in which a certain round of events or phenomena is completed, recurring in the same order in equal succeeding periods. A round, course or period through which anything runs to its completion.'*

Planetary cycles of time

Let's look at the three planetary cycles of time that we are all familiar with. These measures of time are directly related to the revolutionary movement of the earth around the sun and the moon around the earth.

- A day; sunrise to sunrise.
- A month; full moon to full moon.
- A year; vernal equinox to vernal equinox.

What is common to these three cycles is that they:

- are an interval or unit of time, a measure
- are repetitive and regular;
- have common starting and stopping points;
- have opposing and intervening points; sunset/noon, new moon/crescents, equinox/solstice.

It is scientifically accepted that we can calculate the precise position of the planets, but there also needs to be acceptance of the principle that the positions of the planets have an influence on life here on earth.

Here is some information on lunar cycles indicating that there is a growing recognition that the relative positioning of the sun and the moon does create conditions which can affect life on earth. For centuries, people have believed that the Moon does have an effect on human behaviour, but the idea had largely been written off by modern medicine. The word lunacy derives from the Latin *lunaticus*, meaning "moonstruck". In a 2019 BBC article by Linda Geddes on lunar cycles, several medical research projects are presented which suggest there may be some truth to these ancient beliefs about how the lunar cycle can influence people's behaviour.

Dr Thomas Wehr, an emeritus professor of psychiatry at the US National Institute of Mental Health commented on the findings of one such project. *"The thing that struck me about these cycles was that they seemed uncannily precise in a way that one would not necessarily expect of a biological process. It led me to wonder if there was some kind of external influence that was operating on these cycles and the obvious thing to consider was whether there was some lunar influence."*

The Moon affects Earth in several ways. The first and most obvious is through the provision of moonlight, with a full Moon coming around every 29.5 days, and a new Moon following 14.8 days after that. Then there's the Moon's gravitational pull, which creates the ocean tides that rise and fall every 12.4 hours. Given the human body is said to be composed of 75-80% liquids, it is clear this gravitational force can have some effect.

To describe the various phases of a cycle, the wave-form pattern is most effective.

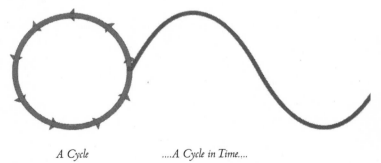

A Cycle   *....A Cycle in Time....*

This pictorial presentation shows the relationship between circular rotation and its corresponding measure in linear time. All the planets have a circular movement around the sun. The measurement of the relative positions of these planets with respect to the planet earth and to each other can be calculated precisely.

When we look more closely at this cyclical wave, we see a steady ascension in the beginning, then the rising rate becomes less steep until there is an evening-out process when a peak point is reached. At the same rate, the downward stage begins until the level is reached where the upward process started. That is the journey of the outward phase. The inward phase then begins following the same pattern but going downward first and then rising until the level which the cycle began is reached.

There has been considerable scientifically oriented research undertaken during the last 50 to 60 years about cycles. In the 1960s in the United States a well-funded *Foundation for the Study of Cycles* came into existence and funded several studies. One of its most productive projects was a book written by Edward R Dewey entitled Cycles, *The Mysterious Forces That Triggers Events.* The main topics of this book are the cycles of business, economy and wars, but it also explores religious membership, marriage and death rates. The span of time included in their research was the period from the 18th–20th centuries, with cycles usually less than twenty years long. The data was gathered primarily in the United States and Europe.

Their research revealed these cyclical patterns:
- The 6 year cycle of Steel Production, 1874–1947.
- The 9.6 year cycle of Wheat Harvesting, 1868–1947.
- The 9.2 year cycle of Stock Prices, 1830–1966.
- The 18.2 year cycle of Immigration to the United States, 1824–1950

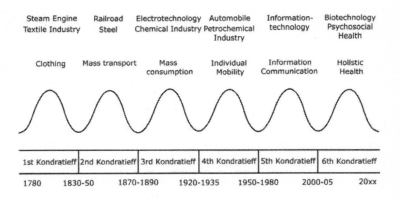

Steam Engine	Railroad	Electrotechnology	Automobile	Information-	Biotechnology
Textile Industry	Steel	Chemical Industry	Petrochemical	technology	Psychosocial
			Industry		Health

| Clothing | Mass transport | Mass | Individual | Information | Holistic |
| | | consumption | Mobility | Communication | Health |

1st Kondratieff	2nd Kondratieff	3rd Kondratieff	4th Kondratieff	5th Kondratieff	6th Kondratieff
1780	1830-50	1870-1890	1920-1935	1950-1980	2000-05	20xx

The Long Waves in the World Economy, Leo & Simone Nefiodow, 2014

A prolific study of business cycles was based on the extensive research of Joseph Schumpeter whose book, *Business Cycles*, was published in 1939. This work relates economic cycles to the evolution of a culture. His study began in the last quarter of the 17th century and also drew on data from the United States and Europe.

In economics, Kondratieff cycles discovered by the Russian economist Nikolai Kondratieff are periods of a wave ranging from 40–60 years. The cycles consist of alternating intervals of high sectoral growth and intervals of relatively slow growth. Economists have empirically proven five Kondratieff cycles since the late 18th century, as shown in the illustration above.

Despite all this useful guidance on the existence of business cycles, there are many people who have difficulty in accepting the inevitability of cyclical patterns. A good example is found in the assumptions made by politicians and business executives around the time of the *dot com boom* in business at the beginning of the 21st century. The assumption made was that the long-observed cycle of *boom and bust* had been eliminated. They were mistaken, as was shown by the financial crisis of 2008, which was brought about by greed and excess; a grasping of people wanting more money and not knowing when to stop.

Cultural Cycles
The main elements of a culture

The Latin source word is *cultus*, which relates to growing and cultivation. A cultured person has been improved and cultivated by education and experience. A dictionary definition says that culture is a manifestation of specific ideas, customs, religions, and social behaviour. Four of the primary elements of any culture are the language spoken, the religion practised, the system of law and the values that are deemed important. As noted, it is important that we look not only at our own cultural history, but also at those of other major cultures in the world in the same timeframe. What is interesting is the relative response of the various cultures to the same existing conditions.

In terms of its application to a culture, there is a time when there is an outward display of fine qualities, successful endeavours and a position of influence in the world. The spiritual tradition of the culture is manifest for most of the period, but gradually this positive state diminishes as the outward cycle enters its final downward stage. In this downward stage the interest and concern for the material world becomes excessive, eventually resulting in a complete loss of discrimination.

The inward phase follows the very same pattern, beginning with a rejection of the concern for the material world and more time and energy expended going within. Using the analogy of the breath, we do not favour one aspect of breath over the other; both are engaged as natural and necessary parts of the cyclical process. The downward phase of a cultural cycle is one which encourages and supports a turning within, using contemplation, meditation and other reflective practices which help bring about a more stable and balanced state. What then arises quite naturally is greater sense of service. These two phases also relate quite closely to left-brain and right-brain theory. Many scientific and psychological studies have been published on the subject and we will explain its relevance to cycles as we proceed.

Those people who engage in these reflective practises on a regular basis gradually find peace and satisfaction within, more so than in the material realm. There is of course physical activity during this downward phase, which ideally can be led by more selfless leaders with fine intention and guided by fine values. External powers like economic wealth and military power will not be as great as in the upward, outward phase. In the final stage of the downward phase there is the inevitable rigidity. However, as the spiritual realm of the culture has been regenerated during this period, a new positive outward renaissance begins.

Let us look at stages of the cycle from a practical perspective. In his book, *The Fate of Empires* Sir John Glubb included in his examination of 11 empires those of the Greek, Roman Spanish, British empires and six other world cultures.

In Glubb's view, the stages of the cycle are:

Pioneers; the energetic pursuit of a new idea

Conquest; the overcoming of obstacles

Commerce; spreading the word

Affluence; success

Intellect; being convinced all is well, when it is not

Decadence; when excess, greed and corruption prevail

Decline and Death; the end

He attributed the basis for decadence and decline to; *"selfishness, too long a period of wealth and power, love of money, and a loss of a sense of duty".* Decadence is characterised by factors including; *"materialism, frivolity and the weakening of religion".* He observed that the negative period in the cultures involved were all marked by; *"rigid forms of government, extensive bureaucracy, poor leadership and a reluctance to change".* Does this sound familiar?

It seems clear from his analysis that a common factor in the move from affluence to decadence is a strong sense of pride. If we are not careful, continued success can confuse our powers of discrimination, inevitably leading to unabated egotistic demands for 'more and more for me'. This results in a life of excess, leading to decadence and decline. This a useful lesson to remember. A statement from Glubb's book that best supports our work:

> *Any useful lessons to be derived must be learned*
> *by the study of the whole flow of human development,*
> *not by the selection of short periods*
> *here and there in one country or another.*

There was a strong awareness in ancient Egypt of the cyclical nature of time. Each cycle started with a creative impulse which needed to be renewed. The daily temple rituals accompanied the sun's rising and the journey across the sky with all its perils and worked to ensure that this was successfully accomplished. There is an ancient prophecy described in a book called *Asclepius*, translated by Clement Salaman, about the final stage of a cycle:

In the final stage the memory of the function of man was lost and as a result the gods would withdraw from earth to the heavens, foreigners pouring into the land would ignore religion, and Egypt would become a desert.

The Cycle of Yugas

Here is a most fascinating approach to cycles, one of a different culture, whose period is in thousands of years and whose impact is said to affect all of humanity. The approach is set out quite nicely in a book, *The Holy Science*, written by a modern Indian sage, Sri Yukteswar.

The purpose of the book as described by the author is *"to remove the barriers and to help in establishing the basic truth of all religions."* It was written because he saw that sufficiently positive conditions existed in the world at that time, as indicated by a system of global cycles followed by his tradition. Their system includes four phases or Yugas, which comprise a 24,000-year cycle. For obvious reasons we will not go into great detail in describing the implications of these phases, but it is useful to learn about another culture's perspective on cycles.

The four Yugas each last for a distinct period of time. The prevalent influences of each stage range from a high degree of wisdom and enlightenment in the first stage down through three other stages, where gradually the human ego plays an increasingly influential role. In the fourth and final stage the ever-shining sun, which represents our true nature, becomes heavily covered over by the clouds of ego-based motives, thoughts, feelings, speech and actions. As with all cycles, once the low point of the cycle is reached, an ascending phase begins.

The technical basis for the measurement of this cycle is the relative movement of the earth revolving around the sun. The key astronomical measuring points are the Vernal/ Spring and Autumn Equinoxes, which are the days in the year when the length of the day and the night are equal all over the earth. On the day of the Spring Equinox the time of daylight equals the darkness of night. After that date, the days begin to get longer in our Northern hemisphere. The Autumn Equinox is when the balance of day and night is again attained, to be followed by a period when the days begin to get shorter.

Now when measuring the relative position of the sun against the backdrop of the stars, the 'precession of the equinoxes' needs to be taken into account. A brief example may help clarify the situation. The view of modern Western astrologers assumes that on 21 March, the date of the Vernal Equinox, the sun is in the first degree of Aries. This is a measure of the position of the sun against the backdrop of the stars' configuration of Aries. Due to the shift in the earth's axis over the years when astronomers today measure carefully the position of the sun on that day, they find it about 24 degrees behind at 6 degrees of the previous sign, Pisces. The Indian system of astrology, called *Jyotisha*, which is used as the basis for our calculations, has been studied and practised for more than 3000 years. It is more accurate than the modern Western astrological system, because *Jyotisha* takes into account this shift. The planetary positions as

27

presented in *Jyotisha* correspond exactly with modern astronomical measurements.

This cyclical period for the Vernal Equinox to take place with the sun in the same relative position totals 24,000 years. This period is divided into two sections; an ascending phase and a descending phase, each being a 12,000-year period divided into four stages or Yugas. Let us look at what is said about the nature of the influences existing during the period of our investigation. The starting point in the current cycle was calculated to be 11,501 BCE when the Autumn Equinox occurred in one degree of Libra, the sign directly opposite Aries. This was the beginning of a descending cycle.

The four *Yugas* are described as follows:

- **Satya Yuga, the Golden Age.** This period is one when the highest level of consciousness is available. Its period is 4,800 years, which is divided into three sections: 400 years of a transition period with the previous period, 4,000 years of the full measure and then another 400-year transition period; thus **400/4,000/400. (11,501–6701 BCE)**
- This same pattern applies to all four stages; 1/10th of the period as an initial transition phase before the main period and another 1/10 as a final transition period.
- **Treta Yuga, the Silver Age.** Fine consciousness is still available, but some element of ego has gained strength, which means individuals take claim for the fine work. Its period is 3,600 years: **300/3,000/300. (6701–3101 BCE)**

- **Dwapara Yuga, the Bronze Age.** Intelligent activity and spirituality still in evidence but guided by personal preferences with a gradual weakening of faith. Its period is 2,400 years: **200/2,000/200. (3101–701 BCE)**

- **Kali Yuga, the Iron Age** The lowest stage where the individual ego dominates, causing stress and tension leading to a breakdown in human relationships and the abandoning of spiritual practices by the majority. A more detailed listing of the qualities of the *Kali Yuga* can be found in various Indian texts. Some of the main ones are that mutual attraction becomes the sole consideration in marital relationship, business becomes tantamount to the practice of fraud, and wealth becomes the main factor in estimating a person's worth. Thankfully this period is only 1200 years: **100/1,000/100 (701 BCE–501 CE)**

According to this system, the descending phase of the *Kali Yuga* cycle began 701 BCE and continued until 501 CE. It is interesting to note that the beginning of the dark *Kali Yuga* cycle was met by the arrival of many wise sages on a global basis as was described in our explanation of the Axial Age. After that, for 1200 years until 1701 CE, a period of the ascending *Kali Yuga* prevailed, before the beginning of the more conscious *Dwapara Yuga*. Its transition period lasted for 200 years until 1901, during which time increased consciousness gradually became available. The main period will continue for 2000 years.

What is encouraging about this view is that after a long period dwelling in the Iron Age, we are now in an ascending phase

29

of the larger and finer cycle of the *Dwapara Yuga,* called Bronze Age, which may enable people from all cultures to overcome some of the negative elements in life that have become so very much engrained in our lives.

The Cycle of a Society—The Platonic View

In *The Republic,* written by Plato there is an interesting description of five states of society, which demonstrate the stages in the downward phase of a cycle. Each state represents the dominant state of the individuals living in the society at that time The process he describes of the weakening of a society is based on a trend, for leaders first and then for many people to become more concerned about their own interests. This desire for me and mine continues to expand causing an even greater degree of selfishness, greed and corruption and the inevitable state of unhappiness.

Plato begins with a state called **Aristocracy,** which he describes as *rule by the best.* The aristocratic leader is a person who is wise and truthful. He or she lives by the highest principles, keeping in mind the Common Good at all times. The guides for life are the natural human values or virtues as they were described by Plato. This message and the leader's living example are powerful influences which are followed by the people.

The next level is a step down. In this state of society, called **Timocracy,** the highest value being one's honour. It has moved away from the full truth and wisdom because leaders of such societies have taken something for themselves. They have taken advantage of their influential and responsible position, and in some way have started making decisions that benefit *me or mine,* at the expense of others. The power is used incorrectly and what has been forgotten is the full commitment to the common good. The advantage gained may be only a small one, but nevertheless the trust of the people has in some way been violated. To compensate, the leaders established honour, keeping one's word as the highest value. This is a person who has high values and lives them-most of the time.

The next level down is when the seeking for personal advantages by the leaders and other wealthy individuals becomes endemic and a real gap grows in the society between the rich and the poor, the haves and the have nots. The leaders become very wealthy and lose real interest in governing, giving their primary attention to making money and exercising power. This state, which is called an **Oligarchy,** manifests when the rich take undue advantage of the poor, of the less fortunate. This corresponds to a person where vices such as greed, lust and anger are beginning to dominate. The individual mind is not strong enough to resist the temptations offered and to live according to principles. There might be some good intention, but the demand to work for me and mine is too strong.

The inevitable reaction to this is a rebellion by the have-nots and a form of society called a **Democracy** emerges. The cry of the masses is for freedom and equality. They all want to have a say in ruling the society as the leaders have proven to be corrupt and not properly reflecting the voice of the people. As such a society proceeds, freedom comes to mean freedom to do anything I want; my personal freedom is paramount. Equality comes to mean that my idea is as good as yours; my values and choices are as good as those of anyone else.

31

At the individual level this state reflects a lack of discrimination, an inability to discern between right and wrong, true and false, good and bad. Everyone is demanding their rights without any attention being paid to their duties. As we have seen it is very difficult to rule a society which is mired in this state. To obtain an adequate number of votes to be elected one needs to cater to a large number of varying demands. In the West we have fully embraced democracy.

Due to a lack of effective leadership and the vast spread of opinions, a state of confusion and frustration manifests. From this state **Anarchy** eventually arises. Law and order are no longer respected as in the past and eventually to bring order and coherence to society a strong forceful leader emerges: a dictator, or as Plato says, a tyrant. The promise is to bring order, which happens, but only through the use of force and in some cases physical violence. Very soon the tyrant becomes the absolute ruler, ruling without needing to consult the will of the people.

It is at this point that Plato suggests that there are two paths that can be followed:

- The tyrant continues to rule autocratically without concern for the common good and eventually the absolute power becomes absolutely corrupt. Such a society collapses and must begin again in a new form.
- The other possibility is that a wise person, seeing the real need, obtains the trust of the tyrant and is able to influence his decisions. Step-by-step order, coherence, reason and true values are re-established.

Anarchy corresponds to the extremely confused mental condition where an individual is unable to make a coherent decision.

This causes considerable stress and tension which can lead to irrational, extreme responses. This, to some degree, is the stress and tension that we have been observing in our current Western democracy which may be moving into this last phase. As can be seen from Plato's description, there is an option which involves a more conscious response.

Brian Hodgkinson, in his majestic historical work of three volumes entitled *The Advancement of Civilisation in the Western World*, poses a challenging question about the current linear view of history and of human development. Unlike many other historians covering Western history, Hodgkinson has studied the history of other cultures and points out where the cultures differ, but importantly where the underlying principles are the same, even if the outward form differs. At one point he refers to the ancient Vedic teaching as presented in works called *Puranas* which set out the qualities of the four *yugas* as they are manifest in the behaviour of people of each age. The descriptions link nicely with the Platonic views of the various levels of society.

One of Brian's observations about the current perspective on life is that only since the time of Charles Darwin, a little over a century ago, have most men believed that we are descended from more primitive forms of life, that we evolve through successive generations and that, as a consequence, human civilisation tends to improve or progress through time. With such a belief is associated the idea that greater knowledge implies greater complexity, that the simple is naïve. For at least five thousand years before the nineteenth century, the general belief was the reverse. Human life was seen as declining; tradition was associated with the memory of better laws and customs; individuals were judged against the standard of the ancient heroes and heroines, the pure and the virtuous.

Hodgkinson poses two interesting questions on this issue:

"Are we, who live through an era of nuclear weapons, drug abuse and widespread neurosis, to assume without question that for five millennia the best thinkers of each age were wrong?"

"Would history not be more accurate if it studied the societies that held such a view against the backdrop of that view, rather than imposing upon them our idea of progress?"

He then offers some of the examples of the characteristics of people from each of the four *yugas* or ages. Each age has a special quality: Iron Age – liberality; Bronze Age – sacrifice; Silver Age – knowledge and Golden Age – meditation. In the Golden Age human life was pure and simple and full of love. Beauty was all around them in nature and what they made was beautiful, for it was not made as work, but as an act of love. Their lives were filled with the happiness natural to all creatures. They had no need to seek happiness in external things, like money or pleasure, for it was ever-present. Love was rarely hindered by thoughts claiming anything for oneself.

What gives the Silver Age its great qualities of justice, virtue and prosperity is the character of the sages and the rulers. There is a great sense of honour and a clear vision of the leaders that they are serving for the good of all. Nothing unreasonable was commanded to be done and protection of the people was a prime priority Every man was brave and every woman virtuous. No one failed to perform their duties. Merchants were unscrupulously honest, and craftsmen were devoted to skill. When those who were not leaders began to operate in ways to better their own personal gain, the inevitable conflicts were dealt with effectively. Two examples given were the rule of Rama in the Indian tradition and the actions of Heracles, who became the Greek model of courage, nobility of character and champion of the oppressed. To point out that even in a lower period like the Iron Age, a ruler of Silver Age qualities can emerge to fill a need. Hodgkinson says that the English king Alfred the Great was such a leader.

The Bronze Age is also marked by heroes, but of mixed qualities, like bronze itself which is an alloy of copper and tin. It is an age dominated by the warrior class with great virtues like courage, strength, and boldness, but intermixed with dark aspects of selfishness, greed, cruelty, lust and arrogance. It was inevitable that war would be a constant feature of an age of heroes, but a thread of wisdom still ran through their lives and manifested as a willingness to sacrifice for the sake of defending their people. An example of heroic leadership touched with a glint of bronze was Winston Churchill. He had both physical and moral courage and was a great inspiration in the face of a major threat to the security of the nation.

Hodgkinson then uses the *Vishnu Purana* as his reference for setting out the conditions of the Iron Age. The darkness is profound. People are surrounded by a thick husk which cuts them off from the light of their true self. Endless selfish desires dominate life, so that they act without reference to reason and almost become automatons, the blind leading the blind. Ignorance and vice control motives, tradition is lost, and society disintegrates. Those who are thought to be wise are merely learned, those that are powerful are merely rich and they abuse their power of authority for more personal gain. Merchants and traders extract all they can from their customers and forget the honest dealing that creates prosperity for all. Standards of craftsmanship deteriorate, and money becomes the only incentive. Virtuous men and women are rare and as a result the family as a unit declines and children are neglected and grow up in ignorance with no spiritual element to their education.

If we try to assess the current state of our society in terms of these three views of cycles, it seems that we live in a fully democratic society which has many of the characteristics of the Iron Age. There is however some Good News in that we have begun an ascension into a more promising Bronze Age *Yuga*. This positive impulse seems to be reflected in the growing recognition that all is not well and what arises is a strong intention to begin living life in accordance with natural values with concern for the needs of others. This response has been observed in many men and women down the ages from all cultures. These fine examples are a more accurate reflection of our true potential and we need to follow their guidance.

Now that we have better idea about the nature of cycles, let's look at the subjects of Astronomy and Astrology to see what specific effect the position of the planets can have on the conditions observed in the cultural cycles of the past and what will the likely effect be going forward.

Astronomy/Astrology

AIR   FIRE

EARTH   WATER

Astronomy

Astronomy involves the measuring of the movements and position of the planets against the backdrop of the starry heavens.
It is a subject that has been studied and applied by all cultures
throughout history. Its basic elements are:

- **Sun, Moon & the Planets**—representing moving ener-
  gies/forces that have an effect on all living beings on
  earth.
- **The Star Configurations**—visible from the earth
  which make up the clockface needed to accurately measure the position of the planets and the planetary configurations at any moment of time.

Plato made Astronomy a required subject of study for the education of rulers. Here is a one statement by him on the subject:

"The sun and moon and five other stars, which are called planets, were created by Him in order to distinguish and preserve the numbers of time." Plato's influence regarding the importance of Astronomy as a subject of study continued until the Middle Ages when it was considered as one of the Seven Liberal Arts, grouped as part of the Quadrivium of mathematically based subjects: arithmetic; geometry; astronomy; and music.

Astrology

The movement of the planets against the backdrop of the stars is like a clock which provides us with mechanical time-the quantitative aspect with no reference to quality of the moment. Astrology adds this further dimension. It uses the same precise mathematical calculations to determine the positions of the planets, including the relative position in relation to all the other planets. It is also attributes to each planet a particular energy or power which, based on the planetary positions, has an effect on earthly life. Many cultures have attached great importance to astrological relationships of the planets and some, such as the Indian, Chinese, and Mayan cultures have developed elaborate systems for predicting terrestrial events from celestial observations. Classical Western Astrology, one of the oldest astrological systems, can trace its roots to 19th–17th century BCE Mesopotamia, from which it spread to Egypt, Ancient Greece, Rome, the Arab world, and eventually to Central and Western Europe. Throughout most of its history astrology was considered a scholarly subject and was common in academic circles, normally in close relation with astronomy, alchemy, meteorology, and medicine.

In the Western culture the middle ages were a time of exploration into the subject since some people had time for luxuries like education. Astrology became one of the highly studied subjects. Cambridge University (1200) had chairs and classes on this star-studded subject. Royal families and courts had their own astrological informants. It was a time of acceptance by many.

While the study and application of astrological laws has been an integral part of all the great cultures down through the ages, there has been a growing separation between the mathematical science of astrology and modern scientific thinking in the West. In addition to not accepting the proposition that the planets have an effect on earthly life, modern Western astrology as noted has been rejected by science because it fails to take account of the fact of the precession of the equinoxes and thus the position of the planets, which are the basis for any predictions, are incorrect. An astrological reference by Shakespeare speaks about an important aspect of the subject.

> *"The fault, dear Brutus, is not in our stars, but in*
> *ourselves, that we are underlings."*
> Shakespeare, Julius Caesar

This points out that while the stars may indicate a strong influence, we as human beings have the ability through the application of our human consciousness to not be unduly influenced. If we do not choose to act consciously, then we will become *underlings.*

In a book entitled *Planetary Influences on Human Affairs* the author, an Indian Astrologer of the 20th century BV Raman, speaks of the negative view of Astrology held by many western scientists. In defence he used the example of Isaac Newton, who studied Astrology in some depth. He had a collection of astrological works in his library and when his friend and pupil Halley protested to him about his regard for Astrology, he replied: *I have studied these things and you have not.* Raman then proposed that such an answer should be presented to modern scientists with the following query:

"Is your disbelief in Astrology based on investigation or only on a passive second-hand acceptance of a fashionable scepticism based on the prestige of science and technology?"

Sri Shantananda Saraswati described the Indian system of astrology in the following way:

"Jyotisha is a journey into the past and the future based on the readings of the planets and stars (known as celestial beings) and their position at the present. Not only do the celestial beings have some influence on human affairs, but the system can chart out what would happen to an individual or a society. Jyotisha is a science, a mathematical science, and if properly studied, it can account for future events to come. Consciousness is the sovereign force, which when applied can negate any of the influences and which will result in fresh new response."

Consciousness is said to be available in the present moment, when the mind is fully present and is not dwelling in the past or imagining what the future will look like. This being in the present is what needs to happen in assessing the state of our own being and of society today. This conscious approach brings true enlightenment and enables us to make the right decisions on how to proceed on our journey.

Two Planetary Clock Faces

The planets and the stars make up our global clock. The seven planets are the hands of the clock and the star configurations represent the numerical indicators of time. From the earth the planets are seen to move in a path across the heavens, which is called the zodiac. There are two systems of star configurations which are used in *Jyotisha* to indicate the time.

The 12-Fold Division of Star Constellations

The twelve signs of the zodiac constitute one astrological clockface divided into twelve equal proportions of 30°, which is also used by the western astrological system. Each of these twelve-star configurations is related to one of the four basic elements. The name of the twelve signs and their elements are:

Air – Gemini, Libra, Aquarius
Water – Cancer, Scorpio, Pisces
Fire – Aries, Leo, Sagittarius
Earth – Taurus, Virgo, Capricorn

The 27-Fold Division of Star Constellations

In *Jyotisha* the primary division of the heavens is based on 27 fixed stars called Nakshatra, thus dividing the zodiac into 27 equal proportions of 13°20. In this system planetary movements can be measured more precisely, including such events as conjunctions.

Cyclical periods of the sun, moon and five main planets

Each of the planets has a specific cyclical period of revolution. The cycle measured against the backdrop of the

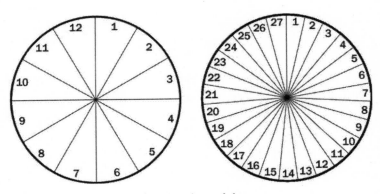

A diagram of the two clockfaces

starry clockface is the time it takes the planet to return to the exact point where it began. Here are examples of the planetary cycles The time shown for the sun is that of the earth's revolution around the sun; the time for the moon it is revolution around the earth and the times for planets are times for the revolution around the sun:

Planet	Period
Sun	365.25 days
Moon	27 days
Mercury	88 days
Venus	225 days
Mars	1.9 years
Jupiter	11.9 years
Saturn	29.7 years

Among the many interactive patterns between planets that have been observed, our interest is in the cycles and sub-cycles that manifest due to the movements of Jupiter and Saturn and their relationship to each other. Taking into account the movement of the earth, the speed of Jupiter's movement relative to the speed of Saturn is the ratio 1.618, which is known as the Golden Mean or Golden Ratio. Here is diagram showing the ratio.

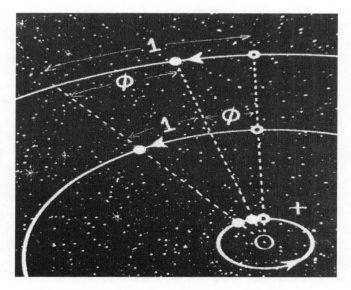

This Golden Mean proportion between numbers gives what is known as the Fibonacci series of numbers e.g.1,2, 3, 5, 8, 13, 21, 34, 55, 89... The division of one number into the next gradually moves to a consistent sum of 1.618 e.g. 55/34 = 1.618. You will note the next number in the series is equal to the sum of the previous 2 numbers e.g. 8+13=21. This Fibonacci series of numbers appears in different aspects of creation, a beautiful example being the numbers of leaves on flowers. Here are just some of the flowers that follow the Fibonacci pattern:

Number of leaves	Flowers
5	Buttercup, Columbine, Larkspur
8	Delphinium, Coreopsis
13	Marigold, Ragwort, Cineraria
21	Aster, Chicory

FIBONACCI 5

FIBONACCI 8

FIBONACCI 13

FIBONACCI 21

An article written in the Guardian Newspapaer in 2005 noted that the famous music composer Johan Sebastian Bach, the genius of the visual arts Leonardo DaVinci, were both strongly focussed on the Fibonacci sequence. The music of Bach and the art of Da Vinci reflect the precise harmony associated with the Fibonacci series of numbers. The reason for these references is to emphasise the point that the relative movement of Jupiter and Saturn does generate a powerful and harmonious pattern of energy.

Conjunctions

Conjunction is a phenomenon that we observe when there is a new moon, when the sun and the moon line up in the same place as viewed from earth. The opposite is a full moon, when they are directly opposite each other and the full light of the sun falls on the moon. Jupiter and Saturn are conjunct, located at the same point on the 12-fold clockface every 20 years.

The conjunctions in the same grouping of astrological signs, either Air, Water, Fire or Earth lasts for around 250 years, The most recent conjunctions of Saturn and Jupiter in Fire signs began in 1723 and continued in Fire signs (Aries, Leo, Sagittarius) until 1921, when the first conjunction in an Earth sign occurred. It is important to note that there is a transition period where the conjunction locations shift back and forth between two elements. For example, in 1940 the conjunction was in a Fire sign, then back to Earth signs in 1960 and 1980, with the final Fire sign conjunction being in 2000. This is called the 'Mutation Period' by Edith Hathaway in her most informative book, *In Search of Destiny* where she writes about the Jupiter and Saturn conjunctions. From 2020 in this cycle the conjunctions will be in Earth signs. Her astrological research has shown that the 20-year Jupiter-Saturn conjunction cycles are pivotal in assessing several factors including socio-political-economic trends. The nature of the influence during that period is based on whether it is in Air, Water, Fire or Earth signs. The conjunctions and therefore the larger cycle will have different themes each time a given element becomes dominant.

The key element of this pattern of conjunctions is that Jupiter and Saturn are conjunct in the same point in the heavens, as measured by the finer 27-fold clockface, every 854 years. They then start a new cycle. Detailed charts of the planetary positions of these conjunctions from 3000 BCE–2160 CE were prepared by Geoffrey Pearce and analysed in depth by Jan Willem van Doorn, two eminent *Jyotisha* experts, to confirm this pattern.

As an introduction to the historical significance of the conjunctions, here is a brief summary of the general qualities of the four stages of an 854-year cycle based on the location of the conjunctions, including some brief examples from the different cultures.

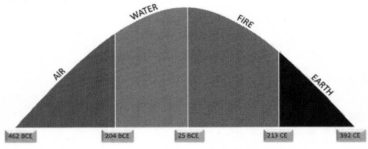

Air periods are characterised by an overcoming of the inertia of the past and the setting in motion through free movement and communication new ideas that meet the needs of the time. It is taking the initiative with a new vision. These ideas form the basis for the cycle and will be manifest in the succeeding stages in a manner based on the qualities of the prevailing element. This Air period is the time of a renaissance, a re-birth. For example, influential new ideas emerged at the beginning of the Western Renaissance in the 13th and 14th centuries. This Air period, from 1246–1524 CE, manifested in response to the rigidity of the Earth dominated Feudal period. An important element of this new impulse was a great sense of individual freedom of expression and growing self-confidence.

Another example during the Air period was the new impulse of the Mongol invasions from the East, under the leadership of Genghis Khan. In little more than half a century, Genghis Khan and his successors created the largest continuous empire that the world had ever known, from the Great Ocean in the East to Poland and Hungary in the West.

Water periods are those which provide great fluidity of movement with new ways emerging to spread the seeds of the new message. There is also a bonding, an acceptance, during this period which increases confidence. In this positive stage, momentum builds like the power of a rushing river.

A good example of the rapid expansion of a fundamental idea is that within one hundred years after the death of Mohammed in 632 CE, when his followers conquered an enormous area that stretched from Central Asia and the Middle East to North Africa and Spain. During this period, they successfully converted many people to their faith.

In an earlier Water period from 283-6 BCE, the Roman Empire expanded in many areas: Sicily; Corsica; Sardinia; Spain; Africa; Macedonia; Western Turkey; Syria; Cyprus; Crete; and many other places. In the Water period from 630–908 CE, the Vikings from Scandinavia penetrated large areas of sea and rivers deep into Europe. They dominated the British Isles, conquered Normandy and entered Paris. The Vikings also penetrated into the Mediterranean area and Turkey.

During the most recent Water period, from 1484–1763 CE, there were numerous overseas adventures: the voyages of Vasco da Gama; Columbus; Vespucci; Magellan; Hudson; Cook; and many others. All the oceans were crossed and all continents were visited, many for the first time. Active in this stage were the Dutch, Spanish, Portuguese, French and English

Fire periods are when the fruits of the initial stages are most fully manifested and enjoyment experienced. They are peak periods of apparent brightness, of wealth, results and active energy. A prime characteristic of the latter stage of the Fire period, however, is excess, due to the inability to discriminate as to the right measure. This state, when the peak has been passed and the inevitable decline has begun, is not easily acknowledged. There exists a false intellectual conviction that 'all is well' and humanity is advancing. A Fire period, which clearly demonstrates this process is then one from 85 BCE–233 CE, the peak period of the Roman Empire. The initial stage ruled by Emperor Augustus and then maintained by a group of good emperors, with the last being Marcus Aurelius, produced positive results. Then, decadence and poor leadership prevailed bringing about the inevitable period of decline.

The next Fire period was from 829–1087 and in the West, there was the presence of Charlemagne, Alfred the Great and the spread of Christianity with fire and sword during the crusades. The most recent Fire period was from 1723 until 2000, including: the period of the industrial revolution; the development of the combustion motor; the rise and mass use of electricity; the rise of fire weapons; the unlimited application of steel and glass in buildings which are both made with intense fire; with the ultimate developments being laser technology and nuclear energy. The Fire based events in the last part of the period, which have caused untold damage to the West are World Wars I and II.

Earth periods are the final concentration and consolidation of the initial impulse of the cycle. There is also an increasing rigidity and a gradual slipping into decay, which blocks further development. The decay begins with depression and insecurity for many people and a searching for new ways by other people. The key initial elements of the cycle are given physical form, and the guidance for the initiation of the next cycle begins to manifest.

A good example is the period from 154–432 CE, which saw a consolidation of the tenets of the Christian religion. The next Earth period, from 1067–1286, was a time when many new physical manifestations of Christianity appeared, the most relevant examples being the cathedrals of Europe. These cathedrals are not only magnificent physical buildings, but they also serve as physical proof of everything that had been attained in art, religion and sciences in that cycle, which during the Earth period is preserved in physical form.

The present Earth period started in 1920, since that time a good portion of the buildings now in the world have been built. As noted there were transition conjunction in Fire signs in 1940 and 2000. A major shift occurred in 2020 when on 21 December an especially powerful Jupiter Saturn conjunction took place on the same date as the Winter Solstice. It happened in the Earth sign Capricorn and marks the beginning of a period of 120 years when the Saturn Jupiter conjunctions will occur only in Earth signs. It will be a period when there will be greater environmental consciousness, more concern for the earth, which is sorely needed.

Geoffrey Pearce commented on this conjunction:

"Capricorn is ruled by Saturn so democratic governments will become more prominent along with people of most nations calling for greater social and economic justice, and the environmental crisis to be addressed."

Another most useful analysis has been provides by Edith Hathaway. Commenting on the Earth period, which including transition conjunctions will last until 2199, she said:

"So far during the Earth period, the global population has grown from 1.9 billion in 1921 to 7.7 billion in Dec. 2019, thus almost quadrupling in some 100 years. This is the largest population leap in world history. It took 126 years to increase from one billion in 1804 to 2 billion in 1927. And we can assume that material prosperity and technical advances have been positive factors in manifesting this reality."

The most relevant point about the continuing conjunctions in Earth signs is the projection that there will be continual subtle support for the Climate Change initiatives which is the most crucial issue facing the world today.

The 854-year cycle
- Cycle I   462 BCE–392 CE
- Cycle II   392–1246 CE
- Cycle III   1246–2100 CE

To clarify the point about the overlap of conjunctions see the summary below. The date of the first conjunctions in an air sign, the indicator of a new cycle, is 523 BCE. Then there is the date of the beginning of the ruling period 462 BCE, which is based on the date when the overlap finishes. From this date the next series of conjunctions will only be in air signs. Then the date when the conjunction occurs in the very same location 854 years later which is 392 CE. The last conjunction in the earth sign, 452 CE, signals the final termination of that cycle. The key for this analysis is the ruling period which as can be seen are all 854 years. These are the dates this book uses for the assessment of the historical events.

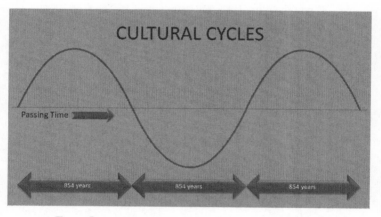

	First Conjunction		*Last Conjunction*
	Air sign	**Ruling period**	**Earth sign**
Cycle I	523 BCE	462 BCE–392 CE	452 CE
Cycle II	332 CE	392 CE–1246 CE	1305 CE
Cycle III	1186 CE	1246 CE–2100 CE	2160 CE

There is consistency in the period of the first conjunction and the last. For these three cycles the periods are 975, 973 and 974 years respectively.

3

CULTURAL CYCLES,
WESTERN EUROPEAN/AMERICAN
CYCLE I

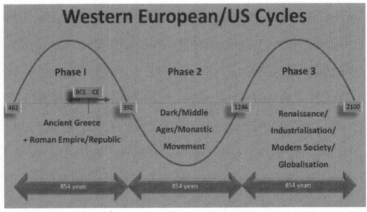

Cycle I: *Greek Power/ Roman Republic, then Roman Empire 462 BCE–392 CE*
Cycle II: *Dark/Middle Ages/Monastic Movement 392–1246 CE*
Cycle III: *Renaissance/Industrial Revolution/Globalisation 1246–2100 CE*

CYCLE I 462 BCE–392 CE

Air Period—a new impulse 462 BCE–164 BCE
- Greek Philosophic Tradition emerges and spreads Socrates/ Plato/Aristotle/Epicurus/Zeno Plato's Academy 388BCE /Aristotle's Lyceum 334BCE
- Greek art, architecture, education flourish
- Greek Military Might Greco-Persian Wars 490–480 BCE / Age of Pericles 46–429 BCE Peace and cultural advancement / Peloponnesian War 431–404 BCE/ Alexander the Great 356–323 BCE and successors who amass one of the largest empires of the ancient world.

Greek philosophic tradition

The Greek philosophic tradition became one of the main spiritual elements of the Western Culture. Alfred North Whitehead, a widely influential twentieth century philosopher and mathematician, commenting on the influence of Plato said, *The safest general characterization of the European philosophical tradition is that it consists of a series of footnotes to Plato.*

The philosophic teachings that preceded Socrates, Plato and Aristotle began with Thales of Miletus, who was very interested in Astrology, and who accurately predicted the solar eclipse of 585 BCE. Also active at this time was Anaximander, who said, *"The material cause and the first element of things was the Infinite which is eternal, ageless and it encompasses all the worlds."* Their work was communicated via the School of Miletus, where many people studied.

They were followed by the very influential Pythagoras, who settled in southern Italy and started a society that was very much like a religious order. One of his main contributions was to establish philosophy as a practical guide, a way of life, and not merely an intellectual theory. Socrates was acquainted with some of his teachings, as was Plato.

During my university education I connected with some of the teaching of Pythagoras in two ways. The first being his beautiful mathematical formulas that showed how to measure many natural aspects of the creation. Here is a prime example, the Pythagorean Triangle:

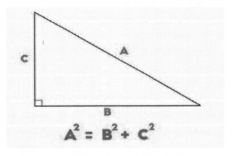

$$A^2 = B^2 + C^2$$

Pythagorean Triangle: bing.com / images

The other connection was via the Greek-Letter Fraternity that I joined, called Sigma Pi. There were many of these organisations present on our campus. We were described as a Pythagorean Brotherhood and one of the key directions we received was a quote from **Pythagoras:** *To Seek the Golden Mean.* That has certainly come to mind on many occasions in my life, the most recent being this study which reveals the relative movement of Jupiter and Saturn corresponding to the Golden Mean.

The great Greek teachers—Socrates and Plato

As the teaching of these two sages has had such an impact on our Western culture, it seems right to highlight briefly some of the key elements of their lives.

Socrates is credited as one of the founders of Western philosophy and the first moral philosopher of the ethical tradition of thought. An enigmatic figure, he made no writings and is known chiefly through the accounts of classical writers, particularly his students Plato and Xenophon. In Plato's Dialogues, which are the most comprehensive accounts of Socrates to survive from antiquity, his method of dialectic questioning in an attempt to discover the truth about any issue is a major feature. He did not claim to have knowledge, but simply continued questioning in a step by step process until the truth was revealed. Depictions of Socrates in art, literature and popular culture have made him one of the most widely known figures in the Western philosophical tradition.

There is an interesting story about a friend of Socrates who asked the Delphic Oracle, *"Who is the wisest person alive?"* The Oracle replied, *"There is no one wiser than Socrates."* When told about this response, Socrates was puzzled in that he claimed that he knew nothing. He then, to confirm his view that he was not the wisest, set about questioning those people considered wise by many people. In his intense questioning what was revealed was that the supposedly wise people really did not know, but they had convinced themselves and others that they did know. Socrates thus came to the conclusion that true knowledge arises when you do not have any preconceived ideas, *"you know nothing."*

Then you can give your full attention to the subject and knowledge can thus arise.

Plato was born at a time when Athens was at war, which was followed by a period of weakness and confusion. Here is Matthew Pye's assessment of Plato's qualities and approach to dealing with the challenges of the time:

> *"Plato was brave enough to think far beyond the conventional wisdom of his day. He was a thinker who was totally committed to looking beyond all of the clutter and opinions to get a proper grip on the reality of a situation. Yet, perhaps the most impressive feature of Plato's method of addressing the problems confronting humanity at the time was the way in which he synthesised all these dimensions of his thought into one fluid and open dialogue. This is sharply relevant for dealing with the climate crisis—our modern world is so complex, diverse and interconnected."*

Plato attempted to help restore order by founding a school of learning, the Academy, the first institution of higher learning in the Western world. Among the many subjects that Plato wrote about and taught in his Academy were the Seven Liberal Arts; the Trivium—Dialectic, Grammar and Rhetoric and the Quadrivium—Arithmetic, Geometry, Music and Astronomy. Other subjects studied were Harmony, Ethics, Reason and Values. Plato described two types of values, which he called Goods: Human Goods/Values; health, beauty, wealth and strength, which are attainable when the Divine Goods/Values; wisdom, justice, temperance and courage are lived. This is the path we are advocating.

The other important contribution that Plato has made to society is his clear description of the system of dialogue used so effectively by his teacher Socrates in discovering the truth about a wide range of issues, both secular and spiritual. In a dialogue input is accepted from all parties with the one proviso, that the aim of the conversation is to discover the truth and not to win the debate. We will look at the dialectic method in more detail when we address the plan for the way forward.

Although the popularity of Plato's works has fluctuated over the years, they have never been without readers and advocates. The so-called Neoplatonism of philosophers, such as Plotinus and Porphyry, who followed at the final stage of the cycle, influenced Saint Augustine and thus Christianity. Marsilio Ficino, in 15th century Florence, became the main proponent of Platonic Philosophy in conjunction with Christian teaching which together provided the spiritual impulse that marked the beginning of the third cycle.

Another important teacher of this time was Aristotle (384–322 BCE) who was a student of Plato. He founded his own school, the Lyceum, and a system of philosophy called the Peripatetic school which covered a wide range of subjects including Logic, Physics, Ethics and Rhetoric.

Greek art and architecture flourished

An indication of the positive of outward stage of a cultural cycle is that artistic expression is refined and beautiful works of art and design are produced which came to be appreciated even in later cycles.

Greek Military Power

The Greco-Persian Wars, also called Persian Wars, were a series of wars fought by Greek states and Persia over a period of almost half a century. The fighting was most intense during two invasions that Persia launched against mainland Greece between 490 and 479 BCE. Although the Persian empire was at the peak of its strength, the collective defence mounted by the Greeks overcame seemingly impossible odds and even succeeded in liberating the Greek city-states on the fringe of Persia itself. The Greek triumph ensured the survival of Greek culture and political structures long after the demise of the Persian empire. In 477 BCE, Athens became the recognised leader of a coalition of city-states that did not include Sparta. This coalition met and formalized their relationship at the holy city of Delos, and thus became known as the *Delian League*. Its formal purpose was to liberate Greek cities still under Persian control, but it soon became the vehicle for expanding the power of Athens throughout the Aegean.

A competing coalition of Greek city-states centred around Sparta also arose and became more important as the external Persian threat subsided. This coalition became known as the *Peloponnesian League*, which became the vehicle for expanding the power of Sparta. These two arch-rivals eventually engaged in warfare which came to be known as the Peloponnesian War (431–404 BCE).

Pericles was a prominent and influential Greek statesman, orator and military general of Athens during its Golden Age— specifically the time between the Persian and Peloponnesian wars. Pericles had such a profound influence on Athenian society that Thucydides, a contemporary historian, acclaimed him as *the first citizen of Athens*. Pericles turned the Delian League into an Athenian empire and led his countrymen during the first two years of the Peloponnesian War. The period during which he led Athens was from 461 to 429 BCE. He promoted the arts and literature, and it is principally through his efforts that Athens acquired the reputation of being the educational and cultural centre of the ancient Greek world. He started an ambitious project that generated most of the surviving structures on the Acropolis, including the Parthenon. This project beautified and protected the city, exhibited its glory, and gave work to the people. Pericles also fostered Athenian democracy.

The Peloponnesian War reshaped the ancient Greek world. The Greeks fought amongst themselves until they destroyed their glorious culture. On the level of international relations, Athens, the strongest city-state in Greece prior to the war's beginning, was reduced to a state of near-complete subjection, while Sparta became established as the leading power of Greece. The economic costs of the war were felt across Greece. Poverty became widespread in the Peloponnese, while Athens found itself completely devastated, and never regained its pre-war prosperity. The war also wrought subtler changes to Greek society; the conflict between democratic Athens and oligarchic Sparta, each of which supported friendly political factions within other states, made civil war a common occurrence in the Greek world.

The energetic leadership within Macedonia began in 359 BCE when Philip of Macedon was acclaimed as King Philip II. He began expanding Macedonia's influence abroad with an aim of restoring Greece to its grandeur by liberating all Greek lands from Persian dominion. This dream even included conquering Persia itself.

Philip's son, Alexander the Great (356–323 BCE) came to power when his father was assassinated. He was only 20 years old, but he continued his father's plans to conquer all of Greece, using both military might and persuasion. After a victory over Thebes, Alexander travelled to Athens to meet the public directly. Despite speeches against the Macedonian threat on behalf of the war party of Athens, the public in Athens was still very much divided between the *peace party* and *the war party*. The arrival of Alexander charmed the Athenian public, which strengthened the peace party so that a peace between Athens and Macedonia was agreed. This allowed Alexander to move on his and the Greeks' long-held dream of conquest in the east, with a unified and secure Greek state at his back. In 334 BCE, Alexander with about 30,000 infantry soldiers and 5,000 cavalry, crossed the Hellespont into Asia. He never returned. Alexander managed to briefly extend Macedonian power not only over the central Greek city-states, but also to the Persian empire, including Egypt and lands as far east as the fringes of India. He managed to spread Greek culture throughout the known world. Alexander the Great died in 323 BCE in Babylon during his Asian campaign of conquest.

Water Period—expansion 283 BCE–14 CE
- Rome defeats the Greeks 275 BCE.
- Roman Republic begins the growth of its empire—defeat of the Carthaginians in 3 Punic Wars (264-146 BCE).
- Major expansion led by the aggressive leadership of Julius Caesar, 61– 44 BCE. Dependencies of Rome increase to include Egypt, Cappadocia and Armenia.
- Christ is born

The Rise of Roman Power

With the fall of Greece, the next great Western power to emerge was that based in Rome who took up the task of expanding the Western culture that had been initiated by the Greeks. The first task was to defeat the internal enemies in Italy and then to subjugate the Greeks. What followed then was the First Punic War (264 to 241 BCE) which was the first of three wars fought between African based Carthage and the Roman Republic, the two great powers of the Western Mediterranean. For 23 years, in the longest continuous conflict and greatest naval war of antiquity, the two powers struggled for supremacy. Rome was victorious in the first war, but this did not deter Carthage from making a fresh challenge.

The Second Punic War (218 to 201 BCE), also referred to as The Hannibalic War, was one of the deadliest human conflicts of ancient times. Fought across the entire Western Mediterranean region for 17 years, it was waged with unparalleled resources, skill, and hatred. It saw hundreds of thousands killed, the destruction of cities, and massacres and enslavements of civilian populations and prisoners of war by both sides. The war began with the Carthaginian general Hannibal's conquest of the pro-Roman Iberian city of Saguntum in 219 BCE, prompting a Roman declaration of war on Carthage in the spring of 218 BCE. Hannibal surprised the Romans by marching his army overland from Iberia to cross the Alps and invading Roman Italy, After the death or imprisonment of 130,000 Roman troops in two years of battles, 40% of Rome's Italian allies defected to Carthage, giving her control over most of southern Italy. Macedon and Syracuse joined the Carthaginian side and the conflict spread to Greece and Sicily.

The Romans gradually defeated Carthage's allies in Europe, ending their rule in Iberia in 206 BCE, and then invaded Carthaginian Africa in 204, inflicting two severe defeats on Carthage forcing the recall of Hannibal from Italy. Hannibal was defeated and harsh peace conditions were imposed on Carthage, which ceased to be a great power and became a Roman client state until its final destruction by the Romans in 146 BCE during the Third Punic War.

Julius Caesar was a Roman politician, military general, and historian who played a critical role in the events that led to the demise of the Roman Republic and the rise of the Roman Empire. Caesar rose to become one of the most powerful politicians in the Roman Republic through a number of his accomplishments, notably his victories in the Gallic Wars, completed by 51 BCE.

During this time, Caesar became the first Roman general to cross both the Rhine River and the English Channel, when he built a bridge across the Rhine and crossed the Channel to invade Britain. Caesar was challenged by the dominant politicians of the day and in response he initiated a civil war. His victory in the war put him in an unrivalled position of power and influence. The Republic expanded and he was eventually proclaimed *Dictator for life*, giving him additional authority. His populist and authoritarian reforms angered many, who began to conspire against him. In 44 BCE, Caesar was assassinated.

Christ is born

A new Teacher/Avatar arrives, who eventually becomes a major influence in the Roman world and in Western society. More on this subject as we proceed.

Fire Period—Summit Reached, Decline Begins 85 BCE-253CE

- Roman Empire, beginning 27 BCE with Augustus; continues to expand until 180 CE. Rome rules lands in Europe, Africa, and Asia.
- Roman Philosophy becomes established, based largely on the Greek Tradition: Plotinus (Neo-Platonist), Cicero, Seneca, Epictetus (Stoic).
- Christian teaching emerges, gradually spreading within the Roman Empire.

Roman Empire

Following the death of Julius Caesar, confusion reigned in Rome, which grew into a Civil War. Through the efforts of Octavian, the war came to an end in 31BCE and in 27 BCE he became Augustus, Emperor of the Roman Empire. From this point on Rome was ruled by Emperors. While there were many advances in Roman culture and philosophic thought during the next 150 years, the main focus was in the expansion of the empire which reached its physical peak in 117 CE.

During the period there were what were called, Five Good emperors who demonstrated positive leadership qualities. They were: Nerva, 30–98, Trajan, 98–117, Hadrian, 117–138, Antoninus Pius, 138–161, and Marcus Aurelius, 161–180. Of these the one that has greatest was Marcus Aurelius. He was also a Stoic philosopher and the last emperor of the Pax Romana, an age of relative peace and stability for the Empire. His personal philosophical writings, *Meditations*, are a significant source of the modern understanding of ancient Stoic philosophy. It includes the thoughts of a philosopher-king, which are based on the moral tenets of Stoicism, learned from Epictetus. These include the view that the cosmos is a unity governed by an intelligence, and the human soul is a part of that divine intelligence and that *it is important not to react to that which you cannot control, but to maintain focus on that which you can.* Some of Marcus's ideas seemed to also relate closely to a version of Platonism, known as Neoplatonism.

Roman Cultural Highlights

Language—The teaching of Latin, and for some, the Greek language as well.

Law—A system of Roman Law is developed. Later attempts are made to introduce Democracy in order to check and balance the rule of the Emperor.

Architecture—Colosseum, Aqueducts, Trajan's Forum, Pantheon, Hadrian's Wall.

Earth Period—Consolidation, Decline, Conclusion 154–362

- Christian teaching advances rapidly, becomes the religion of the Empire.
- Descent begins, 180 CE reign of Commodus.
- Invasions, by Huns, Ostrogoths, Visigoths, Franks.
- Ineffective leadership, Emperors serve short terms, some are assassinated, chaos prevails.
- Empire first split, in 284 CE by Emperor Diocletian— Western Roman Empire centred in Rome, Eastern Roman Empire established in Constantinople.

The Expansion of Christianity

St Paul was one of the prime agents for spreading the teachings on understanding the death and resurrection of Jesus Christ as a central turning point in history. Paul established Christian churches throughout the Roman Empire, including Europe and Africa. However, in all cases the Church remained small and was persecuted, particularly under tyrannical Roman emperors like Nero (54–68), Domitian (81–96), under whom being a Christian was illegal, and Diocletian (284–305).

Emperor Constantine turns the tide

When a Roman military leader, Constantine, won victory over his rival in battle to become the Roman emperor in 306 CE, he attributed his success to the Christian God and immediately proclaimed his conversion to Christianity. Christianity became legalised within the Roman Empire in 313 CE. Constantine then needed to establish exactly what the Christian faith was and called the First Council of Nicea in 325 CE, which formulated and codified the faith.

The conditions which existed during the Earth period from 154–362 CE, are those which signalled the final fall of the Roman Empire. This period is especially important for the Western culture of today as we are just entering the Earth period of our cycle and the conditions that exist now seem to bear a close resemblance to the conditions that existed then. There have been numerous studies about the reasons for Rome's decline and fall.

Here is a description of the characteristics of this period of cultural decline as presented by Edward Gibbon in his classic work, *The Decline & Fall of the Roman Empire:*

- Large disparity between rich and poor
- Extravagant displays of wealth and outward show
- Unhealthy obsession with sex
- Decline of military discipline
- Desire to live off the bounty of the state

An important reference to the period of decadence comes from Boethius (480–525 CE), a wealthy Roman who ran afoul of Theodoric, the Ostrogoth ruler of Rome, was imprisoned and eventually executed. While in prison he wrote a book called *The Consolation of Philosophy*, which was to become one of the most influential books in Europe for hundreds of years. It relates how Boethius was led through a philosophic enquiry into his own state of being and also the state of the current society. He was asked whether the dominant values of the time of the fall of the Roman Empire, namely Wealth, Power, Fame and Pleasure, would bring him lasting happiness. Upon careful reflection he finally concluded that they would not. Do those values sound familiar?

LESSONS LEARNED FROM CYCLE I

One of the most important lessons learned from this cycle is that the state of the society is largely determined by the prevalent values that are dominant at the time The values that are lived by the leaders and a good number of influential people, need to be examined carefully. When natural human values are the motive and basis for life, then a society flourishes in all aspects: intellectually, emotionally and spiritually. What was learned from this cycle is that when success in the material realm becomes the main motive, resulting in the side-lining of morality and spirituality, this will inevitably lead to excess and the decline of peace, happiness, and love. The predominant values become those that drive people to maximise personal gains in the material world. Care needs to be taken about what values are put forth as the best guides for life. Both the Greek philosophic tradition and Christianity offered the same important message that natural values when lived fully are the real source of happiness for all.

The Importance of Contemplation *Theoria and Silence*

When a period of excess arrives, people react in such a way that there is constant physical and mental activity and in this environment the mind gets little rest, causing a significant degree of stress and tension. Consumption of food, drink and other physical stimulants increases beyond measure endangering health. Attention to religious/spiritual practices are dramatically reduced which are an integral part of all cultures.

In response to these negative conditions, a new initiative was launched beginning 200 years before the final fall of Rome. It focussed on more reflective, contemplative practices designed to quiet the mind and emotions so that real peace and contentment, of the type not available in the material world, could be experienced by everyone; *a peace beyond all understanding.*

Contemplation involves simply the opening of mind and heart. It is not the suspension of all activity, but rather a concentration on a single act or thought to connect at a deeper level with the spiritual dimension of our being. Contemplative prayer is a process of interior transformation, moving from a state of incessant desire and movement to one of stillness, peace and divine unity. A form of contemplative prayer was practised and taught by the Desert Fathers of Egypt, Palestine and Syria beginning around the 3rd century CE. This group was started by Anthony, a Christian monk living in Egypt, who with a few devotees retired from society to live alone in caves.

In parallel around 280 Plotinus, a philosopher of the Platonic tradition, was advising people in society to practise '*Theoria: reflective contemplation, a going within, a letting go of the habitual way of seeking happiness in external objects, people and actions.'* The direction given was to become quiet within and to make contact with the eternal peace and happiness that is part of our being. It is always shining, like the sun and we simply need to remove the clouds of excessive thought and feeling and simply be. What arose in the next period were monasteries where groups of contemplatives lived together marked with a number of daily periods of meditation, study and prayer. This new impulse was the beginning of a different type of Renaissance; not one of expanding an active presence in the external world, but rather a quieting of the self and connecting with the inner calm which is a characteristic of our true nature.

This stage of the cycle is the Earth Period, the final of the four stages of the 854-year cycle. At this point the outward flowering of the Western Culture moved into its closing stage and at the same time the seeds for the new inward cycle were sown. The way of life which has been established in the first three stages has become rather firm and rigid, less susceptible to change. This is the Earth stage. As noted, in December 2020 the Earth period of the current cycle came into full effect, so lessons learned about the excesses of this first Western cycle need to be carefully considered.

4

CULTURAL CYCLES
WESTERN EUROPEAN/AMERICAN
CYCLE II

CYCLE II 392–1246 CE

The Dark or Middle Ages/Monastic Movement

During this cycle the European culture went through a period of withdrawal, a going within. It lost its military and economic domination and apparently became a less important player on the world scene. It was actually a time of change to another structure, as the basis of the current European nation states began to take shape. While much of Europe was seen to be in an economic recession, underneath all these external difficulties there was occurring a spiritual renewal—a renaissance. The Christian teaching was establishing itself deeper in the hearts and minds of the people. The monastic movement flourished during this period, as did the idea of service to the community. From the time that Emperor Constantine established Christianity as the 'state religion', the message of Christ expanded rapidly in Europe and became increasingly influential in guiding the way people thought, spoke and lived their lives. A vision arose during this period of an empire united under a Christian ruler. Art was primarily dedicated to the expression of spiritual themes which served as reminders of the Christian teaching for the people. In the latter stages of this period magnificent cathedrals arose around Europe in praise and glory of the Lord. So, while GDP was not very high, other very important aspects of life were on the rise. As noted, the link to the previous cycle was the contemplation, reflection and meditation that had been encouraged by the Desert Fathers, Plotinus and others, aimed at quieting the mind and turning one's attention within to connect with internal peace and happiness.

Air Period—A New Impulse 392–630 CE

- St Basil the Great (330–379) created monastic rules that are followed in the Byzantine Empire.
- John Cassian, (365–435) founded a house for monks in Marseilles and another for nuns. He writes a book, *Institutes,* for beginners in the monastic life and a series of *24 Conferences,* a study of the Egyptian Desert Fathers' ideal of a monk.
- Gradually monasteries formed around Europe which encourage literacy, learning and the preservation of the

classics through the work of fine calligraphers called scribes. Service in the community later became an integral part of their work and as a result, monks were well respected in the community.

- Augustine of Hippo (354–430) created a Rule for the Augustinian order, which spread to Britain in 4th and 5th centuries, including Iona, Lindesfarne & Kildare.
- St Patrick in Ireland, the Start of the Celtic movement (431).
- Franks converted to Christianity (497).
- St Benedict (480–543) founded a monastery at Monte Cassino in 529, and wrote guidelines for monastic life, *The Rule of Benedict.*

The beginning of the inward Renaissance

What is most striking about the first stage of the new inward cycle was the speed with which the movement to greater stillness, silence and inner reflection came about The total loss of economic power meant that there was a dramatic decrease in employment opportunities for young people. Many young men joined a monastery which provided an opportunity to work and serve, under strong spiritual guidance and with a real sense of community.

John Cassian's works were useful in communicating the benefits of quiet reflection and meditation. Here is a quote from his Conference 14 about dealing with problems that arise:

"When we are free from the attractions of all that we do and see, and especially, when we are quietly meditating during the hours of darkness, we think them over and we understand them more clearly."

Here is a quote from Conference 10 which sums up nicely what the monastic effort was all about:

"To gaze with utterly purified eyes on the divinity is possible—but only to those who rise above lowly and earthly works and thoughts and who retreat with Him into the high mountain of solitude. When they are freed from the tumult of worldly ideas and passions, when they are liberated from the confused melee of all their vices, when they have reached the sublime heights of utterly pure faith and preeminent virtue, the divinity makes known to them the glory of Christ's face and reveals the sight of its splendours to those worthy to look upon it with clarified eye of the spirit".

His emphasis on prayer and meditation on the Scriptures was the fundamental attitude of the early monks of Egypt. This is an example of a useful cross-cultural guide to help individuals cope with a difficult situation. It also mirrors to some extent what is currently happening in the West, where people are receiving considerable guidance on quiet reflective practices such as Meditation, Mindfulness, and Yoga from Eastern cultures.

An admirer of John Cassian, Benedict of Nursia, later Saint Benedict, wrote a document, *The Rule*, designed to guide both monks and monastic organisations in enhancing personal development and effectively managing the monastic community for the benefit of all. It added a strong element of order and discipline, which was useful and very gratefully received in this early stage of the monastic movement. The order that he founded became known as the Benedictines.

Although the text of the Rule is quite short and along with practical details about the organisation of the monastery, there is much spiritual teaching plainly expressed.

"*The monk is a disciple, always alert to the word of God: he must therefore be humble and attentive, ready to greet Christ in the stranger or serve him in the old, the young, the sick—anyone he may meet. Purity of heart, as the monastic tradition understands it, prepares us for a closer union with God. The whole point of monastic life is to prepare us for that union and lead us to it.*"

Here is a modern text from the Benedictine Nuns of Holy Trinity Monastery, Herefordshire regarding the content of the Rule:

"*Compared with earlier monastic writers, Benedict is much more moderate in the demands he made on people. The way of life he prescribed allowed the monk (or nun) enough food, drink and sleep without letting any luxury, self-indulgence or, above all, private ownership, creep in. Prayer, work and reading made up the content of the monastic day. Benedict was aware that his Rule would need to be adapted to different times and circumstances, so within the text there is a wide discretionary power given to the superior.*"

Richard Harries, Lord Harries of Pentregarth, commented on the impact of the Benedictine Rule in his book *The Re-Enchantment of Morality-Wisdom for a Troubled World*.

"*Not only has it given rise to the Benedictine order with its thousands of religious houses over the centuries, but new religious orders also have often looked to the Benedictine Rule, even when they wanted to achieve something more austere and less communal. The Rule has stood the test of time in a truly remarkable way.*"

Water Period—Expansion 630–928 CE

- Monasticism expanded further around Europe. Many new orders of priests and nuns were founded, as the appeal of monastic life increased.
- Charlemagne crowned Holy Roman Emperor, 800; the beginnings of new Western Empire.
- Alfred the Great an inspirational English leader ruled from 871–899.
- The rise of Islamic power led initially by Muhammad, the Prophet, founder of the tradition (570–632). Islamic military power and empire grew to include parts of Europe, with Spain being the main focus.

The Monastic Movement

By the ninth century the Rule of Benedict had become the standard form of monastic life throughout the whole of Western Europe, excepting Scotland, Wales, and Ireland, where the Celtic observance still prevailed for another century or two. Monastic scriptoria flourished from the ninth to the twelfth centuries. Sacred scripture was always at the heart of every monastic scriptorium. As a general rule those monks who possessed skill as writers made this their chief, if not their sole, active work. Until the thirteenth century, medieval monks and nuns made most of these books themselves, preparing parchment, mixing inks, laboriously copying texts by hand, and painting exquisite images in the time allotted to work between the liturgical hours.

Monks and nuns increasingly performed many practical services; they housed travellers, nursed the sick, and assisted the poor. The abbots and abbesses were often asked for advice by secular rulers of the day. Monasticism offered society a spiritual outlet and ideal with important consequences for medieval culture as a whole. Monasteries encouraged literacy, promoted learning, and preserved the classics of ancient literature, including the works of Cicero, Virgil, Ovid, and Aristotle. To beautify the celebration of the liturgy, monastic composers enriched the scope and sophistication of choral music, and to create the best environment for devotion, monasticism developed a close and fruitful partnership with the visual arts. The need for books and buildings made religious houses active patrons of the arts, and the monastic obligation to perform manual work allowed many monks and nuns to serve God as creative artists.

Monastic needs and tastes proved as transformative for the art of book design as for architecture in the Middle Ages. Monasteries required books for everyday use in the liturgy, at mealtimes and meetings when books were read aloud, and for private prayer and meditation. An array of fine liturgical texts became available for reading, study and joint discussion, including theological works by Saint Augustine, Gregory the Great, and other intellectuals of the time.

The Restructuring of Europe

With the continued weakness in leadership, the fragmentation of the Roman Empire continued. For the period of the 7–10th centuries we will examine briefly the coming to power of two inspiring leaders, Charlemagne and Alfred the Great.

Charlemagne (Charles the Great, Charles I) was King of the Franks from 768 CE, King of the Lombards from 774, and then in 800 was crowned as the Holy Roman Emperor by Pope

Leo III in an effort to revive the Roman Empire in the West. He was the first recognised emperor in Western Europe since the fall of the Roman Empire three centuries earlier. The expanded Frankish state that Charlemagne founded is called the Carolingian Empire. In contrast to the general decline of Western Europe from the 7th century, the era of Charlemagne was a period of revival. Charlemagne was able to halt the political and cultural disintegration of the early Middle Ages and lay the foundation for strong central government north of the Alps. Partially as a result of Charlemagne's activity, Northern Europe emerged in the late Middle Ages as the dominant economic, political, and cultural force in the West.

When he met Alcuin of York, a well-known scholar of the day Charlemagne knew that he could help him to achieve a renaissance of learning and reform of the Church. At the king's invitation, Alcuin joined the royal court in 781, and later became one of Charlemagne's chief advisers on religious and educational matters. Alcuin was responsible for an intellectual movement within the Carolingian empire in which many schools of learning were attached to monasteries and cathedrals, and Latin was restored as a literary language. The importance of art was emphasised as were the Seven Liberal Arts.

Another influential scholar of the time was the Irish philosopher and theologian, John Scottus Eriugena (810-877), who also became a trusted advisor to Charlemagne. He adopted the Platonic based dialectic method to address theological questions of the day. His apparent challenge to the established meaning in order to gain greater understanding, took considerable courage.

Alfred the Great was known for effectively safeguarding his kingdom against the Vikings and continuing to expand his influence, finally becoming England's ruler. Alfred proposed that primary education be conducted in English rather than Latin, and he worked hard to improve his kingdom's legal system, military structure, and the people's quality of life.

The Church of Rome wielded immense power and its influence extended to almost every aspect of Saxon life. It also had a near monopoly on the acquisition of knowledge, as its official language Latin, could be read and spoken only by church officials and understood by a mere handful of Wessex clergy. This awareness of the acute lack of Saxon books probably led Alfred to have written a series of histories—each compiled in a different monastery, each added to year by year. They became known as the Anglo-Saxon Chronicles. Much of this work is beautifully illustrated and it is often regarded as Alfred's greatest achievement. Another of Alfred's great gifts to posterity was the translation of a collection of great Latin works into his native Saxon tongue.

While the intellectual and spiritual well-being in the monasteries was growing, there were increasingly aggressive actions being launched against Europe, emanating from surrounding regions, and it became necessary for all sections of society, including the religious orders, to take a more pro-active stance. These are the key indicators of an impending Fire period.

Fire Period—Summit Reached; Decline Begins, 829–1107 CE

- Invasions by Saracens, Magyars and Vikings, 793–911.
- Norman invasion of England, 1066.
- Attack by the West on Byzantine Empire, 1084.
- Carthusian order founded in Germany 1084; by 1300 there were 200 houses around Europe.
- The First Crusade, 1096.
- Bernard of Clairvaux, Cistercian order, 1098; 750 houses by the 15th century.
- 1000 monasteries in Britain – 11th century.
- Hospitallers/Knights of St John 1100; military order founded to also assist the sick & pilgrims.
- Knights Templar, 1119, Teutonic Knights 1190; military orders formed for the Crusades.

European Invasions

In addition to the continual Arab threat from their base in Spain, three main groups, Saracens, Magyars and Vikings, launched raids on Europe in the 9th and 10th centuries. The Saracens, Arabs from North Africa, attacked Sicily, Sardinia, Corsica and southern Italy. The Magyars, nomadic tribes from the Hungarian plains, plundered areas of Germany, Northern Italy and France, with many monasteries being victims of their attacks. The most dominant of the invaders were the Vikings, with Danish tribes focusing on France, and the Norwegian tribes on Britain and Ireland. The Swedish Vikings attacked tribes in Russia and founded there the kingdom centred in Kiev. They later formed links with Byzantium.

A very obvious lesson to be learned from the series of invasions experienced is that when a particular region becomes weak and fragmented, it is highly likely that other entities will make some sort of attack to take advantage of the weakened state. It might not necessarily be a military attack; it could be an economic one that gives the victor greater control over the defeated. This could be a useful reminder for the European Economic Union. More on this topic later.

1066 Norman Invasion

The Norman conquest and occupation of England by an army of Norman, Breton, and French soldiers in 1066 was led by Duke William II of Normandy, later styled William the Conqueror. William's claim to the English throne derived from his familial relationship with the childless Anglo-Saxon King Edward the Confessor, who may have encouraged William's hopes for the throne. After the victory and the elimination of William's main rivals, he still faced rebellions over the following years and was not secure on his throne until after 1072. The lands of the resisting English elite were confiscated and some of the elite class were forced to flee into exile. To control his new kingdom William granted lands to his followers and built castles commanding military strongpoints throughout the land. There was little alteration in the structure of government, as the new Norman administrators took over many of the forms of Anglo-Saxon government.

The impact of the Fire element is obvious when one looks at the activities of political rulers and the military, as well as the spiritually inclined monastic communities. The period is full of examples of wars and conflicts within society and within the church. Another indication of the Fire influence is the appearance on the scene of a number of **militarily oriented religious orders.**

Knights Templar, or simply Templars, were a Catholic military order founded in 1119 CE and recognised by the papacy in 1139. The order, which was among the wealthiest and most powerful, became a favoured charity throughout Christendom and grew rapidly in membership and power. Templar knights were among the most skilled fighting units of the Crusades. Non-combatant members of the order, who formed as much as 90% of the order's members, managed a large economic infrastructure throughout Christendom, developing innovative financial techniques that were an early form of banking. This was built on a network of nearly 1,000 commanderies and fortifications across Europe and the Holy Land. The Templars were closely tied to the Crusades and when the Holy Land was lost, support for the order faded.

The Order of Knights of the Hospital of Saint John Jerusalem, also known as Knights Hospitallers, was a medieval Catholic military order. The Hospitallers arose in the early 12th century, at the time of the great monastic reformation, as a group of individuals associated with an Amalfitan hospital in Jerusalem. After the conquest of Jerusalem in 1099 CE during the First Crusade, the organisation became a religious and military order under its own Papal charter, charged with the care and defence of the Holy Land. Following the conquest of the Holy Land by Islamic forces, the knights operated from Rhodes, over which they were sovereign, and later from Malta.

Time Line of the Crusades

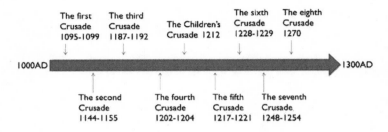

image: bing.com / images

The Teutonic Order was a religious order formed to aid Christians on their pilgrimages to the Holy Land and to establish hospitals. Its members have commonly been known as the Teutonic Knights, having a small voluntary and mercenary military membership, and serving as a crusading military order for protection of Christians in the Holy Land.

The Continuing Expansion of the Monastic Movement

In the later Middle Ages monasteries were often founded by the nobility. Cluny Abbey was founded by William I, Duke of Aquitaine, in 910. Cluny Abbey was noted for its strict adherence to the Rule of Saint Benedict. Gradually nobility became involved in the funding and running of monasteries which would later contribute to their decline. The number of monasteries grew dramatically in all parts of Europe. By the 11th century there were 1000 monasteries in Britain alone. Here are examples of two new orders which grew very rapidly.

1084 Carthusian order, 200 houses by 1300

The order was founded by Bruno of Cologne and included both monks and nuns. Rather than following the Rule of Saint Benedict, the order developed its own Rule called *The Statutes*, which combined hermit - oriented monasticism, living as a hermit, with a form of monasticism that stressed community life. The name Carthusian is derived from the Chartreuse Mountains where Saint Bruno built his first hermitage in the valley of these mountains in the French Alps. The word charterhouse, which is the English name for a Carthusian monastery, is derived from the same source. The motto of the Carthusians is *Stat crux dum volvitur orbis,* Latin for *The Cross is steady while the world is turning.*

1098 Cistercian order, 750 houses by the 15th century

The Cistercian order's founding fathers were a group of Benedictine monks from the Abbey of Molesme in France, who were dissatisfied with the relaxed observance of their abbey and desired to live a solitary life under the guidance of the strictest interpretation of the Rule of Saint Benedict.

The new regulations demanded severe asceticism. They rejected all feudal revenues and reintroduced manual labour for monks, making it a principal feature of their life. Communities of nuns adopting the Cistercian customs were founded as early as 1120–30, but they were excluded from the order until about 1200, when the nuns began to be directed, spiritually and materially, by the monks.

The Cistercians might have remained a relatively small family had not the fortunes of the order been changed by Saint Bernard of Clairvaux, who joined in 1112 as a novice, along with about 30 relatives and friends. In 1115 he became the founding Abbot of Clairvaux, and from that point the growth of the order was spectacular. No other religious body grew so greatly in so brief a time. At Saint Bernard's death the total number of Cistercian abbeys was 338, of which 68 were direct foundations from Clairvaux, and the order had spread from Sweden to Portugal and from Scotland to the countries of the eastern Mediterranean.

What can be learned from that Fire stage was how material success, of even a religious order, can lead to a shift of focus to one of a more outward orientation, greater concern for the material wealth and activity. To serve the community, it was seen to be necessary for monastic orders to bear arms and to acquire wealth so that actions against opponents could be more effectively managed. The restraint and temperance of the monastic life were put aside in favour of a more active participation in the world. While many of their efforts were well motivated, the indicators of growing excess were becoming more evident.

Earth Period—Consolidation; Decline; Conclusion, 1107–1246
- First European Universities Founded 1100–1250.
- Building of Cathedrals/Religious Art 1100s.
- Saint Francis of Assisi (1181–1226) founds the Franciscan order, also to counter excess.

The final stage of a cycle reflects the manifestation of the key elements which characterised the cycle, the ideas and inspirations experienced in the initial Air period. These motivators take on a physical form during the Earth period, but in this final stage there is also a negative aspect which brings on the final decline and end of the period. The final stage of all cycles is characterised by excess and a fixed, but mistaken, view of what is right and good for that moment. Let us now look briefly as some of these developments commencing with the founding of Universities.

Founding of first European Universities 1100–1250 CE

Here are the dates and locations of the first wave:

University of Bologna, Italy 1088.
University of Oxford, England 1096
University of Salamanca, Spain 1134.
University of Paris, France 1150.
University of Cambridge, England 1209.
University of Padua, Italy 1222.
University of Naples Federico II, Italy 1224.

The word *university* is derived from the Latin *universitas magistrorum et scholarium*, which approximately means *community of teachers and scholars*. The term was coined by the Italian University of Bologna, whose traditional founding date of 1088 and is thus considered to be the first university. The origin of many medieval universities can be traced back to the Christian cathedral or monastic schools, which appeared as early as the 6th century and were run for hundreds of years as such before their formal establishment as universities in the high medieval period.

The Building of Fine Cathedrals in the 1100s

The Knights Templar, through the implementation of Gothic architecture constructed some of the most beautiful and long-lasting spiritual monuments in the world, the Notre-Dame Cathedrals. Of these cathedrals, one of the most magnificent architectural marvels and sacred is Notre-Dame-de-Chartres. The 167 stained glass windows of Chartres are unique, dating back to the early 13th century. The usage of this type of window appeared in the early 12th century but vanished in the middle of the 13th century. The luminous nature of this type of window is superior to that of any other and it is far more effective in enhancing the light. Its interior lighting effect is the same, regardless of the degree of light coming from the outside. This special type of stained glass also has the unique power to transmute harmful ultra-violet rays into beneficial light. The secret of how this type of stained glass was created was never revealed or duplicated.

Winchester Cathedral is another good example. William the Conqueror was anointed King at Westminster Abbey, and quickly moved to take control of the Church. He replaced Winchester's last Saxon bishop with his own royal chaplain, Walkelin. The French bishop set about building a huge new church in the Norman Romanesque style. The Cathedral was consecrated in 1093 CE with a great ceremony attended by almost all England's bishops and abbots. Sumptuous works of art were also commissioned. A glorious new font celebrating the work of St Nicholas was installed. In the 12th century, a magnificent illuminated Bible was made for the monks to use in their daily worship. You can still see the Winchester Bible in the Cathedral Library.

New monastic orders

Disenchantment with the materialistic approach that many abbeys had taken and a general desire for a more spiritual observance, led to the founding of new religious orders in the 11th century. It began with the Carthusians in 1082; the Cistercians followed in 1098. The movement continued and two other major orders, the Dominicans and the Franciscans who were founded in the 13th century.

The latter part of the 14th century saw a great decline in the religious life of the friars. The life of the order became fragmented, with several groups being formed, each with its own ideas about the way to proceed.

Saint Francis of Assisi, founded the Franciscan order to counter the prevalent excess in the monastic society at the time. The pattern of its growth, development and decline is another example of a movement that proceeds in a cycle of four stages. It began with the original monastic motivations to seek the Lord's power within, through prayer, contemplation and meditation and to serve the community, but then shifted to a state where the group was acting more freely and independently to gain greater individual wealth and power. Here is an outline of the story.

Stage I

It was probably in 1207 that Francis felt the call to a life of preaching, penance, and total poverty. He was soon joined by his first followers, to whom he gave a short and simple rule of life. In 1209 he and 11 of his followers journeyed to Rome, where Francis received approval of his Rule from Pope Innocent

III. Under this Rule, Franciscan friars could own no possessions of any kind, either individually or communally.

Stage 2

The friars wandered and preached among the people, helping the poor and the sick. They supported themselves by working and by begging food, but they were forbidden to accept money either as payment for work or as alms. The Franciscans worked at first in Umbria and then in the rest of Italy and abroad. The impact of these street preachers and especially of their founder was immense, so that within 10 years they numbered 5,000. Affiliated with them were the Franciscan nuns, whose order was founded at Assisi in 1212, by St. Clare, who was under the guidance of Saint Francis. Clare and her followers were lodged by Francis in the Church of San Damiano, where they lived a severe life of total poverty. They later became known as the Poor Clares or the Order of Saint Clare. During the first years of the Franciscans the example of Francis provided their real guidance for life, but as the order grew it became clear that a revised Rule was necessary. Francis, with the help of several legal scholars, reluctantly composed a more restrained final rule in 1223. This rule was approved by Pope Honorius III. Even before the death of Francis in 1226, conflicts had developed within the order over one important element, the observance of the vow of complete poverty.

Stage 3

The rapid expansion of the order's membership had created a need for settled monastic houses, but it was impossible to justify these if Francis' rule of complete poverty was followed strictly. Three parties gradually appeared: the Zealots, who insisted on a literal observance of the primitive rule of poverty affecting communal as well as personal poverty; the Laxists, who favoured many mitigations; and the Moderates, or the Community, who wanted a legal structure that would permit some form of communal possessions. Something of an equilibrium was reached between these different schools of thought while Saint Bonaventure was in charge (1257–1274). Sometimes called the second founder of the order, he provided a wise, moderate interpretation of the rule which helped the order recover from the growing dissension and fragmentation. During this period the friars spread throughout Europe, while missionaries penetrated Syria and Africa.

Stage 4

With the death of Saint Bonaventure, the internal dissensions of the order flared up anew. The Zealots, who now became known as the Spirituals, demanded absolute poverty. Opposed to them were the Community, or the Conventuals, who stood for a more moderate community life adapted to the needs of study and preaching. Papal decisions favoured the Conventuals, and the Spirituals ceased to be a faction of importance in the order after 1325. The latter part of the 14th century saw a great decline in the religious life of the friars. The life of the order became very fragmented, with several groups being formed, each with its own ideas about the way to proceed.

LESSONS LEARNED FROM CYCLE II

This cycle, from 392 to 1246, began with a rejection of the distorted view that happiness and personal fulfilment would be achieved solely in the physical realm; in money, power, pleasure. The rejection of the external materialistic approach to life resulted in a looking within. During this cycle, the concerted efforts to control the outgoing senses resulted in a spiritually oriented initiative of the Air period, which came to be known as the monastic movement. Hundreds of thousands of people were engaged in contemplation, prayer, and meditation for large parts of the day, working in unified groups of like-minded people. The spiritual dimension of man was explored, using the teachings of Christ as the guide. Christianity grew in strength and influence mainly due to the experience and fine example of dedicated worshippers, both in and out of the monasteries.

Gradually, as the solitary silence and practices began to take hold, the natural inclination was to use one's refined energy in service of the community. That became the work of the monks and nuns living in monastic orders. Their work in the world of service to the society expanded rapidly in their Water period. Greater intellectual development was also part of this expansion. It was important and much time was spent by monks in study. Monasteries helped to establish the acceptance and teaching of Latin in a broader circle so that greater access could be had to some of the fine works of the past. Then a major effort was made to translate many fine spiritual works into local languages such as French and English, to give access to an even wider audience.

What was observed when the internally oriented monasteries went out into the communities was that in some cases, they attracted the financial support of the nobility. This was very useful initially, as the motive was good. Gradually, though, the rich people contributing wanted something for themselves in return. Also, as the monasteries became rich, all the conveniences were provided, which came to be the norm. In addition, with the coming of the Fire period, the actions in the world became more outward and aggressive. During this period there were a number of militarily oriented religious groups formed who actively participated in the warlike crusades. It was also observed that as the monasteries became wealthier, monks started taking advantage of their position. They now expected to be served and, as discrimination slipped, they began going to excess in their consumption of food and drink. Fat monks were common sights in the final stages.

On the positive side what was also observed in the final Earth stage of the cycle was the establishment of institutions of learning to help promote the intellectual development of people and the beautiful design and presentation of places of Christian worship. To enable the continuation and expansion of intellectual development which arose in the monasteries and was initially communicated through the fine books they produced, a movement began in Europe to form universities, centres of study where unity in diversity was the underlying aim. The design and construction of numerous places of worship including majestic cathedrals also came to fruition in this period, along with complementary artistic presentations of the Christian tradition through sculpture, paintings and stained glass.

What has an important bearing on our assessment of the current conditions, was that as Europe slipped into a period of economic decline at the beginning of the 2nd cycle, three other cultures; the Chinese, Indian and Arabic, were entering into an outwardly productive cycle.

5

CULTURAL CYCLES,
WESTERN EUROPEAN/AMERICAN
CYCLE III

CYCLE III 1246–2100 CE
Renaissance, Enlightenment, Industrial Revolution

Air Period—A New Impulse 1246–1544 CE
- A cultural Renaissance inspired by Greek philosophic thought and Christian teaching.
- Florence was a focal point; home of the Medici family and Marsilio Ficino, who became an instrument for the Platonic renewal, including links to Christianity.
- The key focus was the power, freedom and great potential of the individual.
- Flourishing of the arts and science, an expansion of intellectual life.

- Distinct European countries were arising with growing emphasis on nationhood, writing and speaking in their own language, and variations of Christian belief.
- European economy began to expand globally.

The Renaissance

As the Western culture re-emerged from its inward, reflective period, the people of Europe were found to have new energy, new inspiration and aspirations. Their world literally expanded, due to explorations by land and sea. Arthur Farndell, a linguist, historian, teacher and philosopher, has been a great source of guidance on this seminal period.

In the fifteenth century Western Europe received a boost of energy that revitalised it spiritually, intellectually, artistically, and economically. This revitalisation came to be known as the Renaissance, the rebirth of the human spirit, the recognition of the divine within the human. Central to this impulse was the newly awakened interest in the values and achievements of the ancient Greeks, and this interest itself was enhanced by the eruption onto the European stage of the complete corpus of Plato's writings, suddenly available as a whole for the first time in about a thousand years.

This Latin translation of Plato was the work of Marsilio Ficino, under the patronage of the Medici family in Florence. To each Platonic dialogue Ficino added his own commentary. He subsequently translated other Greek writings, together with the *Corpus Hermeticum*, and his works were hugely influential for centuries to come. Following the tradition further, he founded the Platonic Academy of Florence in the 15th century in order to enable a greater understanding of the works, so that intellectual learning could be transformed into living action. In addition to being a scholar and translator, Ficino was a priest, doctor, musician, court advisor, and prolific letter-writer who corresponded with the high and mighty of the time.

After 40 years of work, 11 of 12 books of Ficino's letters are now available in the English translations produced by the *School of Philosophy and Economic Science* in London, where a team of devoted translators, including Arthur Farndell, are working on the final book in the series. These English translations are appreciated by scholars of international renown as well as by those who read them for the spiritual uplift they bring.

As a philosopher, Ficino also forms an important link in a metaphysical tradition that extends from Zoroaster through Plato to at least Hegel. To Ficino the writings of Plato contained the most important knowledge for humanity: knowledge of one's true nature, the divine and immortal principle within. To Ficino it was vital that one had faith in this principle so that it could become a living ideal for the age.

What was also important about this new period was the focus on the individual. The main theme was to extol the natural virtues and qualities of the person. People were encouraged to think and judge for themselves, rather than waiting to be given orders or to consult others before acting. It was a time of growing individual freedom. While people did look back for inspiration to the Greek and Roman times, there was a real impulse to create something new. One group of people who took this on very fully were the artists.

Flourishing of the Arts

Many artists such as Leonardo DaVinci, Michaelangelo, Raphael, Botticelli, and Hans Holbein made a lasting impresssion on European culture. Renaissance art was not only painting, but also sculpture and decorative arts, which also emerged as a distinct style in Italy in about 1400. In parallel there were also developments in literature, music, and science. Renaissance art spread throughout Europe, influencing artists, their patrons and the general public. These developments were the beginning of the transition of Europe to the Early Modern age.

European economy begins to expand

The Renaissance is generally accepted to have started in Italy. Many believe that this was due to its almost perfect location between Western Europe and the Eastern shore of the Mediterranean. Italian cities became important as trade and commercial centres. This wealth helped sustain the political and social changes that were occurring at the time. Rivers were the easiest way to move goods and so towns along the rivers grew as important trade centres also. The Danube, Rhone and Rhine rivers all became important trade routes and the towns along their banks flourished. The importance of the economic and political relationship between the landowners and their tenants of the agrarian economy diminished as trade in other areas increased. Florence became a wealthy city in spite of its inland location away from the major trade routes. Family fortunes were made in banking and industry in Florence, which became the banking centre of Italy during the 14th century. During the 15th century, the Medici bank began opening branches in major cities in Europe. In addition to loaning money, they operated mines, mills and other commercial activities. Cosimo de'Medici owned *The Medici Bank* and accumulated huge profits which he used to finance cultural as well as political activities.

Water Period—Expansion 1425–1782 CE

This was a period where the initial impulse of the Renaissance began to spread to the rest of the world. A pattern evolved where the European countries set out initially to expand trade and bravely sailed in uncharted waters towards new countries. When they found them, a pattern emerged where they not only traded, but gradually assumed control of the territories, a process called colonisation. Efforts to convert the people to Christianity also prevailed during this period. This lasted for more than 300 years, beginning in the mid-15th century. Here are some of the highlights:

- Global trade by sea and land expands dramatically.
- Magellan voyages around the world, 1434.
- Columbus 'discovers' America, 1492.
- Italy's power gradually wanes as countries like Portugal establish trade routes to the East.
- England's colonising of America.
- Spanish take-over of South/Central American lands.
- Dutch voyages and colonisation of Indonesia.
- France expanded presence in Africa.

- European approach – trade agreements, attempts to colonise, then to convert natives to Christianity.
- Reformation & Counter Reformation.
- European Conflicts.

This was a period of global expansion via trade and colonisation for Europe, with several countries being very pro-active. Among the prime movers were Italy, Portugal, Holland, Spain, France, and England, who all made great voyages of discovery. The perspective of the world was opening up dramatically. Trade was also very active with India and China, which started to awaken the West to the scope of these ancient cultures. The awe and wonder lasted only a short time and then efforts started to focus on building up trading relations. Following successful growth in trade, what began for many European powers was a period of colonisation followed by religious conversion programmes and then in some cases total domination of a country. A few examples of that extensive European colonisation process are:

Portugal – Africa; Brazil
Spain – Mexico; South America
Holland – Indonesia; South America
France – Africa; America; Canada
England – America; Africa; West Indies
Italy – Guyana

Italy's economic power was challenged during the late 14th century as other countries began consolidating their power. The rulers of England, France and Spain put policies in place that were favourable to their own middle-class traders and weakened the influence of the Italian middlemen in trade. Italy's influence was further diminished by Portugal's development of a direct sea route to Asia at the end of the 15th century. Until that time Italy controlled the primary route between the Far East and Western Europe. Journeys like Italian-Spanish Christopher Columbus's voyage to the Caribbean Sea and Vasco da Gama's voyage to India intensified national rivalries.

This Water period was clearly one of spreading the message of this new cycle. The sea voyages dominated this period, as the European countries were filled with confidence and wanted to not only advance trade, but also to communicate the message of Christianity. Their collective judgement was that the countries they visited were less cultured and would be better off if they were converted to Christianity. They convinced themselves that helping these people *see the light* was a good service.

Reformation & Counter Reformation

One of the main elements of the European Renaissance was an emphasis on *individual freedom*. This manifested in many ways, but one of the first reactions was resistance against the rigid rule of the Catholic Church. Martin Luther was one of the main protagonists who called for reform of the Church. It was aggressively rejected by the Church, but his approach appealed to German princes who opposed the imperial dominance and so support was offered. This resulted in a movement called Protestantism which spread around Europe. In England this eventually resulted in Henry VIII's break with Rome in the 1530s.

The Catholic Church responded to the criticism and a movement called the Counter-Reformation arose. After a series of meetings organised by the Church from 1545–1563, reforms were implemented. Many of the old religious orders were also reformed and new ones created, the most notable one being the Jesuits under the guidance of their founder Ignatius Loyola. Another major stimulant for change was the implementation of practical printing services directed by Johannes Gutenberg. The first book printed on his press was the Bible in 1455. The translation of the Bible into local languages offered another level of freedom for individuals who, before having access to a local language text, had to depend totally on the Church's interpretation.

European Conflicts

As with any situation where different groups are given freedom and are expanding rapidly, a competitive atmosphere is created. Unchecked, this often leads to conflict, initially within a country and then sometimes to outright war with another country. This is what happened in Europe over the next 200 years. Some of the main examples were:

- The Italian Wars 1494 –1559; warfare in Italy involving France, Spain, England and Germany.
- The French Wars of Religion 1559 –1598 The Protestant community, called Huguenots, fought against those supporting the Roman Catholic Church. The civil war continued until a compromise was reached and a more liberal Catholic became King.
- The Emergence of Spain as a European Power 1491– 1598 The marriage of Queen Isabella of Castile and King Ferdinand of Aragon in 1469 united the two

100

most important Spanish Kingdoms. The subsequent discovery and conquest of the Americas gave Spain great wealth and power. Under the rule of Philip II from 1556–98, Spain projected its power in several directions including against Turkey, the Netherlands, Portugal and England. In 1588 Philip ordered a great fleet, the Spanish Armada, to invade England. They were defeated by the English.

- The Dutch also revolted against Spanish rule and won their independence in 1648.
- Elizabeth I ruled England from 1558–1603. Her finest hour was the defeat of the Spanish which opened up new possibilities for world-wide influence; however, there was resistance. The English government evolved to include a strong parliamentary system designed to act as a check against excessively rigid rule of the monarchy. This was resisted by King Charles I, ruler from 1625–1649, who believed in the Divine Right of kings to rule without any limitations. In 1629 Parliament was suspended for 11 years. This led to the Civil War, which ended with the execution of Charles I in 1649. England then became a Commonwealth or Republic. Battles continued until 1651, which finally brought an end to the English Civil War.

Business growth and development—Capitalism

In parallel there was a rise in capitalism. The birth of businesses such as the English and Dutch East India companies in the early 16th century enabled the wide expansion of trade to new lucrative markets. The British East India company expanded in India and set up bases in Bombay and Calcutta and in 1694 it was granted a monopoly on trade with India. This greater emphasis on business was the foundation for the Industrial Revolution, which was to begin in England in the mid-18th century.

From another perspective, what happened in India in terms of the increasing influence of the British via the business activities of the East India Company took a very negative turn, due to excess. The desire to maximise profits in their trading activities meant that the needs and concerns of the Indian people became less and less important. Even when the British assumed full control of India, making it a part of its expanding global empire, the main priority continued to be making money. For example, as trade in opium proved to very profitable it was expanded and aggressively sold in India and China, damaging the well-being of the people as addiction grew rapidly. In keeping with the distorted view of service held by the European culture, the English made great efforts to convert the Indian people to Christianity. Incorrectly believing that the Indian culture lacked a spiritual tradition, they arrogantly pursued their goal of conversion. A better approach would have been to help the Indian people to discover their own spiritual tradition, including showing the common ground with Christianity.

On a positive note, the removal of the shackles of religious dogma helped widen the view of European thinking in the 16th and 17th centuries. Improvements in technology and the presence of new generations of thinkers like Copernicus, Galileo, Isaac Newton and medical specialists like William

Harvey, physician to Charles I, who gave the first accurate description of blood circulation. These were the initial stages of the scientific movement which continues until today. With people having greater freedom of thought, the availability of books and improved education facilities, including more universities, the seeds were planted for what is called the period of Enlightenment in Europe.

Fire Period—Summit Reached, Decline Begins 1723–2000 CE

It was a very productive period for Europe with the Industrial Revolution playing a major role in expanding wealth creation and increasing international presence. Key to this period is America's role as an economic leader who also exercised a major influence on the cultural norms of the day.

- *Age of Enlightenment* 1700–1800
- *The Industrial Revolution* 1750–1850
- *US Becomes a World Power* 1890–Present

The Age of Enlightenment

The Enlightenment period, also known as the Age of Enlightenment or the Age of Reason, emerged. In French it was called *Le Siècle des Lumières*, the Century of Lights, and in German *Aufklärung*, Enlightenment. It was a period of intellectual and philosophical thinking that dominated the world of ideas in Europe during the 18th century. It was not a single cohesive movement, nor did it have a simple start and finish. It was in many ways a manifestation of the ideas and vision of the

Renaissance, of the Air period. Putting these ideas into practice became quite a task as the trend grew for more freedom of thought. There were many examples of reform, but it was not an easy process.

Enlightenment included a range of ideas centred on reason as the primary source of authority and legitimacy and it came to advance ideals such as liberty, progress, tolerance, fraternity, constitutional government and separation of Church and State. In France, the central doctrines of the Enlightenment philosophers were individual liberty and religious tolerance, in opposition to an absolute monarchy and the fixed dogmas of the Roman Catholic Church. The Enlightenment was marked by an emphasis on the scientific method and reductionism, along with increased questioning of religious orthodoxy—an attitude captured by the phrase *Sapere aude*, 'Dare to know.'

Some of the key ideas of the Enlightenment are those which launched this cycle: *the expansion of social tolerance and personal freedom, the growth of global market capitalism and the rise of science and technology.* These ideas tended to undermine the authority of a monarchy and the Church and eventually paved the way for the political revolutions of the 18th and 19th centuries. A variety of 19th-century movements, including liberalism and neo-classicism, trace their intellectual heritage back to the Enlightenment.

The Age of Enlightenment was closely associated with the scientific revolution. Earlier philosophers whose work influenced the Enlightenment included Bacon, Descartes, Locke, and Spinoza. Some of the other major figures of the period included Diderot, Hume, Kant, Montesquieu, Rousseau, Adam Smith, and Voltaire. Benjamin Franklin visited Europe repeatedly and contributed actively to the scientific and political debates there and brought the newest ideas back to Philadelphia. Thomas Jefferson closely followed European ideas and incorporated some of the ideals of the Enlightenment into the Declaration of Independence (1776). One of his peers, James Madison, incorporated these ideals into the United States Constitution during its framing in 1787.

The Industrial Revolution

The Industrial Revolution is the name given to the enormous changes that took place in technology, farming, mining, manufacturing, and transportation from the middle of the 18th century through to the middle of the 19th century. These changes had a massive impact on people's social and cultural life, as well as their economic conditions.

Here are some of the basic aspects of the Industrial Revolution provided by Paul Goodman in an article that appeared on the online site *owlcation.com* .

10 Industrial Revolution Facts
- It Began in Britain
- It was one of the Biggest Events in Human History
- Machines Replaced People
- More People Lived in Cities
- Economic Conditions Improved for Most People
- Industrialization Caused New Problems
- Production of Clothing and Fabrics was Transformed
- The Steam Engine Improved Transport and Production

- The Industrial Revolution Created a New Economic System
- Some Countries Have yet to Experience an Industrial Revolution

The Industrial Revolution began in Britain and later spread to Western Europe, North America, and around the world. The main thing that happened during the Industrial Revolution was that machines were developed that could perform many of the jobs and tasks that had previously been done by people (or in some cases, animals, such as horses).

Before the Industrial Revolution, societies were largely rural, and people made things at home. Industrialisation meant that more and more people lived in cities, and goods were mass produced in purpose-built factories. The Industrial Revolution generally brought about much better economic conditions for most people, but the poor and working classes often suffered with grim jobs and terrible living conditions.

The Industrial Revolution effectively created a new economic system, known as *Capitalism*. Although the overall effects of industrialisation were positive, there were many bad sides too, including the pollution and waste that was created as a side effect by the machines. Working practices became more regimented and many people worked long hours in factories performing repetitive, and sometimes dangerous or unhealthy jobs.

The fire-based steam engine was one of the most important inventions of the Industrial Revolution. The first practical steam engine was a machine made to pump water out of mines by the English inventor, Thomas Newcomen, in 1712. The steam engine design was later improved upon by the Scotsman, James

Watt. As well as powering the machines used in factories and mines, steam engines were also used in ships and locomotives, which improved transportation dramatically. It is interesting to note that in the Fire period fire-based energy devices became the standard and continued to advance, becoming faster, more powerful and more diversified. What began with the steam engine later morphed into petrol-based engines making transport faster and more flexible via cars, buses, trains and airplanes. Preparing meals went from gas and electric powered stoves to microwaves. Unfortunately, one of the negative aspects of the technological revolution has been the development of weapons, eventually weapons of potentially mass destruction. As happens in the Fire period, people become convinced that what is happening is good and progressive, and so it is now fully accepted that the weapons industry is one of the most prolific and needs further investment to be maintained.

The two world wars were fought in periods when the conjunctions were still in Fire signs. The destruction of European life during that 30-40 year period has been horrendous and has seriously damaged the European culture. What happened in the final stages of the Fire period was the development of atomic and then nuclear weapons. With the lessening of individual discrimination that comes in the final Earth period of decadence and dissolution, the threat of further human destruction is present and cannot be ignored.

United States of America Becomes a World Power

In the 19th & 20th centuries there has been a mass migration to America of 34 million people. free and liberal atmosphere upon which America was established provided ideal conditions for the diverse groups of immigrants.

There were not the fixed rules and expectations of the long-established countries and so people felt freer to develop and express their potential. The atmosphere was such that a feeling of *anything is possible* prevailed. This indeed became the best place where the fulfilment of one of the essential ideas of the cycle, the power of the individual, could be most fully expressed.

I certainly experienced this, being born in America in the 1940s and then passing through my youth in the 50s and 60s. The great potential for growth and expansion created a highly competitive environment. With many people, myself included, believing that anything is possible, it is easy now to see why there was serious competition in all aspects of life. Winners were held in high regard, while losers were ignored. Life was seen as a zero-sum game. There was great pressure to win, which for some acted as a positive incentive, but for others some negative responses arose. People could become quite depressed about not winning and then lose confidence in their abilities. Or an attitude could be assumed that one can do anything needed to win, including lying, cheating, taking drugs to enhance performance.

In the period after the Civil War (1870–1890) the US became the number one economic power in the world, exceeding the economies of India and China with their large populations and well-established trading histories. Key to American growth were inventions in applied technology. From 1860 to 1890, 500,000 patents were issued for new inventions. Companies such as AT&T helped build a good communication network. Scientists such as Nikola Tesla and Thomas Edison (who also co-founded General Electric) invented several electrical devices, providing a huge boost to power plants. There were many others.

Earth Period—Consolidation, Decline, Conclusion 1921- 2100

- The American Century
- Current Cultural Values
- Care for the Environment

The American Century

This term describes the 20th century as the United States largely dominated the politics, economics, and culture of the period. It is comparable to the description of the period 1815–1914 as Britain's Imperial Century. The United States' influence became especially dominant after the end of World War II, when only two superpowers remained, the United States and the Soviet Union. After the dissolution of the Soviet Union in 1991, the United States remained the world's only superpower. That power is clearly now being challenged.

In addition to its political influence, the United States also had a significant economic influence. Many states around the world would, over the course of the 20th century, adopted the economic policies of the Washington Consensus, sometimes against the wishes of their populations. The economic force of the US was powerful at the end of the century due to it being by far the largest economy in the world. It had large resources of minerals, energy resources, metals, and timber, a large and modernised farming industry and large industrial base. US systems were rooted in capitalist economic theory based on supply and demand, that is, production determined by customers' demands.

Earth and Fire Conjunctions

The first conjunction in Earth signs occurred in 1920, but then, as with all the transition periods, there were further conjunctions in Fire signs (1940, 1960 & 2000). From 2020 all the conjunctions will be in Earth signs until 2100. This means that there is not very much history for us to explore during this Earth period, but we will look at some of the trends that provides us an indication of the future direction in the Western European/US cultures.

What can be noted about the period beginning early in the 20th century is the cataclysmic effect of the two wars fought in Europe, marking the end of the Fire period, where millions of young people died, seriously weakening the European culture and its ability to face the challenges confronting it in the 21St century.

Current Western Cultural Values

We should not think that we have to imitate fully what happened in the past, but it is important to understand the prime elements that need to change and also what direction one needs to travel. We have many choices in today's society, freedom in that respect is full. The difficulty, though, is in making the right choices, the right decisions. The basis of our decisions is strongly influenced by our values, that which we hold to be dear. Our strong belief is that by following these values, we will achieve greater happiness, peace and fulfilment.

Values prompt our desires, and this in turn results in actions to attain the object of our desire. For example, one of the main natural human desires is for happiness. If you mistakenly believe that having money will make you happy, then one of your prime values will be wealth and you are likely to base your decisions on what you need to do to acquire more money and then, when embarked on such actions, how to maximise your return.

Most of the world's spiritual traditions define values as aspects of our true nature. Happiness is a natural value which is confirmed by the fact that everyone desires happiness. We make mistakes about what we think will make us happy, but it is clear that there is no one who desires to be unhappy. If we can give sufficient attention to our motives, and do not react mechanically to the popular ideas of the day, then a greater mindful awareness and finer discrimination is possible. The natural values can then act as our moral compass for making decisions.

What are the dominant cultural values in our society today? They are the same as they were at the end of the Roman Empire.

WEALTH, POWER, FAME AND PLEASURE

Ad agencies and media offer many programmes that stimulate desires for these values. The media are continually publishing lists of the 100 richest, the 100 most powerful, the 100 most famous and even the 100 sexiest. People who embrace these values firmly believe that they will lead to happiness, but indications are that this is not the case. A number of quantitative studies taken over the years have shown that beyond the very basic level, increased wealth does not bring increased happiness. An interesting parallel with the corrupt period at the end of the

Roman Empire was highlighted in a 2018 newspaper article about a Roman charioteer who was actually paid more than Christian Ronaldo, today's highest paid footballer. As is the case now, money was then the prime motivator. The problem now, as it was then, is EXCESS. We do not know when to stop. We do not know what is enough. The daily stream of newspaper articles and numerous scientific reports about the increasingly high degree of stress, depression, obesity, violence, broken families, drug addiction, self-harm, participation in perverted sexual practices—the list goes on—all seem to point to the fact that we are not following the right path, as happiness is not being gained.

Dealing with excess, knowing when to say no, is one of the most challenging situations for us today and it must be addressed if a more empathetic, ethical and healthy society is to be developed. This point is confirmed by the Dalai Lama in a conversation with Archbishop Desmond Tutu documented in *The Book of Joy*.

"The ultimate source of happiness is within us. Not money, not power, not status. Some of my friends are billionaires, but they are very unhappy people. Power and money fail to bring inner peace. Outward attainment will not bring real inner joyfulness. We must look inside.

"The problem is that our world and our education remain focused exclusively on external, materialistic values. We are not concerned enough with our inner values."

SUMMARY

What is the state of the Western European/American Culture Today?

- Major Values of the day are wealth, power, fame & pleasure. Excess has become the norm, for example, pornography and marijuana are now rapidly expanding businesses.
- A predominantly materialistic society dominated by scientific dogma that says if something cannot be quantifiably measured, it is illusion, it is not real.
- Increasing atheism with no spiritual education offered to many young people and little practised by adults.
- The collapse of the family as a cohesive unit causing increased stress and tension in young people raised without the love and discipline offered by both parents.
- Highly advanced technologically, resulting in increasing dependence on the internet and social media, with unregulated damaging material available even to young children.
- Continually growing disparity between rich & poor.
- Economically powerful, with the United States still first globally and some European countries still represented in G8, but both are slipping.
- Over-emphasis on my freedom & equality; my rights (not duties) & my idea is as good as yours, leading to a fragmentation of society.

- **Climate Change, which has become a global problem. The West, being the current dominant economic power, needs to make significant changes to its policies and actions that damage nature for the sake of economic gain.**

Another historical view which confirms the situation as presented and adds some other interesting factors comes from a marvellous work by (Lord) Stephen Green, *The Human Odyssey; East, West and the Search for Universal Values.* He too looks at other cultures with emphasis on those that comprise what he describes as Eurasia, a single land mass consisting of Europe, Asia, which in turn includes China and India and the Middle East.

In charting out the human odyssey or journey, here are three points of his presentation that complement the view we are offering, while adding a useful new perspective. They are:

- The impact of urbanisation on all cultures
- The view that China and India will become the major world powers in the 21st century
- The romantic, devotional movement that is emerging in response to the cult of the rational, scientific approach

Urbanisation

It is noted that most Eurasians now live in cities and by the end of the century virtually all will do so. As of 2008 50% of the world's population lived in cities. The rate is growing even more rapidly due to the mass movements in India and China An example given of dramatic growth in urbanisation is the city of

Shenzhen in China, which in 1984 was a rural town with a population of about 20,000. Fast forward to today and you will find a thriving metropolis of more than 10 million people.

The mass movement to a city is as a result of the transition from an agrarian to an urban based economy. In Europe only between 1-3% of the population now work in agriculture. Cities are the place where various aspects of culture seem to flourish, including trade, art and intellectual exchange. What also inevitably seems to occur is an emergence on the social stage of two classes of people, the rich traders and the working class. Generating and keeping the wealth by those involved in commercial enterprises generates an inevitable expanding gap between the rich and the poor, causing revolutions like the proletarian-led revolution of Marx. Democracy then replaces rule by aristocracy and the oligarchs and the rule of the majority becomes the established way. At the same time the wealth is still maintained by the few and the gap widens further. Great emphasis is placed on personal freedom which is the pattern we have seen most clearly in current Western culture. Another aspect of this is the strengthen of nationalisation- emphasis on my nation as opposed to union with others. '*Let's work to make my country great!*' is a familiar call.

Industrial urbanisation has resulted in a major disconnect with nature, which is a natural element of the more agrarian society. We are beginning to experience the global impact on the environment due to the way society has compromised nature for the sake of money and modern personal conveniences. This will be a real challenge going forward.

Climate Change—A Major Challenge

What follows has come from a range of sources, but the primary one is the most relevant book by Matthew Pye, *Plato Tackles Climate Change*. A great deal of research has been undertaken by Matthew and his team of supporters to clearly define the problem and to offer suggestions as to ways to deal with the major issues. Our approach follows quite closely both his definition of the problem and guidelines for the way forward.

Climate Change is an existential threat to human civilisation. This formidable danger has been intensifying in full view—all within our technologically advanced, literate and cultured society. We know the direction that all of the graphs are going in and we know the consequences of inaction and yet, since we resolved to combat the problem in 1992 , with the signing of the United Nations Framework Convention of Climate Change (UNFCCC) treaty, there has not even been one single year in which our greenhouse gas emissions have gone down.

The contradiction between our public declarations and the alarming course of the crisis can be seen at many different levels. The state we are in throws up all kinds of contradictions. The natural world has provided a formidable set of intransigent responses to the limited gestures we have made towards solving the problem.

On the issue of Climate Change, Andrew Marr in his classic work, *A History of the World*, offered a useful perspective as to the problems and the needed response. He highlights as one of the causes of the problems being experienced, the vast increase in the human population. The need for more fresh water and fertile soil to grow crops of food are paramount.

What is making the conditions even more challenging are the extent to which industry is polluting our rivers and oceans. The acidification of the oceans and overfishing are causing an environmental disaster. Add to this the atmospheric pollution being generated in the growing number of large cities which is causing a huge loss of human life. This is another 'failure of success' - excess, not knowing when to stop. The truth is that to cope with the failures of success we will need to change our behaviour and expectations.

Growing Power of China and India

Historically one can see that these two cultures have been very successful in the field of trade and commerce. The increasing shift of their cultures to a more urbanised, technologically driven culture is producing a new generation of well-educated resourceful individuals who will enable their respective economies to grow rapidly. More on this subject as we proceed.

Response to the Rational, Scientific Approach to Life

The other major compromise has been the excessive reliance on scientific thought to explain man's true nature, ignoring the spiritual dimension of humanity. The human spiritual journey as described by Stephen Green highlights how an original sense of unity has fallen into extreme diversity which means the journey is seen as an individual earthly journey which results in the inevitable pain of separation. More people, young and old, are now more willing to reconsider their values and the way forward.

6

CULTURAL CYCLES, CHINESE

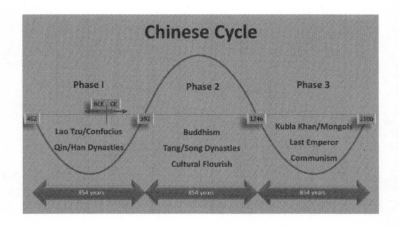

An ancient culture

By way of introduction we should note that there are existing artefacts in China from as far back as 1.7 million years. From that time there has been found a continual stream of artefacts highlighting the progress made in the transition from the ape-man to the modern man.

When I visited a Chinese History museum in Shanghai, I was amazed to see beautifully designed and produced pottery said to have been made 6-7000 years ago. That would be considered recent art in comparison with examples of Chinese Neolithic art from 10-11,000 BCE.

China, which is the oldest continuous civilisation in the world, has a strong tradition of rule by family-based dynasties. This marks out the importance and strength of family to the Chinese culture and their innate desire to be ruled by a single authority. This used to be the Emperor, then the General Secretary of the Communist Party of China and now the President of the People's Republic of China. Both of these factors are still present today.

Another fundamental element of Chinese culture has been harmony with nature. The Yellow River, known as the *Mother River* and *The Cradle of Chinese Civilisation* as its presence helps make possible the nurture and fertilisation of the land, on which China depends for its survival. Currently, due to the pressures of industrialisation, the view is that man must conquer nature.

Due to the vast expanse of land which comprises China there has existed many tribes with varying customs and capabilities, more than 50 ethnic groups. Many small wars were fought among these tribes to try to gain power. The first dynasty of China was the Xia Dynasty, which ruled from the 21st to the 16th centuries BCE. The next was the Shang Dynasty from around 1600 to 1046 BCE, which spread its influence over a much wider area. As it was fitting that the Emperor should have appropriate accommodation, extensive palaces were built during the reign of certain dynasties, especially the Shang. During each of these dynasties there was progress in art, agriculture, trade and the evolution of the written language.

From 1046–770 BCE China was ruled by the Western Zhou dynasty under the rule of 12 kings of 11 generations. From 770–476 BCE has been described as *'Spring and Autumn Period'* and also *'The Warring States Period'*.

Let us now look at the highlights of the three cycles.

CYCLE I - CHINA 462 BCE–392 CE

Air Period—A New Impulse 462 BCE–164 BCE

A great spiritual impulse

What arose in China, as part of the Axial Age, was a series of wise sages which would become the spiritual foundation of the current Chinese Culture. The march of the sages occurred in this sequence: Lao Tzu, Confucius, Mo-Tse, Mencius, Kwang Tse. You could also add a reference to the Buddha (573–483 BCE), for while he was born in India, his teaching truly flowered in China. These teachers and their disciples travelled all over China spreading the word. Some advised rulers, others opened schools or wrote books. The aim was to communicate a different message beyond the struggles for wealth and power that had dominated the Warring States Period. Some very brief highlights of each of the main teachers are:

Lao Tzu (604–515 BCE)

The founder of the Taoism philosophy which in essence teaches the unity of the creation. It is called the Way, an absolute, overriding Spirit, transcending time and space and encompassing the whole universe. There is only One.

Confucius (551– 479 BCE)

Thinking and acting virtuously leads to happiness, a view fully shared by Socrates. He emphasised the need and power of *'ren'* meaning benevolence and said that formalities and rites should be based on *ren*.

A great and lasting work attributed to him is called the Analects. It actually is comprised of individual records kept by Confucius's disciples of conversations between the Master and them, which were then collected and jointly edited by the disciples after Confucius's death in 479 BC.

Mo-Tse (470–390 BCE)

He advocated universal love and non-aggressiveness. He proposed the idea of *'love each other and you will benefit each other'*.

Mencius (370–290 BCE)

He admired Confucius and claimed to be his disciple. He taught that man was born with goodness and attached importance to the company people keep, the external influences. He was against tyranny and advocated a benevolent government as the only true way to rule.

Kwang Tse (369–286 BCE)

He followed the Taoist tradition by advocating conscious detachment from ego-based claims, living in the present moment, which enabled one to *live a peaceful life at any time*. From the end of the 5th century BCE until the imperial unification of

China in 221 BCE was called the age of the Warring States. It was during this period that a transformation took place in the social norms, economics and thought. It was a slow gradual process during the Air period, but it was unmistakably change.

Water Period—Expansion 283 BCE–14 CE
- China united under the Qin Dynasty, 221–206 BCE. The first emperor of a unified China was Qui Shi Huang.
- First Han Dynasty Rules, 206 BCE–9 CE A unified powerful empire emerged with growth in both the economy and the culture.
- The Han Dynasty period saw an expansion of Chinese territory and the establishment of a powerful imperial government.

China united under the Qin Dynasty 221–206 BCE
The first emperor of a unified China was Qui Shi Huang. He unified six powerful states, ordered that written language, weights, measures and currency be standardised, stipulated universal law to be the basis for rule, built the Great Wall of China, several palaces and the Terra Cotta Warriors. He died in 210 BCE and the dynasty collapsed four years later.

Han Dynasty Rules 206 BCE–220 CE
A unified powerful empire emerged with growth in both the economy and the culture. Confucianism became the state religion and Buddhism made its first inroads into China. Initially the capital was located in the western part of China and the

dynasty became known as the Western Han Dynasty. As with all periods in Chinese history unified rule for the long periods proved to be difficult. What emerged around 25 CE was a shift in power to the East and the Eastern Han Dynasty was born. It ruled for about 200 years, expanding the scope of trade, but then continual resistance from other kingdoms caused the dynasty to collapse in disarray.

Fire Period—Summit Reached; Decline Begins, 85 BCE–253 CE
- A shift in power to the East, and the Eastern Han dynasty was born. It ruled for about 200 years,
- The period from 9 CE–220 CE-known as the Golden Age for Chinese art, including music, literature, and poetry as well as the visual arts.

Economic prosperity, trade expands As early as the 4th century BCE commerce began expanding with Mongolia, with kingdoms of Central Asia, with Manchuria and Korea. Economic prosperity grew. During this Fire period there was even greater expansion of trade with silk being its major export. What emerged around 25 CE was a shift in power to the East, and the Eastern Han dynasty was born. It ruled for about 200 years, expanding the scope of trade, but continual resistance from other kingdoms eventually caused the dynasty to collapse in disarray. The period of this Han dynasty was known as the golden age for Chinese art, and included music, literature, and poetry as well as the visual arts. The Han dynasty also witnessed the development of tomb art, where art was created exclusively for funerals.

Earth Period—Consolidation; Decline; Conclusion, 154–362

Following the abdication of the last Han emperor in 220 China split into three kingdoms, the most powerful being the northern kingdom of Wei. Larger by area but much less populated was the kingdom of Wu in the south. For a time they were unified under the Jin dynasty but that did not last long and China eventually became fragmented into what was called the period of the Sixteen Kingdoms. During this period Buddhist writing emerged and many Buddhist scriptures were translated. The legacy of Buddhism in China has led to one of the most extensive collections of Buddhist art in the world.

Lessons learned from Cycle I

The prime influence of the period was the spiritual impulse received at the start, which encouraged people to be quieter and more reflective when making decisions. They were advised to live by natural values and to acknowledge more fully the unity of all humanity. This latter message was especially important considering China's long history of tribal conflicts. The unification of China was a gradual process, which took a long time with many setbacks, but it was proceeding step by step. What also emerged in this period were strong indications of the facility for harnessing manpower to make products that would be attractive in a wide range of markets. Their capabilities for expanding wealth by trade were clearly evident.

CYCLE II - CHINA 392–1246 CE

Air Period: A New Impulse 392–630 CE

The initial stage of this period was marked by continual turmoil, but gradually the Eastern Jin dynasty retained sovereignty over part of the country. What then began was a period of cultural advancement for China, their upward cycle. After more than 400 years of division China was reunited under the Sui dynasty. Buddhism took over from Taoism as the state philosophy. A comprehensive government administrative system was put in place that lasted for almost 1000 years. The ruling emperor was Wei Di, who lived a simple life, was concerned with the needs of people at all levels of society and took steps to expand the economy. Andrew Marr pointed out in *A History of the World* that the Sui dynasty in their brief rule of China, helped to build a rich rice-growing economy. One of the prime developments was the 1,550-mile network of canals, rivers and locks, known as the Grand Canal, which bound the Chinese culture together very tightly. Many believe this construction, completed between 605 and 611, was more important than the Great Wall. Significant trade was made possible and many cities grew up along the route. It made China's economic integration possible. After only three emperors, power was then taken over by the Tang dynasty.

Two periods of change
392–581

The initial stage of this period was marked by continual turmoil. It was later known as 'period of *Five Ethnic Minorities and Sixteen States.* The Eastern Jin Dynasty did retain sovereignty over part of the country. The next stage was the beginning of the cultural advancement of China, their upward cycle.

581–618

China was reunited under the Sui Dynasty. Buddhism took over from Taoism as the state philosophy. A comprehensive government administrative system was put in place that lasted for almost 1000 years. The ruling emperor Wei Di, who lived a simple life, was concerned with the needs of people at all levels of society and took steps to expand the economy. After only three emperors, power was then taken over by the Tang Dynasty.

Water Period: Expansion 630–928 CE

- The Tang Dynasty which lasted for almost 300 years marks a highpoint in Chinese culture.
- The Tang Code of Law was introduced
- Advances in Buddhism - links made to India, classic texts obtained and translated, confirmed as the spiritual guide for the Chinese people.
- An era of peace, prosperity and greater inclusiveness
- The Hanlin Academy founded, to encourage and promote the study of Arts and Science
- Many Japanese monks came to China to learn Buddhism. In 754, Jian Zhen becomes founder of the Japanese religion, Zen Buddhism.
- In 907, Liang Dynasty takes control, 15 reigns in succession.

The Tang dynasty, lasting almost 300 years, marked a highpoint in Chinese culture. The imperial sphere of influence reached Central Asia for the first time. The Tang Code of Law was developed in 624 and Buddhism continued to be the spiritual guide for the Chinese people of this period. Due to the era of peace and the long-term merging of nationalities, the society at the time became open and inclusive, with women playing an important role in society.

The national strength of Tang and the prosperity of economy was unprecedented in Chinese history. Their capital Chang'an became the biggest cosmopolis in the world at the time and an important link to the Western economy. Located at the Eastern end of the Silk Road, it experienced a continual flow of goods coming in from the West. In 750, the Hanlin Academy was founded, to encourage and support the study of Arts and Science. It continues to operate in China today.

Among the cultural communications with other countries, religion was the most active. Xuan Zang, a Tang monk who had learned Sanskrit, went to India and brought back 650 Buddhist classics texts, which he translated and distributed. Many Japanese monks came to China to learn Buddhism. In 754, Jian Zhen, a Tang dignitary, went to Japan to spread Buddhism and became the founder of the Japanese religion, Zen Buddhism. In 907, a Tang general dethroned the emperor and ascended the throne himself, changing the title of his reign to Liang. This led to a period where 15 reigns appeared in succession.

Fire Period: Summit Reached, Decline Begins 829–1107 CE

- In 960 the Song Emperor, Taizong, defeated all others and unified the country
- A high point of Chinese classical culture, including: a flowering of art; literature; scientific innovation.
- Neo-Confucianism adopted as the official state ideology.

The Song emperors presided over a period of economic expansion and technological innovation. One of the highlights of this period was the advancement in technology, building on four great Chinese inventions: the compass, gunpowder, paper making, and printing. They had all been invented hundreds of years before, but this period produced greatly refined versions, which were to become the inspiration for the West many years later.

Agricultural productivity was greatly improved by bringing more land under cultivation. New commercial crops were produced including sugar, tea, bamboo and hemp. Traditional crafts such as silk making, papermaking and ceramics flourished. Improved roads and canals boosted internal trade and with the invention of the compass, China was encouraged to sail further and trade over much greater distances.

All this mercantile activity required a more sophisticated financial system. The Song government inaugurated the first Chinese banks, minting many coins each year and eventually introducing the world's first paper money.

Earth Period: Consolidation, Decline, Conclusion 1107-1246
- Tribes of Mongols move into various parts of China
- Genghis Khan appointed leader of a Mongol Khanate who starts to attack and plunder the neighbouring regions.
- Genghis Khan's successors led Mongolian forces against the ruling Jin dynasty.

Tribes of Mongols lived in various parts of China and in 1206 they organised a clan conference and appointed Timujin as the leader of a Mongol Khanate. He was called Genghis Khan, and he started to attack and plunder the neighbouring regions. In 1219, he led a force of 200,000 men into an area that was part of India. After Genghis Khan died in 1226, his successors led Mongolian forces against the ruling Jin dynasty and destroyed them, thus severely weakening the Chinese Empire.

The Mongols made two further expeditions to the East, taking Russia, marching into Persia, and then Hungary and Austria between 1235 and 1244. From 1253 to 1259 they marched into Iran, Syria and Egypt. For a time both East and West were under one centralised rule, which actually promoted a high degree of economic and cultural exchanges.

Lessons learned from Cycle II

This was clearly an upward cycle for the Chinese culture with many aspects of its culture, including: economic; artistic; language; and education, all under the guidance of rulers who were guided by one of the three spiritual traditions; Buddhism,

Taoism, and Confucianism. Trade with the West via the Silk Road had opened up their view of other cultures, an important learning experience. The loss of power and control of their destiny at the latter stages of the period created an atmosphere of uncertainty, which is how they entered the period of the third cycle.

CYCLE III: CHINA, 1246–2100 CE

Air Period: A New Impulse, 1246-1544 CE

- The grandson of Genghis Khan, Kubla Khan, ruled Mongolia and China from 1260-1294.
- Large construction projects were undertaken, including the building of a new capital, present day Beijing.
- In 1279, the Yuan Dynasty exterminated the Southern Song and thus unified the country under a single ruler.
- The handicraft industry and domestic trade continued to do well in the early stages.
- Marco Polo visited China and wrote extensively about the true nature of the Chinese culture.
- Mongol rule lasted until popular uprisings brought down the Yuan dynasty, replaced by the Ming Dynasty.

This was the beginning of an inward or downward cycle for the Chinese culture. It is during this period that the general public in the West have come to know the Chinese and have formulated an often-mistaken view about their qualities and capabilities, without taking into account their achievements of the more distant past.

The grandson of Genghis Khan, Kubla Khan, ruled Mongolia and China from 1260-1294. Large construction projects were undertaken, including the building of a new capital, present day Beijing.

In 1279, the Yuan Dynasty exterminated the Southern Song and thus unified the country under a single ruler. The handicraft industry and domestic trade continued to do well in the early stages. Among the visitors to China at this time was Marco Polo from Italy, who made extensive tours of China and wrote an informative book, *Journey to the East and Records of Knowledge About the East*, in an attempt to arouse people in the West to the true nature of the Chinese culture. In his view, Beijing deserved the title of; 'capital of the world.' Mongol rule lasted until popular uprisings brought down the Yuan dynasty, which was replaced by the Ming dynasty.

Kublai Khan later sent huge armies to attempt to defeat Japan, Myanmar and Java, but they failed in the end. From 1294, when Kublai died, a period of fierce internal struggles took place, which saw the short reigns of nine emperors in 40 years. Towards the end of the Yuan Dynasty the whole nation was thrown into disorder with various warlord regimes taking up power.

Water Period: Expansion 1425-1782 CE

Ming Dynasty, 1368–1644
- Ming Dynasty (1368–1644) led by Zhu Yuanzhang won several decisive battles with warring factions and brought a greater sense of unity to the country.

- A search continued for an enlightened leader to help guide Chinese society to true peace and prosperity.
- Admiral Zheng was in charge of the largest navy in the world at the time which made many expeditionary voyages, some lasting more than two years.
- Ming Dynasty suffered a number of defeats forcing the Ming government to make continual compromises.

In 1368, Zhu Yuanzhang proclaimed himself Emperor of the Ming Dynasty. After winning several decisive battles with warring factions, he was able to bring a greater sense of unity to the country. To arrogate all the power to himself, Zhu Yuanzhang eliminated a large number of people who might pose a threat to his authority. By these actions he demonstrated that he was not the type of enlightened leader who was needed to help guide Chinese society to true peace and prosperity. This was the ideal put forth by their three spiritual guides of China; Confucius, Lao Tzu and Buddha.

Admiral Zheng

He was in charge of the largest navy in the world at the time. He mustered a vast fleet of more than 200 ships, so large they could each carry 1000 passengers. Zheng commanded expeditionary treasure voyages during the period from 1405 to 1433, many lasting more than two years.

Detailed maps were made of these voyages, many of which found their way into the hands of Western explorers who followed many years later. During these exploratory tours of the world he made stops in India, Arabia and Africa and offered tribute to the natives as a way of learning more about the state of life in these locations and to set in motion cultural and economic exchanges. One of his other functions was to publicise the power and influence of the Ming Dynasty. The Ming Dynasty suffered a number of defeats by various Mongol-based tribes, forcing the Ming government to make continual compromises. In the late 1500s, as trade by sea grew, battles also broke out with Japanese pirates, yet another level of conflict which was gradually weakening the might and the will of the Ming Dynasty.

While all this was happening, there was quietly going on in the background a period of cultural enlightenment. What emerged was a new school of thought called *The Theory of the Mind.* The essence of this school of philosophy are the concepts of *innate knowledge* and *mind is reason.* It was a move towards a new view of the individual, stressing the fineness of man's nature and offering respect for individual thinking. This was far removed from the common Chinese view that the individual must be obedient and follow the directions of the leader.

Fire Period: Summit Reached, Decline Begins 1723-2000

Qing Dynasty, 1644–1911
- Qing Dynasty takes power, but the overall power of China weakens
- First Opium War, 1840 Western countries forced China to open its doors by smuggling opium into the country.

- The Second Opium War, 1856–1860 involving the British, French, Russia and the United States.
- China relegated to a semi-colonial status of the Western powers.

Following a peasants' revolt, which captured Beijing and overthrew the Ming Dynasty, the Qing Dynasty took power, a position it would hold until 1911. Due mainly to weak incompetent leadership, China became embroiled in continual internal struggles, which weakened its overall power at a time when Western powers were starting to make in-roads into the East, initially for the purposes of trade, but later to exert their authority and to colonise to build their empires.

First Opium War, 1840

Western countries forced China to open its doors by smuggling opium into the country. In 1840, the British naval fleet seized Xiamen, Shanghai and other port cities and sailed up the Yangtze River to attack Nanjing. In 1842, the Qing government was forced to sign a treaty which ceded Hong Kong to the British as well as having to pay a huge sum of money. Later the US, France, Spain and Italy used force to obtain major trade concessions.

The Second Opium War 1856–1860

This conflict involved the British and French allied fleet supported by Russia and the United States, forced more concessions including the loss of large areas of territory. China was relegated to a semi-colonial status of the Western powers. In an attempt to learn from the Western capitalist countries, the

Qing government set up a Westernisation Movement designed to study and adapt Western economic, political, educational and military methods. The movement, which continued for more than 30 years, failed to achieve its aim of establishing greater prosperity.

Earth Period: Consolidation, Decline, Conclusion 1921-2100

- A major revolt occurred which brought down the Qing government and the Republic of China was founded.
- Communist Party of China (CPC) founded in 1921.
- Challenging time from 1937–1945, when China struggled against Japanese aggression at great financial, cultural and human loss.
- The People's Republic of China founded in 1949 which signalled the beginnings of dramatic economic growth.

The Revolution of 1911

Reacting to a plan to give authority for railway construction in China to foreign companies, a major revolt occurred which brought down the Qing government, ending more than 2000 years of dynastic rule in China. The Republic of China was founded in 1912. Following unjust treaties imposed on China after the First World War, a national protest arose, a movement involving people from all walks of life. Among the new ideologies investigated were the theories of Marxism and Leninism.

Communist Party of China (CPC)

This was founded in 1921, with Mao Zedong as its leader and through sustained effort became the ruling party in China. There followed a challenging time from 1937–1945, when China struggled against Japanese aggression at great financial, cultural and human loss.

The People's Republic of China 1949

This signalled the beginnings of dramatic economic growth for China as the government established a pattern of 5-year plans to grow the economy and to regain a place as one of the world's powers. One period of great turmoil was experienced in the 1960s, when Mao Zedong erroneously initiated a cultural revolution to discard all Chinese cultural history, called 'The Old'. The reaction against the movement grew in strength and in 1978, a new leader was appointed, Deng Xiaoping, who was an inspiration and an agent for great reform that has put China back on track to becoming a major power in the world. An economic study carried out by Price Waterhouse Coopers in 2017, entitled *The World in 2050*, predicted that China, currently the second largest economy in the world, will be number one by 2050, if not sooner.

LESSONS LEARNED FROM CYCLE III

It had been a difficult time for China, as the ancient system of Dynasty rule was not able to cope with the changing world order. Initially, there were many internal conflicts between various sects, each seeking to maximise its power and control. The influence of their spiritual guides continued to be present in the early stages of the cycle to encourage the leaders to look beyond their own self-interest. What made matters difficult for China was the influx of Western power into their domain. The Western powers were in a positive phase of their cycle in the 16–19th centuries and when in conflict with China, they prevailed. As noted, there are overlap periods between the changes in the stages of a cycle. What is happening now is an awakening of the energy and confidence of China so it can move from its more passive cycle to one where its rich culture can once again be manifest.

Current Chinese challenges—Absolute Rule

President Xi Jinping has been granted ruling power for life, an attempt to replicate absolute rule of the Emperor that has dominated China's history. While the right to rule is there, the agreement and support of the people is not as uniform as it was in the past. The power of the individual is growing in China, admittedly slower than in other cultures, but it is happening. One of the reasons it is becoming an issue is the availability of global technology enabling people in even remote rural areas of China to learn about what is happening in other parts of their country and around the world. Even as recently as 40 years ago discipline was imposed on the rural areas through the presence of regional leaders of the Party who represented the absolute authority. The amount of information communicated to these areas was limited. This has changed.

One area where the Chinese Government is not fully controlling is access to online information. They are making a strong attempt to stifle debate and free intellectual exchange, but the odds are against them being able to continue along the lines of absolute rule. Thirty years ago, the democratic challenge that had a bloody end in the streets of Tiananmen Square is now strongly censored by the Government. There will be more challenges and gradually there will be changes, but the rigidity of the earth period will make it a long drawn-out affair.

China's population

With a population estimated at 1.4 billion, China ranks as the world's most populous country. With the world's population approximately 7.6 billion, China represents 20 percent of the people on Earth. However, policies the government has implemented over the years may well result in China losing that top ranking to India. One example which demonstrated the attempt to exercise absolute control was the one-child rule which was created in 1979 by Chinese leader Deng Xiaoping to temporarily limit communist China's population growth. When the one-child policy was adopted, China's population was about 972 million. China was expected to achieve zero population growth by 2000, but it actually achieved that seven years earlier. It finally ended in 2015 when some of the negative impacts were finally acknowledged. The average age in China is now 37 years, resulting in a lack of young people needed to do much of the practical work and an increasing burden and cost in caring for older people.

As a result of the one-child rule the amount of elderly in the population, which was 14 percent in 2015, is expected to grow to 44 percent in 2050. This will put a strain on social services in the country and may mean that it invests less in bolstering its economy. The other negative impact was that many parents preferred to have a boy as their only child, who they felt would be better able to support them in later years. As a result, the ratio of male births to female births is much higher in China than the world average. In recognition of the negative impact the rule was changed in 2016 to become the two-child rule.

In a recent 48 Group Club *China Global Impact* newsletter, this text appeared about recently passed legislation on a number of tax incentives for community-based elderly care, childcare and household services:

> *Between June 2019 and the end of 2025, earnings of the above-mentioned services will be exempted from value-added tax (VAT) and enjoy a 10 percent deduction in taxable income. Those providing real estate or land for the relevant services will be exempted from deed tax, property tax, urban land use tax and six types of fees including registration fee for real estate.*

Economic Growth & Control

As noted, China is predicted to become the number one global economic power by 2050, within the current cycle. Currently, according to the IMF report, the United States is the world's largest economy with a GDP of $20.4 trillion. Since China's transition to a more market-based economy through privatisation and deregulation, the country has seen its ranking increase from ninth in 1978 to second place in 2018, with a GDP of $13.4 trillion.

It is interesting to note that the European Union countries combined have GDP of more than $18 trillion, more than China. To continue its growth in world trade, a weaker European

Union would benefit their case. The weakness is also making investment in European countries more attractive. While it is not expected that the Chinese will try to colonise the West as they proceed to greater power, they will exercise more economic control. Countries like Spain, Greece and Italy have already been targeted.

China's Belt and Road Initiative (BRI) is a policy aimed at improving China's connectivity with the rest of the world. It is intended to help close the development gap between wealthy Beijing and China's eastern states, and the underdeveloped west of China. The idea is to promote development and economic cooperation along five corridors out of China: land routes through Central Asia to Europe; to the Middle East, and Southeast Asia; and sea routes connecting Chinese ports to Europe and to the South Pacific. At its simplest, it is a policy for Chinese investment in infrastructure including ports, rail, bridges, oil and gas pipelines, and roads within China, across Europe and Asia and throughout the Indo-Pacific area. Outside of China the BRI has been interpreted as a means of Beijing buying influence among its poorer neighbours. There are some concerns about developing countries involved in the BRI taking on unsustainable levels of debt in the form of Chinese concessional loans for major projects making these countries beholden to China.

Another similar example of China's long-range economic planning is the huge investment it is making in Africa. About 10 years ago I was told of China's 20-year plan for economic development in Africa. With a population of more than I billion, a vast supply or natural resources and a great need for improved infrastructure, they are an ideal prospect. In a BBC television news show in 2016 a reporter interviewed an African businessman regarding the active economic intervention of China in Africa who said that this is the same approach taken by European powers for hundreds of years. He then said, *"The only difference being that the Chinese are not trying to convert us."*

One observation made by a fellow businessman who has experience in the Chinese market is that a socialist market economy does not need the constant growth in GDP and in profits that a capitalist market economy needs. Democracy with Chinese characteristics will develop slowly, and the socialist market economy will be the main feature instead of separate state-owned-enterprises and private sector businesses. They will become more unified.

In recent years there has been a growing recognition of the future economic potential of countries other than the dominant Western countries. The current prime players are called the BRICS; Brazil, Russia, India, China and South Africa. At the gathering of the leaders of these countries in 2017, President Xi Jinping applauded the degree of collaboration. He quoted an ancient Chinese proverb: *"A partnership forged with the right approach defies geographical distance; it is thicker than glue and stronger than metal and stone."*

China's Spiritual Tradition

An important question about China is when and how their very fine spiritual tradition will be regenerated. During the inward cycle, which China has been engaged in for more than 700 years, that is the time for refreshment of the spiritual tradition. As we have seen in the current cycle in India, where there have been over the last two hundred years many examples of sages offering spiritual teaching both in India and globally as well. In China the three traditions of Buddhism, Taoism and Confucian philosophy are deeply ingrained in the Chinese culture and despite the current Communist aversion to spirituality they will gradually become manifest in this Earth period of the cycle, in response to the growing rigidity.

7

CULTURAL CYCLES, INDIAN

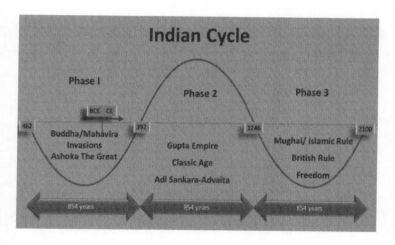

INDUS VALLEY CIVILISATION

Modern excavations and research reveal that the Indic tradition has an unbroken cultural continuity that goes back at least 5000 years. Vedic India is one of the oldest documented civilisations on earth and through its religion, culture and Sanskrit language, has had a profound influence on Europe and much of the world. Considered a cradle of civilisation, the Indus Valley Civilisation, which spread and flourished in the north-western part of the Indian subcontinent from 3300 to 1300 BCE, was the first major civilisation in South Asia. A sophisticated and technologically advanced urban culture developed in the Mature Harappan period, from 2600 to 1900 BCE. This civilisation collapsed at the start of the second millennium BCE and was later followed by what was called the Iron Age Vedic Civilisation.

The Vedic Period

The Aryan influence, some scholars claim, gave rise to what is known as the Vedic Period in India (c. 1700–500 BCE) characterised by a pastoral lifestyle and adherence to the religious texts known as the Vedas. Society became divided into four classes (*varnas*) now popularly known as 'the caste system'. The highest class is comprised of the *Brahmana* (priests and scholars), then the *Kshatriya* (warriors and kings), *Vaishya* (farmers and merchants), and the *Shudra* (labourers). There is now an even lower class, the *Dalits*, or those formerly described as untouchables, who handle meat and waste, though there is some debate over whether this class existed in antiquity. At first it seems this caste system was merely a reflection of one's occupation, but in time it became more rigidly and mistakenly interpreted to be hereditary and therefore one could not change caste or marry into a caste other than one's own.

The native spiritual tradition of India is the deepest and broadest in history. It is important to note that Hinduism is different from the typically understood Western view of religion. There is no one single historical point of origin, scripture or prophet which is generally associated with a religion. It is rather an exploration and a rich repository of the varieties of spiritual experiences. It is grounded in acceptance of the ceaseless journey of the *pilgrim soul* as a matter not of belief, but of fact, and not of humans limited to a single life.

While the beliefs that characterised the Vedic Period are considered much older, it was during this time that they became systematised as the tradition of *Sanatana Dharma*, the Eternal Order, which is described as the basis of Hinduism. The name Hindu is believed to derive from the Indus or Sindus River, where worshippers were known to gather, hence *Sindus*, which became *Hindus*.

The underlying tenet of *Sanatana Dharma* is that there is an order and a purpose to the universe and to human life, and, by accepting this order and living in accordance with it one will experience life as it is meant to be properly lived. While *Sanatana Dharma* is considered by many to be a polytheistic spiritual tradition consisting of many gods, it is actually monotheistic, in that it holds there is one supreme reality, *Brahman*, the Self, who because of an absolute nature, cannot be fully apprehended save through a deep internal silence, when the body, mind and emotions are all still. It is at this point that there is realisation of the unity between *Brahman* and our pure, perfect internal nature, called *Atman*. It is *Brahman* which decrees the eternal order and maintains the universe through it. This belief in an ordered universe reflects the stability of the society in which it grew and flourished.

During the Vedic Period governments became centralised and social customs integrated fully into daily life across the region. It is unclear when some of the great religious and literary works of the *Puranas*, the *Mahabharata*, and *Ramayana* were actually written, but it seems very likely that it was during the first inward cycle of our study i.e. the period from 462 BCE to 392CE.

CYCLE I: INDIA, 462 BCE–392CE

Air Period—A New Impulse 462–164 BCE
- Buddhism and Jainism were introduced into India by Buddha (563–483 BCE) and Mahavira (550–450 BCE). Much work was also started on the development of Hindu law books, epic literature and six systems of philosophy, including the *Sankhya* system introduced by Rishi Kapila.
- India was invaded by the Persian Empire led by Cyrus, 530 BCE.
- The invasion of Northern India by Alexander the Great, 327–325 BCE.
- India was ruled by the Mauryan Empire, 322–185 BCE. The highlight of the period was the rule of Ashoka the Great (269–232 BCE).
- Buddhist and Jain influence at its highest level 200 BCE

−200 CE.

- Versions of sacred scripture such as *Bhagavad Gita* were produced in Sanskrit.
- Gupta Dynasty begun its rule of India from 3rd century CE, the beginning of a new era.

A New Spiritual Impulse

In the sixth century BCE, the religious reformers, Mahavira (540–468 BCE) and Buddha (563–483 BCE), broke away from mainstream interpretation of *Sanatana Dharma* to eventually create their own religions of Jainism and Buddhism. The pragmatic teaching of the Buddha caused a doctrinal revolution as discounting scriptural authority, divine realms, and the supernatural in favour of seeking salvation through reflection, meditation and the complete erasure of delusion and false identity. The message from Mahavira was also concerned with less dependence on the material realm, which could be helped by practising personal austerities. Both approaches introduced monastic institutions to Indian society. The Buddhist injunction against killing was extended by the Jains to the whole animal kingdom, including insects.

Buddhism

Now a world religion, which arose in and around the ancient Kingdom of Magadha, now Bihar, and is based on the teachings of Siddhartha Gautama who was deemed a *Buddha* (Awakened One). Buddha's teaching strives to help overcome false identification and break away from the cycle of rebirth. Buddha advocated a Middle Way, one which was aimed at steering a path between the extremes of worldliness and asceticism. It offers an Eightfold Path of ethical living applicable to all, a spiritual way which does not require the intervention of a priest or prayers to gods. Buddhism spread outside Magadha in the Buddha's lifetime. With the reign of the Buddhist Mauryan Emperor Ashoka, the Buddhist community split into two branches: the *Mahasamghika* and the *Sthaviravada*, each of which spread throughout India and split into numerous sub-sects. During this period of an inward cycle, Buddhism was a major contributor to the spiritual rejuvenation of India and although in a later cycle it was less popular in India, it then rose up to become a major element in the Chinese spiritual tradition.

Jainism

Mahavira was originally born as Prince Vardhamana in North-east India, the son of King Siddhartha and Queen Trishala, who were members of the *Kshatriya* (warrior) caste and followers of the teachings of Parshva. When Prince Vardhamana reached thirty years of age, not long after the death of both his parents, he left the royal palace to live the life of an ascetic, or a *sadhana* (one who renounces all worldly pleasures and comforts). He spent twelve and a half years subjecting himself to extremely long, arduous periods of fasting and meditation. Eventually his efforts bore fruit, and he attained enlightenment, and therefore was later called Mahavira (from *maha*, great, and *vira*, hero).

From that day forward Mahavira taught the path he had discovered to other seekers. His teaching formed an aspect of the Jainism tradition which exists till this day. Mahavira added the principle of chastity to the four Jain principles already established by Parshva in the 8th/9th century BCE i.e. no violence, no lying, no stealing, no possessions. He created a large and loyal monastic/ascetic/mendicant community inspired by his teaching. Over the next centuries the Jain community grew and spread to central and western parts of India.

These changes in religion were part of a wider pattern of social and cultural upheaval which resulted in the formation of city states and the rise of powerful kingdoms, such as the Kingdom of Magadha under the ruler Bimbisara. Increased urbanisation and wealth attracted the attention of Cyrus, ruler of the Persian Empire, who invaded India in 530 BCE and initiated a campaign of conquest in the region. Ten years later, under the reign of his son, Darius I, northern India, the regions corresponding to Afghanistan and Pakistan today, was firmly under Persian control and the inhabitants of that area subject to Persian laws and customs. One possible consequence of this was an assimilation of Persian and Indian religious beliefs which some scholars point to as an explanation for further religious and cultural reforms.

Persia held dominance in northern India until the invasion of Alexander the Great in 327 BCE. One year later, Alexander had defeated the Achaemenid Empire and conquered part of the Indian subcontinent. Again, foreign influences were brought to bear on the region, giving rise to the Greco-Buddhist culture which impacted all areas of culture in northern India from art and religion to dress. Statues and reliefs from this period depict Buddha, and other figures, as distinctly Hellenic in dress and pose.

Water Period—Expansion 283 BCE–4 CE

- The Mauryan Empire; Chandragupta's son, Bindusara, reigned between 298 and 272 BCE.
- His son was Ashoka the Great (304–232 BCE), under whose rule the empire flourished at its height.

The Mauryan Empire—Ashoka the Great

Following Alexander's departure from India, the Mauryan Empire (322–185 BCE) rose under the reign of Chandragupta Maurya (322–298 BCE) and by the end of the third century BCE, it ruled over almost all of northern India. Chandragupta's son, Bindusara, reigned between 298 and 272 BCE and extended the empire throughout the whole of India. His son was Ashoka the Great (304–232 BCE), under whose rule the empire flourished at its height. Eight years into his reign, Ashoka conquered the eastern city-state of Kalinga, which resulted in a death toll numbering over 100,000. Shocked at the destruction and death, Ashoka embraced the teachings of the Buddha and embarked on a systematic programme advocating Buddhist thought and principles. He established many monasteries and provided many public works for the sake of the community, such as free hospital care, wells and drinking water for cattle, which were acts of social compassion. He followed the Buddhist guidelines which advocated a moral political economy. His ardent support of Buddhist values eventually caused a strain on the government both financially and politically. Even his grandson, Sampadi, heir to the throne, opposed his policies. By the end of Ashoka's reign, the government treasury was severely depleted through his regular religious donations and, after his death, the empire declined rapidly.

Fire Period—Summit Reached, Decline Begins 85BCE–253 CE

- In Northwest India, a philosopher-king arose in the form of Menander, (165/155–130 BCE).
- More invasions, which splintered the country into many small kingdoms.
- Increased trade with the Roman Empire.
- A wise king of this era was Kanishka, whose prosperous empire, stretched from Central Asia to the south of India.
- Literature began to develop a more classic form with greater attention given to Sanskrit.
- Under Kanishka's direction efforts made to integrate the teachings of Hinduism and Buddhism.

End of the Age of Invasions; Beginning of the Gupta Dynasty

In the northwest of India, a Philosopher-King arose in the form of Menander (115-90 BCE), from the Bactrian Greek colony which was the Greek residue in India following the exploits of Alexander. Menander was converted to Buddhism, expanded their area of control and applied many of their principles in his rule. He did, however, continue to engage in warfare and was finally killed in battle.

A further phase in the age of invasions was initiated in the first century CE by the Kushans, who emerged from the Mongolian heartlands. This era also saw the increase of trade with Rome following Augustus Caesar's conquest of Egypt in 30 BCE. Egypt had been India's most constant partner in trade in the past. A wealth of fine sculpture from this period has been found. Some of it had a Hellenistic look to it, which was explained as a cultural product of the extensive Kushan trade with the Roman Empire.

The most well-known and wise king of this era was Kanishka, whose prosperous empire, stretched from Central Asia south into India as far as Benares. The areas of Gandhara and Mathura were rich trading locations where art flourished. Literature began to develop a more classic form and Sanskrit, in which Kanishka himself is said to have composed a long poem, acquired a definitive role. The reputation of great Buddhist scholars such as Asvagosha and Nagarjuna became part of the Kushan legacy. Chanaka, said to have been the first luminary of Ayurveda, was Kanishka's physician.

Hinduism was quietly practised in many parts of India. Under Kanishka's direction a council was called to try to resolve the differences between Hinduism and Buddhism. What emerged was a version of Buddhism called Mahayana, the greater vehicle. It incorporated Vedantic mysticism and popularised the practice of yoga. This became more in evidence in this final Earth period. Sanskrit also came into greater prominence, replacing the Pali language, which was the language of earlier Buddhist literature.

Earth Period: Consolidation, Decline, Conclusion 154-362
- The end of Kushan rule.
- The beginnings of the Gupta Empire with first ruler being Sri Gupta. The fruits of his rule became manifest in the initial period of the next cycle.

The Kushan rule came to an end as a result of the invasions from the Sassanid dynasty of Persia in the third century CE. In this period the seeds were planted for the rise of the Gupta Empire, with the initial rule by Sri Gupta from 240 to 280 CE. As Sri Gupta is thought to have been of the *Vaishya*, merchant class, his rise to power in defiance of the caste system was unprecedented. The fruits of his rule will be discussed in the next stage when the outward cycle begins.

Lessons Learned from Cycle I

This inward cycle, like those of other cultures, involved a quiet and continual effort to regenerate and develop further the spiritual dimension of the culture. Great variations arose as to the ruling empires, with strong foreign intervention at times that influenced trade as well as the development of the arts, language and literature. The increasing role of Sanskrit during this period is an important aspect of Indian cultural advancement, which we will discuss in more detail as we proceed. While the Vedas were clearly from an earlier period, as were the initial versions of sacred works such as the *Puranas, Upanishads,* and classical spiritual stories such as the *Mahabharata* and *Ramayana,* it seems that during this first cycle versions of these works emerged in Sanskrit which were accessible to a wider audience. Here is some background on the development of one of the most important spiritual contributions of the Indian culture to the world, the *Bhagavad Gita, The Song of the Lord.* It has been translated into 80 languages worldwide, so its impact has been global. It is one chapter in the *Mahabharata* which is the longest single poem in the world with over 100,000 verses Historians formerly postulated an "epic age" as the milieu of this spiritual jewel, but now recognise that the texts went through multiple stages of development over centuries. The existing texts of these epics are believed to belong to the post-Vedic age, between 400 BCE and 400 CE.

Introduction to the Teaching of the Bhagavad Gita

The guidance offered in the *Bhagavad Gita* is designed to help one live a happy, productive and peaceful life, as well as at the same time discovering our true nature. This essential nature, which is said in the *Gita* to be the same for all, can be reached through different paths. This view, that there are many paths to the same goal, is an inclusive approach, differing from some religious and philosophic traditions who espouse exclusivity; ours is the only right way, we are right-you are wrong.

The *Gita* addresses three main spiritual paths which reflect the inherent nature of the human being. They are the:

- Way of Knowledge (Jnana Yoga)
- Way of Love/Devotion (Bhakti Yoga)
- Way of Selfless Action (Karma Yoga)

A fourth way is also examined, one which is accessible by followers of any path:

- Way of Meditation (Dhyana/Raja Yoga)

In the *Gita*, **Krishna,** the living embodiment of the omniscient omnipresent Lord, fulfils this role. Representing all of us, the people of the society, is **Arjuna**, a great warrior who is confused and very uncertain about how to proceed. He has a lot of questions which are the same questions asked by all of us. The place where the teaching of the *Gita* is revealed is a battlefield. The war being fought came at a time when discrimination and wisdom were in decline and, according to Indian tradition, when this happens an Avatar, a Divine Teacher, is born to remind the people of the main principles of life. The symbolism of the battlefield is an analogy of the common human struggle. The specific challenges are:

Forces of ignorance	vs	*Forces of light & knowledge*
Ego-centric decisions	vs	Full discrimination
Habitual/mechanical action	vs	Conscious action
Me against them	vs	We, we are one
Duality of pleasure & pain	vs	Equanimity
Transient	vs	Eternal
Vices-lust, greed & anger	vs	Love, justice & freedom
Untruth	vs	Truth
Vengeful War	vs	Harmlessness

Arjuna explores with Krishna the nature of the obstacles blocking his path and the different ways he can remove them and thus serve society more fully and at the same time realise his full potential. Remember, Arjuna represents all of us.

We are reminded on numerous occasions during their conversation that our essential nature is one of Unity. The only reason that this is not recognised, accepted and lived is that the knowledge is covered over by ignorance, like the clouds which cover and block access to the ever-shining sun. We create our clouds through our ideas about the creation; the names and forms we impose on objects; the likes and dislikes which establish a fixed attitude towards people, things, events etc. We become attached and identified with these ideas, taking them for reality. The mind is therefore the cause of the ignorance, but once it becomes purified it becomes the instrument for liberation. The mind becomes purified through letting go of the false and accepting that which is true and real. This can only be achieved when the mind is still, a topic that is returned to again and again. Understanding and practicing i.e. living the guidelines offered by the *Bhagavad Gita,* is an important part of the Way Forward in today's world.

CYCLE II: INDIA, 392–1246 CE

Air Period—A New Impulse 392–630 CE
- Gupta Empire (240–550) ruled, the Classic Age of India.
- Science and art began to flourish in this period.
- Buddhism, supported by the Gupta empire, coexisted with Hinduism.
- Harshavardhan (590–647) ruled the region for 42 years, a patron of the arts and a devout Buddhist.

The Gupta Empire Rules
During the Gupta period India was united in peace and prosperity, and there was a flourishing of scientific and artistic endeavours. The period called the Classical Age of India refers to the time when much of the Indian subcontinent was united

under the Gupta Empire. This period was marked by extensive achievements in science, technology, engineering, art, dialectic, literature, logic, mathematics, astronomy, religion, and philosophy that crystallised the elements of what is generally known as Hindu culture.

The *Puranas* of Vyasa were compiled during this period and the famous caves of Ajanta and Ellora, with their elaborate carvings and vaulted rooms, were also begun. Kalidasa the poet and playwright wrote his masterpiece *Shakuntala* and the *Kamasutra* was also written, or compiled from earlier works, by Vatsyayana. Varahamihira explored astronomy at the same time as Aryabhatta, the mathematician, made his own discoveries in the field and also recognised the importance of the concept of zero, which he is credited with inventing.

The Gupta period marked a watershed of Indian culture. The Guptas performed Vedic sacrifices to legitimise their rule, but they also patronised Buddhism, which continued to provide an alternative to Brahmanical orthodoxy. The military exploits of the first three rulers—Chandragupta I, Samudragupta, and Chandragupta II—brought much of India under their leadership and helped unify the culture. Chandragupta I, who ruled from 320 to 330, provided an era of peace and security which enabled the culture to begin to grow. His successor Samudragupta, who ruled from 330 to 386 with great wisdom, brought together smaller states and made them into a cohesive unit, the Gupta Empire.

While Samudragupta did not impose any particular religion, he did actively encourage people to lead an honest and principled life. He also actively promoted the arts, literature, science, music and the study of the Sanskrit language. The latter work then gave people of the time greater access to the fine Indian spiritual teaching which was not seen as religious dogma, but as philosophic guidance with a practical application.

Chandragupta II (380–415), also known by his title Vikramaditya, was one of the most powerful emperors of the Gupta Empire in northern India. He continued the expansionist policy of his father Samudragupta and extended the Gupta empire from the Indus River in the west to the Bengal region in the east, and from the Himalayan foothills in the north to the Narmada River in the south. He surrounded himself with poets as well as members of religious orders. The noted Sanskrit poet Kalidasa, one of India's greatest, was part of his court. All religions enjoyed equal rights and privileges and from time to time he would invite learned people from different religions to meet for discussions which would enable each to better understand and appreciate the other.

Science and political administration also reached new heights during the Gupta era. Strong trade ties made the region an important cultural centre and established it as a base that would influence nearby kingdoms and regions in Burma, Sri Lanka, maritime Southeast Asia, and Indochina.

As the founder of the Gupta Empire defied orthodox Hindu thought, it is not surprising that the Gupta rulers advocated and propagated Buddhism as the national belief and this is the reason for the plentitude of Buddhist works of art, as opposed to Hindu, at sites such as Ajanta and Ellora.

Water Period—Expansion 630–928 CE
- Flourishing of science and spirituality.
- The 8th century, a spiritual renewal led by Adi Sankara.

The Gupta empire was replaced by the rule of Harshavardhan (605–647 BCE) who ruled the region for 42 years. A literary man of considerable accomplishments, Harshavardhan was a patron of the arts and a devout Buddhist who forbade the killing of animals in his kingdom. He did, however, recognise the necessity to sometimes kill humans in battle. He was a highly skilled military tactician who was only defeated in the field once in his life. Under his reign, Northern India flourished, but his kingdom collapsed following his death.

In 712, the Muslim General Muhammed bin Qasim conquered Sind, a province in the west of India and eventually established himself in the region of modern-day Pakistan. The Islamic Sultanates rose in this area and spread northwest. The disparate world views of the religions, which now contested each other for acceptance in the region and the diversity of languages spoken, made the unity and cultural advances, such as were seen in the time of the Guptas, difficult to reproduce.

Revitalising of the Indian Spiritual Tradition—Adi Sankara

In the 8th century, Adi Shankara travelled across the Indian subcontinent to propagate the doctrine of *Advaita Vedanta*, a philosophy of Unity and Non-dualism (*Advaita A*=not, *dvaita*=two; not two, one). He wrote commentaries on the ancient Sanskrit scriptures called *Upanishads* and other sacred texts such as the *Bhagavad Gita* and *Brahma Sutras* by the time he was 16 years old. He then travelled around the country debating with and converting religious and philosophy proponents of other schools of thought. In the four corners of the Indian subcontinent he founded *mathas* or 'monasteries,' each to be run by one of his four main disciples. The system of four disciples or teachers, Shankaracharayas as they were called, continues today.

By the 8th century symbols of Hindu gods became more in evidence, with a corresponding reduction of Buddhist symbols of worship. Although Buddhism did not disappear from India for several centuries, its position was weakened within the culture, which eventually led to its decline.

Sanskrit—The Spiritual Language

When the Gupta kings decided not to encourage any particular religion and instead gave respect to all, this allowed the depth and beauty of Sanskrit to be re-discovered. The past glory of the language was not only revived using the works of Panini and Patanjali, but earlier Sanskrit classic literature like the *Ramayana* and *Mahabharata* were given a new emphasis, making them relevant for the current period. A language derives its value not merely from its logical and grammatical structure, but also from the richness of its literature. The word *Sanskrit* means refined, cultivated, systematised. It is a language of such quality and depth that numerous studies over the past five to six hundred years have shown that is the source language, the model, for many Indo-European languages including Greek, Latin, German and English.

An American teacher of Indian subjects, David Frawley, who has written more than thirty books on topics such as the Vedas,

Hinduism (*Sanatana Dharma*), Yoga, Ayurveda and Vedic astrology, had this to say about Sanskrit: "*Sanskrit is the oldest most continually used language in the world. By the most conservative accounts it has been used continuously since 1500 BCE. The language as we know it today came into existence due to the efforts of Panini around 500 BCE when it became the sacred language of both Hinduism and Buddhism.*"

Fire Period—Summit Reached, Decline Begins 829–1107 CE

- The 8th–12th centuries, rule by several dominant dynasties, including the: Rashtrakutas, Cholas, Chalukyas, Pallavas, Pratiharas, and Palas - the Golden Age of India.

During the period from 750 to 1310 India flourished under two dominant dynasties, the Rashtrakutas and the Cholas. Trade flourished as Indian products were in great demand in the East and the West. This period, which witnessed a Hindu religious and intellectual resurgence, is known as the *Golden Age of India*. During this period, aspects of Indian civilisation, administration, culture, and religion spread to much of Asia, while kingdoms in southern India had maritime business with the Middle East and the Mediterranean. Indian cultural influence spread over many parts of Southeast Asia.

In the early medieval period Indian mathematics influenced the development of mathematics and astronomy in the Arab world and the Hindu numerals were introduced. The Hindu-Arabic numerals, a positional numeral system, originated in India and were transmitted to the West through the Arabs during this period. Early Hindu numerals had only nine symbols, until 600 to 800 CE, when a symbol for zero was developed for the numeral system. The Islamic presence in Spain in this period acted as a transmitter of Indian wisdom to the West. In-depth knowledge about mathematics, astronomy and medicine was eventually translated into Latin and spread throughout Europe. During the period of the next cycle the image of India as a country of knowledge and spirituality grew.

Earth Period—Consolidation, Decline, Conclusion 1107-1246

Muslim forces began the domination of parts of India which lasted for six centuries Islam arrived in India using the sword in the 11th century and by 1200 Muslim forces dominated Northern India, winning control of the Indus and Ganges plains, marking the start of six centuries of Muslim dominance. In 1192 Muslim based forces attacked India and began to rule parts of north India in the 13th century when the Delhi Sultanate was founded in 1206 by Central Asian Turks. This period also saw the emergence of several powerful Hindu states, notably Vijayanagara, Gajapati, Ahom, as well as Rajput states, such as Mewar.

Lessons Learned from Cycle II

This was a period of great cohesion in India which resulted in a large period of peace and prosperity, during which time some of India's finest cultural gifts were made manifest. The work of Adi Shankara was instrumental in uplifting the Vedantic spiritual tradition, so that going forward it would be the guiding element for Hinduism, which is the current description of the

Indian spiritual tradition. Buddhism gradually became less and less influential in India, but as mentioned thrived within the Chinese culture.

The manifestation of fine consciousness in the worldly activities during this period is an important lesson for India to acknowledge. The conditions that existed at the beginning of Cycle II are similar to those in evidence today, at the final stage of Cycle III. This should give the Indian people greater confidence that their time for serving a more influential role in the world, grounded in spiritual principles, is on the way.

CYCLE III INDIA 1246–2100 CE

Air Period—A New Impulse 1246-1544 CE
- Rule of the Delhi Sultanate; two prominent rulers being Ghiyas ud bin Balban 1296–1316; and Mohammad bin Tughluq 1325–1351.
- Attack by Mughals led by Timur
- Vijayangara, the last great Hindu Kingdom in India 1365–1565.
- Lodi Sultanate, 1451–1526.
- Mughals displaced Lodis as rulers of Delhi and Agra, 1526.

The decline of empire and the coming of Islam
A new Muslim dynasty, the Khaljis came to power in 1290 and extended their rule southwards. The Delhi Sultanate reached its greatest extent under Muhammed ibn Tughluk who reigned

from 1325-1351. In 1398 the Turko-Mughal warlord Timur invaded and sacked Delhi, further weakening the state. There were more Turko-Mughal invasions between 1414 and 1421 and by 1451 power in Delhi was assumed by the Lodis, a dynasty from Afghanistan. The Lodi Sultanate was subsequently destroyed in 1526 by Babur, the founder of the Mughal Empire which was to reign until the 18th century.

The 15th century saw the advent of Sikhism. The early modern period began in the 16th century when the Mughals conquered most of the Indian subcontinent. The Mughals suffered a gradual decline in the early 18th century, which provided opportunities for the Marathas, Sikhs and Mysoreans to exercise control over large areas of the subcontinent.

Water Period—Expansion 1425-1782 CE

- Babur's son, Humayun, carried on as ruler and conquered Hindustan before his death. The empire then passed to his son, Akbar
- Reign of Mughal Emperor Akbar, supporter of the arts and religious toleration, 1605.
- Rule of Shah Jahan, Mughal architecture peaks, Agra Forts, Taj Mahal, 1627–1658.
- British East India Company is formed, 1651.

Muslim conquests and rule on the Indian subcontinent

Like other settled, agrarian societies in history, those in the Indian subcontinent have been attacked by nomadic tribes throughout its long history. In evaluating the impact of Islam on the subcontinent, one must note that the northwestern subcontinent was a frequent target of tribes raiding from Central Asia. In that sense, the Muslim intrusions and later Muslim invasions in the 18th century were not dissimilar to those of the earlier invasions during the first millennium. What does, however, make them different is that, unlike the preceding invaders who assimilated into the prevalent social system, the successful Muslim conquerors retained their Islamic identity and created new legal and administrative systems that challenged and usually in many cases superseded the existing systems of social conduct and ethics. They also introduced new cultural codes that in some ways were different from the existing cultural codes. This led to the rise of a new Indian culture which was mixed in nature, though different from both the ancient Indian culture and later westernised modern Indian culture. At the same time, it must be noted that the overwhelming majority of Muslims in India are Indian natives converted to Islam. This factor also played an important role in the synthesis of cultures. However, the continual growth of Muslim dominion resulted in the destruction and desecration of some politically important temples, cases of forced conversions to Islam, the imposition of taxes, and some loss of life for the non-Muslim population.

Akbar, who reigned from 1556-1605, not only rebuilt the empire, but expanded its frontiers right across northern India. Their conquest in 1572 of Gujarat, with its seaports and then in 1576 rich fertile Bengal, laid the foundations for the empire's long-term economic strength.

The relative peace maintained by the empire during much of the 17th century was a factor in India's economic expansion. Burgeoning European presence in the Indian ocean, and its increasing demand for Indian raw materials and finished products, created still greater wealth in the Mughal courts. There was more conspicuous consumption among the Mughal elite, resulting in greater patronage of painting, literary forms, textiles, and architecture, especially during the reign of Shah Jahan.

Among the Mughal UNESCO World Heritage Sites in South Asia are: Agra Fort, Fatehpur Sikri, Red Fort, Humayun's Tomb, Lahore Fort and the Taj Mahal, which they is describe as, *"The jewel of Muslim art in India, and one of the universally admired masterpieces of the world's heritage."* British influence in India began in this period with the introduction of the East India Company whose initial role was to manage British-Indian trade relations. In the next period its influence went well beyond that.

Fire Period—Summit Reached, Decline Begins 1723-2000 CE
- British domination begins -East India Company gradually assumes more control
- British Raj, 1818-1947.
- The First War of Indian Independence, 1857-58, full independence achieved in 1947.

British Intervention in India

The British presence in India began as a commercial enterprise called the British East India Company, a trading organisation, which was active on the subcontinent since its founding in 1600. By the middle of the 1700s, it turned India into what historian Philip J. Stern calls *'the company state.'* The 19th century witnessed the peak of Britain's colonial era, when

India was considered the crown jewel of a huge empire on which, as a contemporary phrase put it, *the sun never set.*

The India that the British encountered at the time was not a unified country, but a patchwork of principalities, and colonial control came gradually through treaties and alliances. British control over India shifted dramatically in the mid-19th century. In the first half of the century, the British East India Company effectively ran British India as its own domain, but in 1857 an armed mutiny of Indian soldiers serving under the British flag changed everything. In the rebellion's aftermath, the British government took direct control of the administration of India, establishing the India Office and a secretary of state for India in London, and appointing a viceroy and provincial governors to govern in India itself.

Through the second half of the 19th century, the amount of India's territory under either direct or indirect British control grew as officials signed treaties with local princes. Under the agreements, the land was considered British territory, but the princes continued to rule, albeit with interference from British officials and under constant threat of removal if they stepped out of line. Some princes became tremendously wealthy under the British regime; the Nizam of Hyderabad, for example, became the world's richest man.

India's economy also changed significantly over the century as a result of British influence. The East India Company established plantations in India to grow commercially attractive commodities such as tea and cotton for export. While the British made more Indian land available for agriculture through irrigation projects, the emphasis on cash crops impaired food production and Indians suffered through several famines in the 19th century. It was the continual demand to make money that prompted the actions of the British presence in India. The needs and concerns of the Indian people were of little concern to the ruling elite whose main focus was *maximising* its financial gains. A good example of this was the growth of the opium trade which destroyed the well-being and life of many people in India and China but made a lot of money for the British traders.

Following the establishment of the India Office in 1858, the British government improved other aspects of the Indian economy. By 1904 the British had laid 28,000 miles of railway track, an important avenue of commerce for India. Gradually the self-confidence of the Indian people grew and thanks to the persistent efforts of Mahatma Gandhi and other brave souls.

Indian culture - increasing links with the West

In the 17th century European missionaries, travellers and traders came to know the Indian languages. In 1699 CE a German Jesuit priest, Fr Johann Ernst Hanxleden, wrote the first Sanskrit grammar text in a European Language. In 1785 the *Bhagavad Gita* was translated into English by Charles Wilkins who was one of the first members of the Asiatic Society, founded by Sir William Jones in that same year. One of the main activities of the Asiatic Society was to collect the old manuscripts of India. From the 19th century the *Bhagavad Gita* began having an impact on Western Culture. Here are some quotes from some prominent Western intellects:

Ralph Waldo Emerson:

I owed a magnificent day to the Bhagavad Gita. It was the first of books; it was as if an empire spoke to us, nothing small or unworthy, but large, serene, consistent, the voice of an old intelligence which in another age and climate had pondered and thus disposed of the same questions which exercise us.

Henry David Thoreau:

In the morning I bathe my intellect in the stupendous and cosmological philosophy of the Bhagavad Gita, in comparison with which our modern world and its literature seem puny and trivial.

Albert Einstein:

When I read the Bhagavad Gita and reflect about how God created this universe everything else seems so superfluous. We owe a lot to the Indians, who taught us how to count, without which no worthwhile scientific discovery could have been made.

Aldous Huxley:

The Bhagavad Gita is one of the clearest and most comprehensive summaries of the perennial philosophy ever to be done. Hence its enduring value, not only for the Indians but also for mankind.

The appreciation of this fine work stimulated further interest in the West to find out more about what was increasingly seen as a very fine culture and not just a developing country whose people would benefit from learning more about our western culture.

Earth Period—Consolidation, Decline, Conclusion 1921-2100

- Indian Independence
- Economic Development
- Spiritual Regeneration

An Independent India

The killing of unarmed people in Amritsar by British soldiers in 1919 and other extremities of repression led to the first civil obedience campaign led by Mahatma Gandhi in 1921 which was guided by his passive resistance strategy consisting of 'non-violent non-cooperation.' It was called *Satyagraha* which means 'holding onto truth.'

This was the first of three major and evenly spaced campaigns (1921, 1930, 1942). Bounded by the two world wars, the transition drew its first impetus from India's contribution to preserve the empire which help gain British support for the recognition of India's national identity.

Gandhi launched a Satyagraha against the tax on salt in March 1930. The highlight was the Salt March where, together with 78 volunteers, he marched 388 kilometres from Ahmedabad to Dandi in Gujarat to make salt himself, with the declared intention of breaking the salt laws. The march took 25 days to cover 240 miles with Gandhi speaking to often huge crowds along the way. Gandhi was jailed in anticipation of a protest that he had planned. The protest at Dharasana salt works went ahead without its leader. This went on for hours until some 300 or more protesters had been beaten, many seriously injured and two killed. At no time did they offer any resistance.

With the outbreak of World War II, the nationalist struggle in India entered its last crucial phase. Gandhi hated fascism and all it stood for, but he also hated war. The Indian National Congress, on the other hand, was not committed to pacifism and was prepared to support the British war effort if Indian self-government was assured. The proposal was not accepted. Once more Gandhi became politically active and in 1942 there was a firm demand for the immediate British withdrawal from India—what became known as the Quit India Movement.

In mid-1942 the war against the Axis Powers, particularly Japan, was in a critical phase, and the British reacted sharply to the campaign. They imprisoned the entire Congress leadership, including Gandhi and his wife and set out to crush the party once and for all. A new chapter in Indo-British relations opened with the victory of the Labour Party in Britain 1945. During the next two years, there were prolonged triangular negotiations between leaders of the Congress, the Muslim League under Mohammad Ali Jinnah, and the British government, culminating in the Mountbatten Plan of June 3, 1947, and the formation of the two new dominions of India and Pakistan in mid-August 1947.

Economic Development

Economic development in India in the first stage of independence followed socialist-inspired guidelines, including state-ownership of many sectors. India's per capita income increased at only around 1% annualised rate in the three decades after its independence. Since the mid-1980s, India has slowly opened up its markets through economic liberalisation. After more fundamental reforms since 1991 and their renewal in the 2000s, India has progressed towards a free market economy. In the late 2000s, India's annual growth reached 7.5%.

Spiritual regeneration

What happened in India spiritually during the current cycle is not unlike what happened in the west during its Dark Ages, i.e. the monastic movement. Quietly, without great publicity or claims, an inspiring spiritual regeneration has been going on in India for almost 200 years. Because of the increased facilities for global communication there has been a passing on of the teaching of several Indian sages, not only to the Indian population, but also to many people in the West. Here is a list of just some of the 19th and 20th century Sages of India known in the West, who have gradually revitalised the Indian spiritual tradition and communicated to people around the world.

Swaminarayan (1781–1830)

A yogi, and an ascetic whose life and teachings brought a revival of central Hindu practices of dharma, ahimsa and brahmacharya. He, who is believed by followers to be a manifestation of God, developed a good relationship with the British Raj. He had followers not only from Hindu denominations, but also from Islam and Zoroastrianism. He built six temples in his lifetime and appointed 500 sages to spread his philosophy.

Dayananda Saraswati (1824–1883)

A social leader and founder of the Arya Samaj, a reform movement of the Vedic dharma. He was the first to give the call for Swaraj as *India for Indians* in 1876. Denouncing the idolatry and ritualistic worship prevalent in India at the time, he worked towards reviving Vedic ideologies.

Lahiri Mahasaya (1828–1895)

A yogi and teacher who revived the yogic science of Kriya Yoga when he learned it from his guru Mahavatar Babaji in 1861. Lahiri Mahasaya was also the guru of Shri Yukteswar. Mahasaya is a Sanskrit spiritual title translated as *large-minded.*

Ramakrishna (1836–1886)

A mystic and saint of 19th century Bengal. He experienced spiritual ecstasies from a young age, and was influenced by several religious traditions, including devotion toward the goddess Kali, Tantra (shakta), Vaishnava (bhakti), and Advaita Vedanta. Reverence and admiration for him led to the formation of the Ramakrishna Mission by his chief disciple Swami Vivekananda.

Swami Vivekananda (1863–1902)

A devoted disciple of Sri Ramakrishna, who was a key figure in the introduction of the Indian philosophies of Vedanta and Yoga to the Western world. He is credited with raising interfaith awareness and bringing Hinduism to the status of a major world religion during the late 19th century. He is perhaps best known for his speech which began with the words, "*Sisters and brothers of America* .," in which he introduced Hinduism at the Parliament of the World's Religions in Chicago in 1893. He toured the west before returning to India to help in the re-awakening of the Indian people to their true potential. In a book, Rebuild India, he set out a collection of his ideas on the subject. Here is one quote which sets out a clear direction:

'The national ideals of India are Renunciation and Service. Intensify her in those channels. And the rest will take care of itself.'

Sri Aurobindu (1872–1950)

A philosopher, yogi, guru, poet, and nationalist. He joined the Indian movement for independence from British rule and for a while was one of its influential leaders. He later became a spiritual reformer, introducing his visions on human progress and spiritual evolution.

Rama Tirtha (1873–1906)

Also known as Swami Ram, he was a teacher of the Hindu philosophy of Vedanta. He was among the first notable teachers of Hinduism to lecture in the United States, travelling there in 1902. During his American tours Swami Rama Tirtha spoke frequently on the concept of *practical Vedanta* and education of Indian youth.

Ramana Maharshi (1879–1950)

A calm and quiet spiritual teacher with a very devoted following. He said that his most important teaching was done in silence. He meant that when people were in his physical presence, their minds were affected. In some cases the effects were astonishingly strong.

Paramahansa Yogananda (1893–1952)

A yogi and guru who introduced millions of Indians and Westerners to the teachings of meditation and Kriya Yoga through his organisation, the Self-Realization Fellowship. In 1946, he published his autobiography, titled *Autobiography of a Yogi* which is on the list of the "100 best spiritual books of the 20th Century."

Krishnamurti (1895–1986)

A philosopher, speaker and writer who in his early life was groomed to be the new World Teacher, but later rejected this mantle and withdrew from the Theosophy organisation behind it. He stressed the need for a revolution in the psyche of every human being and emphasised that such revolution cannot be brought about by any external entity, be it religious, political, or social.

Anadamayi Ma (1896–1982)

She was born, Nirmala Sundari (Immaculate Beauty) in an obscure village in the Bangladesh area of India. She lived a simple life with no possessions nor attachments and called no particular place her home. She was constantly on the move throughout her long life, especially during the final 50 years of her life when she travelled throughout India. People were drawn to her presence and the blissful divine nature of her personality changed them irreversibly and set them on a spiritual course. Though she remained passive, unobtrusive, and mostly silent, ashrams and organisations sprang up in her name, organised by her devotees to provide venues for contact with and care of the multitudes.

A C Bhaktivedanta Swami Prabhupada (1896–1977)

A spiritual teacher and the founder-preceptor of the International Society for Krishna Consciousness (ISKCON), commonly known as the 'Hare Krishna Movement.'

Nisargadatta (1897–1981)

A guru of nondualism who belonged to the Inchagiri Sampradaya tradition. The publication in 1973 of his book, *I Am That*, brought him worldwide recognition and followers, especially from North America and Europe.

Eknath Easwaran (1910–1999)

A spiritual teacher, author, as well as a translator and interpreter of Indian religious texts such as the *Bhagavad Gita* and the *Upanishads*. In 1961 he founded the Blue Mountain Center of Meditation and Nilgiri Press, based in northern California.

Shantananda Saraswati (1913–1997)

A spiritual teacher of the Advaita tradition, founder of the art sanctuary, Temple of Fine Arts and later the Shankaracharya of the north, located in the Jyotir Math. He engaged in direct conversations with a number of Western leaders of spiritual movements. He only answered their questions and did not try to convert them. When he died, his successor **Vasudevanada Sarasvati,** continues to provide spiritual guidance.

Chinmayananda Saraswati (1916–1993)

A spiritual leader and a teacher who inspired the formation of Chinmaya Mission, a worldwide non-profit organisation, to spread the knowledge of Advaita Vedanta. Chinmayananda is known for teaching *Bhagavad Gita,* the *Upanishads,* and other ancient Hindu scriptures.

Maharishi Mahesh Yogi (1918–2008)

Known for developing the Transcendental Meditation technique and promoting Meditation in the West, he became the leader of a worldwide organisation that has been characterised in multiple ways including as a new religious movement and as non-religious. He became known as Maharishi meaning *great seer*.

Mother Meera; 1960–present,

Mother was born in the state of Andhra Pradesh, Southern India. Today, she now lives in a small village in the German countryside. There, and during her travels around the globe, she gave her unique blessing of Darshan. The free transmission of light, love and grace as a mother's gift to the world.

LESSONS LEARNED FROM CYCLE III

India is gradually gaining self-confidence after being under the control of other countries for hundreds of years. The ability to become a more unified culture is big challenge, given the historical patterns of independent regions, the large number of local languages still spoken, and the big differences between Indians living in the dynamic modern urban areas and the vast majority still living and in much poorer rural areas.

It is the teaching of the great teachers who have been active during this cycle that will begin to make a difference in both the revitalisation of the Indian spiritual tradition and the provision of useful guidance to the West. The teaching will enable people of all faiths to re-discover the essence of their spiritual traditions by going beyond the rigid rules and regulations that have become dominating factors in this cycle. Key to the future success of India in preparing for its next upward cycle is the way the government and the families of India deal with the current generation of young people. There are currently around 500 million people 25 years old or younger living in India. One estimate is that by 2020 this group would represent 40% of the world's population of people that age. The lower birth rates in the United States and Europe has resulted in a number of countries with an average age of 40 years old. The one-child policy in China has resulted in their average being in the high

30s. As many of the Indian population of young people live in rural areas, it is not an easy proposition to educate and train them to perform useful functions in the economy. It is one of the top priorities of the Indian government who realise that if this tremendous potential energy of their youth cannot be channelled wisely, then it could turn negative and thus be highly damaging for the Indian culture, and for the world.

In 2018 The Center for Soft Power, part of the India Foundation, was launched to promote India's cultural exports, an area that they view is of increasing global significance. It is also an indication of a growing internal confidence. The Center, apart from carrying out research, also proposes to promote various elements of India's soft power such as Ayurveda, meditation, language & literature, yoga, art, music, performing arts, cinema, cuisine, design, and handicrafts. At their first conference in December 2018 I was invited to give a presentation as part of the Language and Literature Panel about the teaching of Sanskrit at St James School in London. Sanskrit has been taught to students in that school since it was founded in 1975. The links of Sanskrit to English and other European languages, its comprehensive grammatical system and the fine spiritual works written in Sanskrit were the main motivators for the brave founders of St James school to take that step into the unknown. I have for several years been supporting that endeavour including the coordination of an arrangement with Motilal Barnasidass, one of India's oldest and most respected publishers, to publish the ten Sanskrit text books written by the St James's Sanskrit teachers. Since 2013 they have published more than 50,000 copies of the books. The essential message of my presentation was a thank you to India for the benefits that 1000s of children have received in learning the Sanskrit language and reading its fine literature. The audience was encouraged to use this fine cultural jewel more fully. I personally was impressed with the various presentations that reflected a growing confidence in the Indian cultural heritage.

Within the spirituality domain are various systems of Meditation and values-based guidelines for daily life. One characteristic of the Indian spiritual teaching is its inclusiveness, such that they do not make demands for others to convert to their system. In parallel with the promotion is the practice of these fine cultural activities by a growing number of Indians, especially from the younger generation. This is exactly what is needed to help India successfully deal with the complex Earth period that we are now in.

Here is part of the text of a letter received by Sri Mrinalini Mata of the Self Realisation Foundation from Dr Karan Singh, a member of the India's Upper House of Parliament and former Ambassador to the US:

"We are indeed going through a very troubled period in human history. On one hand, science and technology have achieved amazing results, which could benefit humanity; on the other hand, the forces of fanaticism and violence have also raised their head and are creating havoc around the world.

I agree that in the midst of the present turmoil, we all need to deepen our inner perception and move towards spiritual growth."

179

8

CULTURAL CYCLES, ARABIC

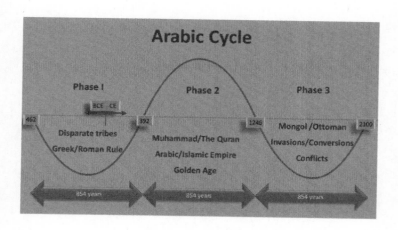

Arabic Cycle

Phase I

BCE CE

462

Disparate tribes

Greek/Roman Rule

854 years

Phase 2

392

Muhammad/The Quran

Arabic/Islamic Empire

Golden Age

854 years

Phase 3

1246

Mongol/Ottoman

Invasions/Conversions

Conflicts

2100

854 years

ARABIC ISLAMIC CULTURE

While this culture began in an Arab state and the common language of the culture is Arabic, the main uniting element is the Islamic religion. Growth of the culture from the beginning embraced the Middle East, North Africa, parts of India and even parts of Europe. Today there are many independent countries that profess to be Islamic. In our assessment we will refer to the culture as Arab, but there will also be many instances where the term Islamic Culture is used.

As the culture was quite fragmented during the time of Cycle I an overall summary is simply provided.

CYCLE I: ARAB, 462 BCE–392 CE

- Pre-Islamic Arab culture, which was a disparate group of independent tribes following a range of religions; a mix of polytheism (mainly), Christianity, Judaism and Iranian Zorastrianism.
- In the Mediterranean area, the Arab population was first under the rule of the Assyrians, then under other local empires, followed later by Greek and then Roman rule, thus exposing the people to a range of cultures.
- Tribes in Africa and the Arabian Peninsula also were expanding at this time due to extended trade in the area. The greater part of Arabia was a steppe or desert with inhabitants who spoke various dialects of Arabic.
- With the downfall of Rome and the establishment of the Byzantine empire many wars erupted with the Sassanian Empires, causing confusion and unrest for the Arabic speaking people.

The known history of the Arabs began in the mid-9th century BCE, which is the earliest known record of the old Arabic language. The Arabs appear to have been under the vassalage of the Neo-Assyrian Empire (911–612 BCE), and the succeeding Neo-Babylonian (626–539 BCE), Achaemenid (539–332 BCE), Seleucid and Parthian empires. After Alexander the Great conquered Iran in 333 BCE, Greek ideas began to spread through the area, as did the teachings of Mani, the founder of Manichaeism. Arab tribes began to appear in the Southern Syrian desert from the mid-3rd century CE onwards and this became the early centre of the Arab population. Roman rulers gave certain freedoms to the area. Caesar Augustus 27 BCE -14 CE, Tiberius 14-37 CE, and Hadrian 117-138 CE, all visited Palmyra and in 200 CE, it was proclaimed a free city as part of the Roman province of Petraea. It was primarily an agrarian society, producing grains, fruits, wine and oil, which were traded widely in the area. The Arab people were exposed to both the Greek and Roman cultures and in the early 4th century, and when Christianity became an established Roman religion, its influence was also present. There were also many Jewish communities in the area, so this early period of the culture was quite fragmented.

LESSONS LEARNED FROM CYCLE I

The main lesson is that a tribal based society, with no common religious or philosophical basis, language or laws, has not yet evolved into a coherent culture. The considerable change and confusion in society became a real prompt and impulse to find a better solution. A more cohesive culture was needed.

CYCLE II: ARAB, 392–1246 CE

Air Period—A New Impulse 392–630 CE

- Arab population expanded in several areas, including: the Arabian Peninsula; and the Middle East; i.e. Iran, Iraq, Syria and Africa.
- The inhabitants of the Arabian Peninsula, who spoke various dialects of Arabic, followed different ways of life; nomads who raised camels or sheep, known as Beduins, cultivators of food, craftsmen and tradesmen.
- Families grouped into tribes led by strong tribal leaders was how the society was structured.
- Muhammad received his first revelation in 610 and two years later began his prophetic mission to consolidate Arab culture under Islam.

The exposure to the ruling Western cultures and the positive responses received regarding their craftsmanship and trade gave the Arabic culture an increased degree of confidence. While they were a fragmented society there was a growing positive attitude about their role in the world.

Mecca had become a thriving mercantile city, but as with all commercial ventures where success is measured by wealth alone, there was discomfort. The excessive greed was seen to be compromising the established tribal land family values. Karen Armstrong's book, *Islam, A Short History,* noted that a spiritual restlessness grew in Mecca and throughout the peninsula at this time. Arabs knew that Judaism and Christianity, which were practised in the Byzantine and Persian empires, were more sophisticated than their own pagan traditions. Some people had come to believe that the High God in their tradition, *Allah* - meaning God - was actually the deity worshipped by the Jews and Christians, but they had not received any specific guidance about how to live their lives to please God. In addition to the spiritual uncertainty, there were increasingly more violent conflicts among the tribes as competition mounted.

It all changed when Muhammad, an Arab businessman, had an experience that heralded a major change in the world. During the holy month of Ramadan in 610, Muhammad embarked on his yearly act of devotion and retired to a cave on the summit of Mount Hira, where he prayed and fasted. One evening he awoke to find himself overwhelmed by a powerful presence. He heard the words of a new Arabic revelation sounding in himself. For the first two years he kept quiet about his revelation, but after the encouragement and support of his family, he began to speak about the guidance he had been given.

The message he offered was simple and not a new doctrine. He believed that he was merely reminding people about the faith in the One God, *Allah.* He did say that it was wrong to build a private fortune, but good to share wealth and create a society where the weak and vulnerable were treated with respect. He warned that if the tribal leaders did not change their motives and actions, their culture would collapse. Not a message that many of the wealthy wanted to hear, but he did attract many people as a following.

This was the basis of a new scripture, called the *Quran,* which means 'recitation'. The approach for the communication of the scripture was by listening to public readings of its chapters—

surah ~ because most of the followers, and Muhammad were mostly illiterate. The *Quran* was revealed to him verse by verse during a 21year period, often in response to a problem or a question from the growing following. The new spiritual tradition was called *Islam,* meaning *'surrender, obedience and peace'. Islam* is derived from the word *Salam* which is used as a term of greeting or a gift when a Muslim meets another person. Muslims were people who made this submission of their entire being to *Allah* and his demand that human beings behave to one another with justice, equity and compassion. Social justice was an important value of Islam and one of the first duties was to build a community — *ummah* - characterised by practical compassion and the fair distribution of wealth. The *Quran* insisted strongly that; *"there shall be no coercion in matters of faith"* and commanded Muslims to respect the beliefs of Jews and Christians, whom the *Quran* calls; *ahl-al-kitab or 'people of the book',* as it continues to do today.

This major new impulse which manifested through Muhammad and his followers was the main element of the upward cycle of the Arab culture. It was not only the basis for the new cycle that had begun, but it was to continue to be the underlying factor in the succeeding cycles. In Mohammad's brief period of life following the revelation, there were several obstacles to overcome. It began with objections to his preaching by those people in charge of the community in Mecca, who began persecuting him and his followers. He was invited to live in Medina and with about 70 Muslim families in 622, he embarked on a *hijrah* - a 'migration' - from Mecca to Medina. This *hijrah* is said to mark the beginning of the Muslim era.

What followed was a series of intense battles between the forces of Mecca and the Muslim community. Finally, after several defeats, the Muslims soundly defeated the army of Mecca and Muhammad brokered a peace treaty between Mecca and Medina. When Mecca violated the treaty, Muhammad marched towards Mecca with a large army, as many Arab tribes had joined his side. Mecca, sensing defeat, opened the gates and the city was taken without bloodshed and without any demands that the people converted to Islam.

Water Period—Expansion 630–928 CE
- Muhammad died in 632; Arabic expansion began; By 700 the Arab empire had expanded from the Atlantic Ocean to the plains of Northern India and frontiers of China. Sunni and Shi'a conflict about rulership began, which continues today.
- Invasion of Spain in 712, part of which they ruled until 1492. Further Arab expansion in Europe stopped at Poitiers in 732.
- Abbasid Caliphate expanded the empire 750– 936, which was also a period of great intellectual and artistic achievements, among them were the translation of Western works into Arabic, including: Euclid's *Elements*; *The Dialogues of Plato*; Ptolemy's *Astronomical System*; in depth studies of chemistry, physics, astronomy, mathematics (algebra discovered); design and building of mosques.

Muhammad's death in 632 stimulated a major disagreement within the culture about the appropriate ruler. By that time almost all the tribes of Arabia had joined his *ummah*, 'community', as confederates or as converted Muslims. This unification of the Arab tribes was an important step in enabling a significant expansion of the community in the upcoming Water period. Conversion was not a requirement while Muhammad was alive, because he was open to working with different tribes, Jews and Christians, but it later became part of the system.

The first four leaders, *caliphs*, had to deal with considerable resistance from many tribes who valued highly independent rule as opposed to being led by a single ruler. The successors were able to quell the resistance and increase the degree of unity of the tribes. As a result, they were able to send forces into Iraq, Syria and Egypt, where they achieved significant victories, including their conquest of the entire Persian empire. They were also victorious in Palestine, conquering Jerusalem in 638, and by 641 they controlled all of Syria, Palestine and Egypt. Within a century after the death of Muhammad the Islamic Empire extended from the Pyrenees to the Himalayas.

The essence of the internal arguments about leadership that arose was whether or not a member of Muhammad's family, - *sunni* - someone fully conversant with the Islamic teaching, should rule or whether the ruler should be the relative of another family, *shii*. Ali ibn Abi Talib a cousin of Muhammad took command as the fourth Caliph after the assassination of the third due to internal conflicts. Ali was an efficient, powerful tribal leader who was able to effectively guide the massive empire that had been created, adding to the argument that someone other than Muhammad's family should rule. The fifth Caliph

Muawiyah (661–680), added further complexity by moving the capital of the empire to Damascus. The beliefs of these two main warring factions came to be known as Sunnism and Shi'ism, and the conflict continued.

Muslim expansion into Europe began in 711, when a campaign was launched in Spain against the ruling Visigoths. By the end of the campaign most of the Iberian Peninsula, except for small areas in the northwest such as Asturias and the Basque territory - was brought under Islamic rule. Muslim forces later attempted to move across the Pyrenees Mountains towards France but were defeated by the Frankish Christian Charles Martel at the Battle of Tours in 732.

Andrew Marr speaks of the period of the early 8th century as the beginning of 'Islam's Golden Age'. Castles, mosques and cities ruled by Islamic rulers challenged the idea that 'Europe' and 'Christian' meant the same thing. He pointed out that the Arabs who were advancing through Spain were in fact a vivid mix of peoples. Some were from Arabia and Yemen, others from Syria and others still were Berber people of North Africa who had only recently converted to Islam.

In 750 the Umayyad dynasty, whose empire extended for five thousand miles and who had been the undisputed successors of the Prophet, were toppled in a bloody revolt by the Abbasids. This was a major step in the internal conflict of Islam which would become even more viral when the capital of the Muslim world was moved from Damascus to Baghdad, a shift to the East. This created a dividing line with the Al-Adalus caliphate ruling in Spain.

One interesting issue addressed in Marr's book was how the Abbasids saw themselves as inheritors of the learning of the ancient Greeks and also of the Persians and of the Hindu Indians. They claimed that the Christians of Byzantium had forgotten and shunned the great classic heritage, turning instead to a heavily ritual based view of worship.

In practical terms Christianity at the time was clearly not a unified religion, with severe conflicts between the rival Greek and Latin churches. There was strong belief in the European people of the need to convert the heathens of other spiritual traditions and to bring them into the Christian family. This ideal was to materialise in the outward European cycle with the European global expansion by sea to trade, colonise and then convert.

Islamic rule in the Iberian Peninsula lasted for varying periods ranging from only 28 years in the extreme northwest - Galicia - to 781 years in the area surrounding the city of Granada in the south east. This part of the Islamic Empire added contributions to society such as libraries, schools, public bathrooms, literature, poetry, and architecture. This work was mainly developed through the unification of people of all faiths. While the three major monotheistic religious traditions certainly did borrow from one another in Muslim-ruled Spain, benefiting especially by the blooming of philosophy and the medieval sciences in the Muslim Middle East, there was a certain degree of peaceful co-existence of Muslims, Jews, and Christians during this latter part of the Islamic outward cycle.

The Five Pillars of Islamic, Sharia Law

Sharia is the moral code and religious law of Islam. *Sharia* deals with many topics addressed by secular law including crime politics and economics as well as personal matters such as hygiene diet prayer and fasting. Here are the five:

- *Shahadah*; none should be worshipped except Allah and his messenger Mohammad
- *Salah*; offer prayer five times a day
- *Zakat*; give alms to charity
- *Hajj*; take a yearly pilgrimage to the House of Allah in Mecca
- *Fasting*; fast in the month of Ramadan

Fire Period—Summit Reached, Decline Begins 829–1107 CE

- *Quran* text released in 935. Islam spread to many other cultures including Mughal, Persian, and Turkish Ottoman. Sufism, the mystical aspect of Islam, became more popular and accepted.
- Islamic Art flourishes
- An Islamic Golden Age- spiritual growth and expansion
- Interaction between cultures - communications and exchanges with the West

The peak Fire period occurred during the rule of the Abbasid – *sunni* – Caliphate (750–936), which resulted in a great renaissance in Baghdad and other cities of the empire. It was at this time that a coherent body of Islamic law known as *Sharia* was formed.

Islamic Art

What has been fascinating to see is how quickly the Islamic culture moved from a predominantly agrarian culture to one that provided some of the finest examples of art, science and architecture of the period, the scope and quality of which are still admired today. Islamic art developed from many sources: Roman, Early Christian art, and Byzantine styles were taken over in early Islamic art and architecture; the influence of the Sassanian art of pre-Islamic Persia was also of paramount significance; Central Asian styles were brought in with various nomadic incursions; and Chinese influences had a formative effect on Islamic painting, pottery, and textiles. There are repeating elements in Islamic art, such as the use of geometrical floral or vegetal designs in a repetition known as the arabesque. The arabesque in Islamic art is often used to symbolise the transcendent, indivisible and infinite nature of God.

Typically, though not entirely, Islamic art has focused on the depiction of patterns, because it was and is still today, feared by many Muslims that the depiction of the human form is a sin against God, forbidden in the *Quran*.

Islamic arches, similar to columns, followed a style similar to Roman architecture and became quite prominent in Islamic architecture during the 8th to 10th centuries. Islamic art of the period also made very notable achievements in ceramics, both in pottery and tiles for walls, which in the absence of wall-paintings were taken to heights unmatched by other cultures.

Early pottery is often unglazed, but a new technique, opaque-glazing, was developed by the Islamic potters. Examples can be found as blue-painted ware in Basra, dating to around the 8th century. From the 9th century onwards the distinctive Islamic tradition of glazed and brightly coloured tiling for interior and exterior walls and domes developed.

For most of the Middle Ages Islamic glass was the most sophisticated in Eurasia, exported to both Europe and China. Islam took over much of the traditional glass-producing territory of Sassanian and Ancient Roman glass, and since figurative decoration played a small part in pre-Islamic glass, the Islamic approach was fully accepted. As with many of the other aspects of art, the benefit of increased trade was achieved as well as increasing respect in the West for this new burgeoning culture.

Spiritual growth and expansion

Classical Greek philosophy produced a wide range of original works from Ancient Greece (e.g. Aristotle) to those Greco-Roman scholars in the classical Roman Empire (e.g. Ptolemy). Though these works were originally written in Greek, for centuries the language of scholarship in the Mediterranean region, many were translated into Syriac, Arabic, and Persian during the Middle Ages. As the Arab caliphates absorbed Greek/Roman knowledge, the medieval Islamic world gradually became the dominant intellectual centre in the Mediterranean region. As was noted in the presentation of the European cultural pattern, subsequent Western efforts at Latin translations of the Greek classics began in the 15th,century, the beginning of their ascending period, primarily through the efforts of Marsilio Ficino.

One of the most interesting descriptions of the Islamic view on spiritual knowledge and experience was found in a book *The History of the Arab Peoples* by **Albert Hourani**.

"It was in the ninth century that the way to knowledge of God and the nature of that knowledge were first expressed in systematic form. In the writings of al-Muhasibi the way of life of the seeker after true knowledge was described, and in those of al-Junayd the nature of the experience which lay at the end of the way was analysed. At the end of the path, the true and sincere believer may find himself face to face with God in such a way that God's attributes replace his own, and the individual experience disappears, but only for a moment. After it he will return to his own existence, and to the world, but carrying with him the memory of the moment, of the nearness of God, but also his own transcendence."

This beautiful description of a true spiritual experience is very similar to those presented by other major traditions such as the teachings of Vedic Advaita, Christianity, Taoism and Buddhism, and one gets a real sense of the unity that exists between all of them. This more in-depth understanding seems to come to a culture in both the peak period of the ascending period when the bright intellect connects with clear reason and also in the peak period of the descending cycle when there is turning inward and there is an experience of a quiet unmoving state where the heart is open.

Interaction Between Cultures

This exchange of knowledge and experience between cultures is one of the characteristics observed where the cultures were in close contact. This is particularly relevant in today's global world where there is bound to be a useful exchange of knowledge among cultures moving from the outward to the descending inner phase of the cycle and those beginning their ascending outward phase. Science in the medieval Islamic world was developed and practised during the Islamic Golden Age, spanning the period from the 9th to the 12th centuries. Islamic scientific achievements encompassed a wide range of subject areas, especially astronomy, mathematics, and medicine. Other subjects of scientific inquiry included chemistry, botany, geography, cartography, ophthalmology, pharmacology, physics, and zoology.

Astronomy was a major discipline within Islamic science. Effort was devoted both towards understanding the nature of the cosmos and to practical purposes. Astrology was studied to enable the prediction of events affecting human life and selecting suitable times for actions such as going to war or founding a city. Sufism, which traces most of its original precepts to Muhammad through his cousin and son-in-law Ali, is based on the principles of Sunni Islam. They represent the mystical dimension of the Islamic religion in the same way as do the Christian mystics like Meister Eckhardt, the Taoists of China and the Advaitists of the Indian spiritual tradition. Although Sufis were opposed to dry legalism, they strictly observed Islamic law and belonged to various schools of Islamic jurisprudence and theology. With the gradual decline of the Islamic culture in the 12th & 13th centuries, they became more prominent.

Here is a brief list of some of the more notable contributors to the flourishing of Islamic culture in their period of ascendency. The reference for these descriptions is *Doctrina Arabum*, the programme of the exhibition held at the Bodleian Library Oxford in 1981.

Al-Khwarizmi (750–847)

He was famous for introducing Indian numerals and methods of numbering into the Islamic world. By the 13ᵗʰ century both were used throughout Europe and known as Arabic numerals. His other major contribution was Algebra, in Arabic *al-jabr*, which came to Europe through the Latin translation of his book.

Al-Farabi (Alfarabius) (870–950)

He was one of the finest Muslim philosophers who lived in the Middle East. He wrote on a variety of topics with more than 100 works attributed to him. He was influential in the development of Islamic philosophy. He studied the teachings of Aristotle in some depth in the Islamic world and was known as *the second teacher*. Some of his works were translated into Latin and then studied in Europe.

Al-Battani (850–922)

He was a pioneer astronomer who accurately determined the length of the solar year. He contributed to the *Tables of Toledo*, used by astronomers to predict the movements of the sun, moon and planets across the sky. Some of his astronomic tables were later used by Copernicus, which was another example of the natural exchange of knowledge between cultures.

Ibn Sina (Avicenna) (980–1037)

A philosopher and physician who by the age of eighteen had mastered all the then known sciences and by twenty-one wrote his first book on philosophy. One work, *Shifa*, includes four books on: logic, physics, mathematics and metaphysics. His philosophic approach attempted to reconcile faith and reason.

Ibn Rushd (Averroes) (1126–1198)

He studied theology and law and became a judge in Seville and Cordova, he wrote works on philosophy including a treatise on the harmony of religion and philosophy, and extensive commentaries on the works of Aristotle. The versions of his works translated into Latin and Hebrew were important in introducing Aristotle into Europe.

Maimonides (1135–1204)

A philosopher, physician and a celebrated authority on Jewish law. Born in Cordova, he then settled in Cairo, where he practised medicine and served the Jewish community. His major work, *Guide for the Perplexed*, was written for the enlightenment of his local co-religionists, but then its Latin translation was used extensively by European scholars such as Albertus Magnus and Duns Scotus.

Earth Period—Consolidation, Decline, Conclusion 1107-1246

The Earth period of this cycle was filled with war and conflicts, much of it brought about by a renewed and more vigorous Western culture. The Byzantine Emperor sought help from Western Christendom in the 11th century to curb Muslim invasions. This began a period of Crusades, as described in the Western European history of this period, which lasted for more than 200 years resulting in a dramatic decrease in Islamic influence.

LESSONS LEARNED FROM CYCLE II

This was a marvellous example of how a common religion, language and law unites even disparate groups of people, enabling the manifestation of the finest of human qualities. Individual self-confidence of the Arab people grew during this period such that spiritual, intellectual, artistic, and economic achievements, not imagined in the previous period, were realised.

What was especially interesting to acknowledge was how Islamic religion united Arab and other language-based cultures such as the Turkish, Mughal, North African and Middle Eastern countries who operated as one and thus became a true global power. It is a good lesson for the Western culture at this time who are becoming more and more focused on individual nationalistic concerns and thus losing the power of a united culture.

In *Colossus: The Rise and Fall of the American Empire*, historian Niall Ferguson noted that in Edward Gibbon's classic, *Decline and Fall of the Roman Empire*, he posed a challenging question: "*If the French had failed to defeat the invading Muslim army at Poitier in 731CE, would all of western Europe have succumbed to Islam?*"Then Gibbon commented, *"Perhaps the interpretation of the Koran would now be taught in the schools in Oxford and her pupils might demonstrate to a circumcised people the sanctity and truth of the revelation of Mahomet."*

Regarding the implications of the lack of cohesiveness in Europe and the growing power of the global Islamic community, Ferguson said, "*Time and the birthrate favour a Muslim Europe within 50 years.*"

The positive outward cycle was coming to a close. The inevitable rigidity of the Earth period set in weakening the overall strength of the culture. What happened in the next downward cycle was consistent with observations about the other cultural cycles.

CYCLE III: ARAB, 1246–2100 CE

Air Period—A New Impulse 1246-1544 CE
- Mongol invasions from the Far East resulted in clashes with Muslim forces.

The clashes with the invading Mongols continued from 1220 to about 1500. Muslim power was checked, however, at some point many Mongols converted to Islam, continuing to spread the religion.

Water Period—Expansion 1425-1782 CE
- During the 15th and 16th centuries the greater part of the Muslim world was integrated into three great empires; the Ottomans, Safavids; and Mongols.
- All the Arabic-speaking countries were included in the Ottoman Empire, with its capital in Istanbul, except for parts of Arabia, the Sudan and Morocco. The empire also included Anatolia and South Eastern Europe.
- Islamic religion continued to expand in other non-Muslim cultures including the Safavid Empire of Iran.

In the Ottoman Empire Turkish was the language of the ruling class and military, which was largely drawn from converts to Islam coming from the Balkans and the Caucasus. The empire was a bureaucratic state with a single administrative and fiscal system. This was the last expression of a universal world of Islam. During this period the religious law was observed, the holy cities of Arabia were guarded, and it was also a multireligious state, giving a recognised status to the Christian and Jewish communities. A strong Arab Ottoman culture developed.

Islamic religion continued to expand in other non-Muslim cultures. The two most prominent conversions in the period from the 16th–18th centuries were the Ottoman Empire centred in Turkey and the Safavid Empire in Iran. These three empires continued to flourish until the 19th century, when they all declined dramatically under the pressures exerted by the increasingly dominant Western European and later the United States powers.

In the 18th century the balance between the Ottoman central and local governments changed, as did the relations with the states of Europe. The Ottoman Empire had expanded into Europe in the earlier centuries, but now with growing European power, it was under threat from the north and west. With growing trade and economic competition, the Ottoman power was clearly in decline.

Fire Period—Summit Reached, Decline Begins 1723-2000 CE
- In the 18th century the balance between the Ottoman central and local governments changed, as did the relations with the states of Europe. With growing trade

and economic competition, the Ottoman power was clearly in decline.

- The Saudi Dynasty emerged as a power in 1744 and in 1932 became the Kingdom of Saudi Arabia. With the discovery of oil in the mid-20th century their economy expanded greatly.

- Conflicts continued to erupt between the various countries of the Middle East and Africa, resulting in the death of millions, which also weakened economies and caused a great migration to countries in the West, where opportunities to live a more productive life seemed to be the only viable possibility.

- During the 19th century, the three empires which had embraced Islam declined dramatically under the pressures exerted by the increasingly dominant Western European and later American powers.

- The first major conflict was between France and the Arab speaking country of Algeria (1830-47). Attempts were made by the Ottoman rulers to engage with Europe, but a balanced arrangement could not be made. In due course Egypt, Tunisia, Morocco and Libya fell under European control.

- While the religious and legal culture of Islam continued to be preserved, there was a growing inclination to copy the Western ideas and methods, which seemed to be the way forward at the time. The Western society, which had been transformed by the industrial revolution, was now the major world power.

- Conflict between the Ottoman Empire and Russia led to the Crimean War in 1853, which resulted in Britain and France supporting the Ottoman Empire.
- Europe continued to support the Ottoman Empire to a degree because it provided a more stable environment in which increasing trade could be carried out. Gradually, more countries under Ottoman control sought greater freedom. The idea of a democracy, a representative government, was gaining strength.
- With the outbreak of the First World War in 1914. the Ottoman Empire entered the war on the side of Germany and Austria against England, France and Germany, and its own land became a battleground.
- By the end of the war, the Ottoman Empire had lost its Arab provinces and eventually Western allies dictated terms which were documented in the Treaty of Lausanne in 1923 The result was the creation of the Republic of Turkey.
- The political structure within which most Arabs had lived for four centuries had disintegrated. There was a great deal on confusion in the Arab controlled states of Africa and the Middle East as Western influence continued to grow.

The 19th century was the age when Europe was a dominant power in the world and increasingly conflicts arose with the Islamic communities. The first was the conflict between France and the Arab speaking country of Algeria (1830-47). Attempts were made by the Ottoman rulers to engage with Europe, but a balanced arrangement could not be made. In due course Egypt, Tunisia, Morocco and Libya fell under European control. While the religious and legal culture of Islam continued to be preserved, there was a growing inclination to copy the Western ideas and methods, which seemed to be the way forward at the time. The Western society, which had been transformed by the industrial revolution, was now at a peak of power and prosperity.

The Ottoman Empire

The Ottoman Empire became weaker as conflicts arose regarding trade and attempts by European powers to gain influence and control on Middle Eastern and African countries. Conflict between the Ottoman Empire and Russia led to the Crimean War in 1853, which resulted in Britain and France supporting the Ottoman Empire, but at a price. Europe continued to support the Ottoman Empire to a degree because it provided a more stable environment in which increasing trade could be carried out. Gradually, more countries under Ottoman control sought greater freedom. The idea of a democracy, a representative government, was gaining strength.

In 1876, a constitution was approved and a parliament was elected who met in Turkey, but it was suspended soon thereafter by the new sultan, Abdulhamid II, who ruled from 1876 until 1909. In 1908, a revolution supported by the army restored the constitution. This internal conflict encouraged some of the countries of the Empire like Romania and Bulgaria, to declare formal independence. The empire continued to erode as it acquired a huge debt to be able to sustain its economy and with both Europe and Russia taking control of certain territories and the demand for independence from other countries, power was waning fast.

With the outbreak of the First World War in 1914. the Ottoman Empire entered the war on the side of Germany and Austria against England, France and Germany, and its own land became a battleground. By the end of the war, the Ottoman Empire had lost its Arab provinces and eventually Western allies dictated terms which were documented in the Treaty of Lausanne in 1923 The result was the creation of the Republic of Turkey. The political structure within which most Arabs had lived for four centuries had disintegrated. There was a great deal on confusion in the Arab controlled states of Africa and the Middle East as Western influence continued to grow.

Earth Period—Consolidation, Decline, Conclusion 1921-2100

- A changing world profile in the 20th century.
- The culture of Nationalism and greater emphasis on individual freedom which are firmly established in the West put pressure on the Arab countries to change.
- Efforts made to promote Islamic religion and the Arabic language.
- United States and Russia becoming the dominant superpowers after the Second World War.

The 20th century brought about many changes in the structure of the countries of the world and also a significant increase in the migration of people between cultures. In addition to the movement between countries, there was the increasing movement of people from rural countryside to urban areas. Muslim people who migrated to Western countries had to adjust to the local customs and traditions, such as the veiled woman were soon being ignored.

The culture of Nationalism was now firmly established and replaced the more cohesive culture, which resulted from a number of countries being part of a unified Empire. This emphasis on more individual freedom was the characteristic of the Western cycle of this time and it was under this influence that the Arab countries now had to live. The response to pressures imposed by the ruling Western powers resulted in efforts to reinvigorate the Islamic religion and the Arabic language, two crucial elements of the culture. In several of the countries in the 1930s, such as Syria, Palestine and Egypt, Muslims and Christians lived together with the emphasis being on their common national bonds.

The Second World War once again changed the power of the world with the United States and Russia becoming the dominant superpowers. In several Islamic countries, there was an end to French and British rule and attempts were begun to set up effective independent governments. It has not been an easy proposition as many conflicts have arisen between those powers who supported a strong dominant leader versus those supporting a more democratic type of government. The conflict continues today.

In the last half of the 20th century there were many examples of violent responses from the Arab countries. There were some attempts to develop a closer union of Arab countries, but they were not successful. There has been, however, a coming together of Arab people around the world on the issues of the Islamic religion and other common elements of their culture.

The 21st century has seen a sharp increase in violent reactions within the Islamic world. Riots and protest demonstrations have occurred in almost all the Arab countries, driven by demands for a change to rigid and ineffective leadership. In addition, there were, and continue to be, examples of Islamic loyalists using the most violent means against the West, to try and gain independence from a power which they see as corrupt. This particular type of response has caused many people in the West to reject the Islamic view. At the same time, there has been an integration of millions of Muslim people into Europe, the United States and India. In India the Muslim population is estimated to be 193 million, about 14 percent of the total population.

As noted, from 2020 the Jupiter and Saturn conjunctions will continue to be in Earth signs for more than 100 years, indicating the nature of the final phase of the 854-year cycle. For the Arab culture this is the final phase of their inward cycle, which as we have seen has been marked by long periods of control by other cultures. While that has been going on externally, there has been quiet work going on in regenerating the understanding and application of the fine principles of Islam.

LESSONS LEARNED FROM CYCLE III

Hopefully an important lesson learned by the Islamic culture is that the greater good for all can be achieved through peace and not warlike activities aimed at achieving self-serving goals. What is needed are more Islamic leaders who espouse the philosophy of peace. Here are some current examples of just such guidance.

This is an extract from *Peace and Humanitarianism in Islam* by Moulavi S H Athambawa.

"The adherents of the religion of Islam are called Muslims. A Muslim is meant as a person who is peaceful. He is loving of others and makes others peaceful. He is sincere and straightforward. Islam is a religion that actually spreads peace and justice in the world and paves the way for human beings to live peacefully and prosperously. As to the nature of human beings they may follow any religion, may belong to any race, may have any complexion or may speak any language. We are all brothers and sisters."

This fully inclusive view is an important one that needs to be embraced by all races and religions. There is an acknowledgement that a tendency exists among the Arabs to discriminate the non-Arabic speakers and treat certain classes with less respect. It was noted that Muhammad, addressing more than 100,000 people in his last *Haj* sermon, denounced such practices while stressing the importance of racial equity. In his final sermon he reinforced women's rights and stressed that they must be treated with great honour, trust, and kindness.

Mirza Masroor Ahmad is the Head of the worldwide Ahmadiyya Muslim Community. They have seen the dangerous state that the world is in and are trying to discover ways that the world can avert disaster and chart a course to peace and prosperity. Mirza Masroor Ahmad has addressed a large group of United States Congressmen, the Houses of Parliament in London, the military leadership in Germany, and the European Parliament in Brussels highlighting in his addresses the importance of finding a way to world peace.

He has acknowledged many of the issues which we have presented about the negative conditions existing in society and feels we need to shift our focus. Many of the letters he has written to world leaders are included in a book he has written, *Peace and World Crisis and the Pathways to Peace*.

The Voice of the Quran

Here are three of the most relevant quotes from the Quran which are highlighted:

There should be no compulsion in religion. (ch2: v57)

Regarding avoiding envy of the wealth of others which is a cause of increasing restlessness in the world:

And strain not the eyes after what We have bestowed on some classes of them to enjoy for a short time-the splendour of the present world- that We may try them. (ch20: v132)

About justice and equity:

O ye who believe! Be steadfast in the cause of Allah, bear witness in equity; and let not a people's enmity incite you to act otherwise than with justice. Be always just, that is nearer to righteousness. (ch5: v9)

Islam is currently divided into some 45 independent states but is united by one of the strongest of the great world religions in terms of the cultural hold on its followers. It is my view that with the coming of the Earth period there will less fiery responses and more efforts on the part of all cultures for greater understanding, mutual respect and peace so that energies of all can be directed in a more positive way.

9

THE LESSONS LEARNED
AND THE WAY FORWARD

In the next four chapters we are going to objectively examine the state of the Western European/American culture using the lessons learned from our historical analysis, acknowledge some of the major existing negative conditions and then set out some guidance on how we can more effectively address these issues. We will conclude with a recommended approach of applying natural human values to how we think, relate to others and act in service of the common good. A strong resolve is needed to follow these guidelines, which if undertaken, will enhance the journey for people of all cultures.

Each of the last three chapters will highlight 3 steps on the journey.

THE LESSONS LEARNED

In a rather late stage of the development of this book I met with the majestic work written by Karen Armstrong, *The Lost Art of Scripture*. What is most attractive about this book is that it examines in great depth the spiritual traditions of the four cultures that we cover in in our historical assessment. The spiritual beliefs and practices, an integral aspect of all cultures, do change over time and this is what is presented by Karen with keen insight.

One of the main elements of her analysis is the two-fold aspects of human brain which is well accepted by the scientific community today. The common definition of the **left-brain** is that the left side of the brain is seen to be responsible for performing tasks that have to do with **logic,** such as in science and mathematics. The **right-brain** is described as the right side of the brain, which performs tasks that have do with **creativity and the arts.**

An excellent summary of the practical qualities on each side is offered by Iain McGilchrist in his book, *The Mastery of His Emissary: The Divided Brain and the Making of the Western World.*

The Left Hemisphere
- The general
- Prefers what is known & familiar
- The abstract, theoretical, virtual
- Mechanistic
- Unscrupulous
- Inner life a distraction

- Rigid, linear, predictable
- Analytic, abstract language
- Logic

The Right Hemisphere

- The particular
- Attuned to anything new
- The concrete, sensory & personal
- Empathetic
- Truthful
- In touch with inner life
- Tentative, flexible, exploratory
- Imaginative, metaphoric language
- Humour & irony

There are also broader definitions. The right-brain is such that it includes intuitive thinking, and emotional responses, such as, empathy and compassion. It also has a more comprehensive vision of reality and is able to bring about a transformation from a more mechanical existence. This power helps give access to the spiritual dimension of our being, a realm, the existence of which is not readily acknowledged by the scientific community.

The failure to acknowledge the spiritual dimension of humanity, due to excessive emphasis on the intellectual realm, is one of the main reasons for the decay of any culture. If the spiritual realm, that which is beyond personal thought and feeling, is not acknowledged, we become inescapably bound up in a world that we create ourselves, our mental and emotional images, i.e. our individual ego-based world.

The full capability of the left-brain is also broader than just mechanical logic. It has the power of discrimination, to correctly determine the difference between right and wrong, good and bad, real and unreal. This is best described as the power of Reason, which goes far beyond logic.

The 'perennial philosophy' accepted by many cultures in the past, states that the world is pervaded by and finds it full understanding in a reality that exceeds the reach of the intellect. The strong left- brain oriented view of our modern culture just cannot accept that there is anything beyond the intellect. It was with the coming of the Enlightenment period in the West that there was a major shift to 'a total dependence on empirical and objective insights.'

It is our view that when the main focus falls on the left-brain, this is indicative of the outward physically oriented cycle where great advancements in science, technology, and the economy are manifested. In the earlier stages of these outward cycles the spiritual realm also flourishes as a result of the contemplative connection of the previous inward cycle, but it quickly gets reduced in priority in favour of energy and attention being directed towards gains in the physical and mental realms.

When the outward cycle comes to its final stage the excessive focus on the material realm is recognised by some who have a firm foundation of right brain intuitive knowledge and they begin taking the necessary steps to prepare for the next right-brain oriented stage. We saw this in the West as the Roman Empire began its final collapse in the 3rd century. Key agents were the Desert Fathers, John Cassion and neo-Platonist, Plotinus. The inward cycles result in the periods of greater contemplation, meditation, compassion and service, such as were observed during the monastic movement in the West. These inward focused periods enable a connection of what is beyond the mind. There is real transformation where the right- brain is fully engaged. This journey of transcendence is possible for all human beings which is why all spiritual traditions provide guidance on this way to the experience of Reality.

The transition from the right-brain to a more left-brain orientation occurs in the move from an inward cycle to an outward one. While the reflective period and fine service of humanity was very productive, the nature of a cycle shows that in the final stage the quiet environment become too fixed and rigid. That is another form of excess. The result is that there is an impulse to break free from the limits. The Renaissance period of the 13th-14th century in the West is an excellent example of the move towards a more left-brain mentality. That cycle resulted in a majestic outward flow of Reformation, Enlightenment, Industrial Revolution and the Rule of Scientific Thought.

The Coming of the Inward Cycle

As the West is in the last stage of an outward cycle, the preparations have naturally begun for the next 854-year cycle which will be characterised by a greater emphasis on our inner self, a going within, a flowering of the mystical aspect of a spiritual teaching.

All spiritual traditions have an element of 'mysticism' The aim is the soul's mystical union with God which can be achieved by simple prayerful contemplation of Holy Scripture called Lectio Divina. The Sufis are the mystical realm of the Islamic culture, the Kabbala of Judaism, the Tao teaching of Chinese culture, and the Advaita teaching of the Indian tradition. In Christianity there are numerous examples including the Desert Fathers of the 2nd century, Meister Eckhardt, Hildegard of Bingen and St Francis of Assisi.

Mysticism derives from the Greek verb *muo* 'to close' which involves a closing down or reducing analytical and propositional activity i.e. the left-brain orientation. Once the mind is emptied the holistic vison of the right hemisphere has free play. In India the recitation of a mantra in meditation is used to achieve the transition from the left to the right brain i.e. to a more intuitive form of consciousness. What naturally manifests in terms of human behaviour is a greater sense of empathy and compassion, a greater concern for others. The Golden Rule, to treat others as you would want to be treated, manifested in all the world's spiritual traditions during the inward reflective periods of time.

During the inward period of the Chinese culture beginning in 462 BCE, the views of Lao Tzu expressed in his classic work *Tao Te Ching* speaks of transcendent reality as 'The Way' which is beyond rational thought. Lao Tzu's guidance on how a wise person should live involves turning back when anything in life reaches an extreme.

What is needed for that to happen is that we must relinquish our obsession with our ego-based self, me, and cultivate compassion and empathy, i.e. real concern for others. This is the real essence of true enlightenment.

A great Confucian thinker of this same period, Xunzi (340-245 BCE), who was also greatly influenced by Taoism, believed that it was possible for anyone, by the daily practice of benevolence (*ren*) and righteousness (*yi*) to achieve personal transformation. He was convinced that the Way could be comprehended by the quieting of the mind, so that it became 'empty, unified and still'.

As we noted the Indian Vedic spiritual tradition is of great depth and has in various forms been practiced for 1000s of years. The inward cycle which began in India in 462 BCE saw the manifestation of some of its finest scriptures including the *Upanishads* and the *Bhagavad Gita*, which is one chapter of India's great epic poem of more than 100,000 verses, the *Mahabharata*. The works are the guides for the realisation of one's true nature, which is the same for all. That essential nature is said to be pure, perfect and complete. For the sake of communication, it is called by various names; Brahman, Atman, One Consciousness. The unity of all beings is the main tenet of the Advaita system. It is not possible for the human being to achieve this realisation only through the use of the intellect. The ultimate source, be it known as God, Brahman, the Tao, cannot be known in that way. It can be experienced when the mind is still and the heart is also still and fully open. For that to happen, as has been said in Taoism, we must let go of all the ego-based ideas and feelings that cover over the ever-shining sun of our true nature. This requires disciplines such as quiet reflection, mainly on fine scripture, and meditation. Also noted is that the way to the transformation is enhanced by the performance of one's duty (*Dharma*) which is natural law. All the cultural traditions offer what we call values or virtues as the basis for a dharmic life. While there are some differences in emphasis, the virtues or values are universal. Good examples are love, justice, courage, compassion, temperance, wisdom, patience, determination, respect and humility.

Matthew Pye offers a view on how the correct application of the four divine virtues advocated by Plato; wisdom, courage, temperance and justice is needed to address the current climate change issues. *'We will need to use our intelligence with wisdom, our spiritedness with courage and our desires will have to be moderated. And when they all come together, it generates the fourth, justice. The virtues lie at the hub of Plato's thinking and they provide us with a powerful set of concepts for us to move ahead with in the struggle for climate justice—not just at a surface level, but also at a deeper and fully sustainable level.'*

During this inward period in India the teachings of both Buddha and Mahavira had a major impact. Jains and Buddhists both insisted that it was compassion, inner equanimity and harmlessness (*ahimsa*) that liberated one from the suffering (*dukkha*) inherent in existence.

Lessons from the Christian tradition about the benefits of the right brain dominant inward cycle have also been presented in our historical perspective. A major influence was the teachings of Origen (185-254 CE) who believed that the culture had fallen to a low level as a result of *'rejecting the divine and making ourselves the centre of our world.'* He advocated the reading and reflection on scripture, engaging both the mind and the heart *'The human heart is no small thing, for it can embrace so much.'*

Augustus (354-430 CE), bishop of Hippo in North Africa combined his Christian beliefs with the teachings of Plato. Like Buddhists, Jains and Confucians, Augustine insisted that scripture was pointless if it did not lead to compassionate

216

thinking and behaviour. Augustine insisted that scripture taught nothing but charity and that during meditation a monk deliberately turned his *intentio* away from ego towards his fellow human beings. '*The impact of scriptural study is not complete unless it drives the practitioner to work for a more altruistic and compassionate world.*'

The scriptural revolution in the Middle East, which had begun in the first century CE with the works of the Mishnah and the New Testament, culminated in Arabia during month of Ramadan in 610 by the revelations experienced by Muhammad. From that point the outward period of the Arab tradition began and it was not until the latter stages of that outward cycle did the more inward view of Islam emerge taken forward by the Sufi element of the Islamic tradition. Abu Hamid al-Gazzali (d 1111) the greatest Islamic scholar of the time brought the Sufi teaching to prominence. Al-Gazzali realised that the Sufi contemplative rituals helped people to develop an internal spirituality, an esoteric knowledge that transcended the conceptual.

The Persian poet Jalal al-Din Rumi (1207-1273) founder of the Sufi Order, known as the *Whirling Dervishes*, made some of the more complex Sufi ideas accessible to ordinary Muslims through the artful use of poetry. Here is some encouraging guidance, '*You were born with potential. You were born with goodness and trust. You were born with ideals and dreams. You were born with greatness. You were born with wings. You are not meant for crawling, so don't. You have wings. Learn to use them and fly.*'

SUMMARY

The key elements of our findings are that the West today has reached the final stage of the left-brain oriented outward cycle which has produced great advances of intellectual prowess, but due to excessive emphasis on this process without a suitable balance of right brain intuitive experience, the time has come for a change. It is clear that the need for change is not recognised by many, especially those who have benefited greatly from results of scientific advances, the freedom of democracy, the dynamism of the capitalistic system and the great recognition received from achieving the ego-based values of wealth, power, fame and pleasure.

The first step is therefore to present the factual case based on the lessons learned from well documented historical studies and modern statistical data highlighting the deficiencies in our culture, including the high degree of mental illness, the breakdown of the family unit and the extensive erosion of our environment, mainly for the sake of economic gain and personal pleasure.

When this case is made, then drawing upon the guidance from the spiritual traditions of the four cultures, we will describe the inward oriented practices that help to bring us to a more still and balanced state. From this quiet state we will be able to see life more clearly and make better decisions. When practiced with the right dedication and resolve a real connection with our inner most being is possible. Such an experience is beyond the mind and emotions and in fact is only possible if the mind and heart are still and quiet. These practices include forms of contemplation, meditation and a greater degree of silence which need to become an integral part of our daily life.

When this happens there will be a greater recognition of the true values that are part of the natural law that governs humanity. As we acknowledge that our true nature is like the sun, always shining, we will recognise that the natural human such as love, truth and justice are simply rays of the sun. They manifest naturally the power and consciousness in its full measure.

The final stage is work for the common good, to use our intelligence, energy and loving nature to serve others. How we serve will depend on our talents, our position in life and also our willingness to serve needs as we become aware of them. For that to happen the focus has to be more on We then on Me. When this happens, an intuitive knowledge can be availed which will reveal what is needed and how best to respond for the common good.

Then we will address specifically climate change which is one of the most important issues facing our society today which can no longer be treated as an afterthought to our societies. We cannot busy ourselves with getting on with the usual business of growing our economies and only making a gesture towards it as it goes by. We have done this for more than 30 years and mainstream science now affirms the fact that we are now entering into the end game. Climate laws must be the first ordering principle for how we think about all of our other economic and social ambitions. We need a complete understanding of the problem and a systematic response to it.

Let us now look at these three stages of the way forward in more detail.

10

NINE STEPS
THE FIRST 3:
ACKNOWLEDGE THE PROBLEM—
SEE IT!

THE WAY FORWARD

In the next three chapters we are going to attempt to objectively examine the state of the Western European/American culture using the lessons learned from our historical analysis, acknowledge some of the existing negative conditions and then look at ways we can prepare to more effectively address these issues. Bishop Richard Harries addressed this issue and several other important ones in a talk he gave at the 2020 World Confluence of Humanity, Power and Spirituality organised by the Kanoria Foundation of India. Here is his perspective on honest self-examination:

"Above the entrance to the oracle at Delphi in ancient Greece were carved the words 'know thyself'- a very difficult thing to do, as I am sure we would all agree. But it is where any serious Christian spirituality must begin, with honest self-questioning. So much harm in the world is done by the way we deceive ourselves. We avoid looking at our real reasons and motives. Sometimes this is because it is too painful.

We need to question ourselves-not to make ourselves feel bad, or to beat oneself up-none of that, but simply trying to be honest and realistic and in so doing avoiding deceiving oneself and jumping into ill-considered words or actions. And it is this knowledge which can keep us humble, knowing I am one with all other frail, fragile human beings"

To be able to conduct such an objective self-examination the mind and the emotions need to be in a steady state. More quiet time is thus recommended as the next stage in out journey.

We will conclude with a recommended approach of applying natural human values to how we think, relate to others and act in service of the common good. A strong resolve is needed to follow these guidelines, which if undertaken will enhance the journey for people of all cultures. Each chapter will highlight 3 steps on the journey.

I. Acknowledge the State of Western Culture Today

At the conclusion of the presentation on the Western European/American cycles, the following observations were listed regarding the state of the culture today:

- Major values of the day are wealth, power, fame and pleasure. Excess has become the norm, for example, pornography and marijuana are now rapidly expanding businesses.

- A predominantly materialistic society dominated by scientific dogma, which says if something cannot be quantifiably measured, it is illusion; it is not real.
- Increasing atheism with no spiritual education offered to many young people and little practised by adults.
- The collapse of the family as a cohesive unit causing increased stress and tension in young people raised with- out the love and discipline offered by both parents.
- Highly advanced technologically, resulting in increasing dependence on the Internet and social media, with damaging material available to young children.
- Economically powerful, dependent on the continual growth of consumerism - we need to consume more if the economy is to grow. The result is excess.
- Over-emphasis on my freedom and equality; my rights - not my duties - and my idea is as good as yours, leading to a fragmentation of society.
- Continually growing disparity between rich and poor.
- Climate Change, which is a global problem. The West, being the current dominant economic power, needs to make significant changes to the policies and actions that are damaging nature for the sake of economic gain.

These conditions and others militate against realising our true potential and, if unchecked, will cause further stress, tension and unhappiness. It is important that these negative factors be acknowledged, as well as the need for change. We need to look carefully at the idea that our culture is advancing technically and economically and therefore the future looks bright. We can make a mistake about a positive interpretation about the light ahead in the future.

> *The light at the end of the tunnel*
> *is just the light of an oncoming train.*
> **Robert Lowell**

This is not to say that there are not fine and beautiful ideas and values in Western society. They do exist and reflect the finest qualities of the Western cultural and spiritual heritage. However, we would be in denial if we did not acknowledge the debilitating factors that exist today and try to address them.

Here are some perspectives which have appeared in the UK media over the last 2-3 years. One study published in the journal *Royal Society Open Science*, that asked a nearly 500,000 people in 109 countries about their values and attitudes. One of the conclusions drawn was that people who do not practice any form of religion tend to be wealthier. The alternative to religion is called 'secular rationality.'

In an interview between writer Pankar Mishra, and Matthew Taylor, the Chief Executive of the RSA (Royal Society for the Encouragement of Arts, Manufactures and Commerce), the subject of liberal democracy was discussed. While it was agreed that the main ideals of a liberal democracy; equality and the dignity of all, should be cherished, Pankaj claims that they have been compromised by an alliance between the wealthy, big business, i.e. the agents of capitalism, and politicians, saying and doing what is needed to obtain and remain in office. The result is a state of social and economic inequality and a high degree of competitiveness, which "*wears on people on a daily basis.*"

Another point mentioned was the emphasis on the nation state which demands a stringent kind of loyalty that tends to block the sense of solidarity with humanity. The example is given of the degree of American nationalism being provoked by President Trump which generated greater intolerance with people of other nations and cultures. It leads to an incorrect assumption that multiculturism destroys societal cohesion.

A perceptive view of the situation that exists in the United States today is presented in the book *Divine Harmony* by Dr Mary Doak, professor at the University of San Diego in California. She makes the point that a sense of community has been lost due to emphasis on the wrong priorities; "*looking for joy in the wrong places*". Her observation about life in the United States is that the search for the good life has taken a decidedly individualistic and materialistic turn, with the relentless marketing of products promising personal happiness. So many pleasures are available from countless items, many available from a pharmacy, promising to make lives easier, more comfortable, more fun, more interesting. From every direction people are encouraged to have and to do more, quicker, easier. The essential message of her book is a call to community to help individuals cope with the crisis.

A mechanical pattern about using quantity to measure quality has been emerging during the years in all aspects of life, from classrooms to boardrooms. Success is currently measured by quantitative results; be it examination grades; business profits, yearly earnings, the price of our car or house, etc. The result of this obsessive focus is that people feel justified in lying or paying a bribe to secure a business deal, or in cheating to get better exam results. In business, using numerical targets as the measure of success is commonplace and, in many organisations, they are the only measure. The problem with this is that all too often ethical or moral values, like honesty, patience and service are being put aside to make the numbers work. Another problem is that when basing one's life on achieving quantifiably measured results, personal pride arises on success and depression comes with failure, two aspects of the ego.

Here is a response from the Indian teacher Shantananda Saraswati when asked about the importance of a family in a culture. *"The ultimate unit for economic considerations is the family, which accounts for all individuals bound together with love, affection and sacrifice. Happiness of a family depends upon the cultural, religious and philosophical traditions of a society. When they become weak, the disintegration of family begins. Individuals become greedy for security. Once general greed takes over, the economic structure begins to crack."*

In addition, children raised without the love, affection and discipline become subject to even greater degrees of stress and tension. This is all too common in our apparently wealthy western societies.

In our scientific age, the thinking seems to be that unless there is quantitative measure, conclusions as to the usefulness and benefits cannot logically be made. What scientific, materialistic thinking is ignoring is the spiritual dimension of the human being, which cannot be analysed or quantifiably measured, but it can be experienced and can been seen in a person's behaviour. It is not separate from the physical, intellectual and emotional aspects of our being, in fact it includes and enfolds all of them.

2. ACKNOWLEDGE THE MISTAKES WE MAKE ABOUT VALUES

Let us look more closely at the current ideas about values in society and the lessons which can be learned from our observations about the past when these values were also prevalent.

We need to first be clear about the meaning of values and how they influence the way we live. A value indicates that which a person holds dear in the heart, that which is of great importance. When the term 'natural values' is used, it refers to manifestations of our true nature, like the rays of the sun coming from the ever-shining sun. All traditions, secular and spiritual, acknowledge the existence of natural human values, sometimes called virtues, and provide guidance on their importance and how to live by them. This is a 'valuable' point because we are seeking a way to communicate a common message to all cultures. Natural human values thus offer a common ground and is therefore one important aspect of the recommended way forward. Here are quotes from a sage of the East, Confucius and a wise one from West, Socrates, who agree on the principal that living to natural values is the way to true happiness.

"Wisdom, compassion, and courage are the
three universally recognized moral qualities of men"
Confucius

226

"The true philosopher loves truth and wisdom and the joys of the soul above all else; consequently he will be temperate, gentle, sociable, intelligent, and harmonious.

Socrates

Choosing the wrong values

Natural values, when lived, bring peace and happiness, which is what we all seek. Such values are instinctively appreciated by all human beings, however due to our full freedom of choice, other materially-oriented values, such as wealth, power, fame and pleasure are often chosen in preference under the delusion that they will bring peace and happiness. As we have discussed, in themselves these materialistic values are not wrong, but all too often the continual desire to have their fruits such as money and pleasure becomes dominant and become the normative basis for our decisions.

The consequences of basing our decisions on the wrong values are stress and tension, which are being experienced globally by adults and children. What is seen as a need for all of us, especially young people, is to be reminded more often about the importance of natural values and the guidance that has been offered through the ages about how to live these values. Experience has shown that by putting the natural values into practice, we will be better able to resist the temptations and withstand the mounting pressures to succeed in the material realm of life. If we can resist excess, our personal wellbeing and happiness will be greatly enhanced and we also will be more ready to help other people.

The statement made by John F Kennedy in his inaugural address as President of the US in 1961 is especially appropriate. *"Ask not what you country can do for you - ask what you can do for your country."*

We mistake continual activity for fullness of life

It is natural and good for life to be full. A life which is empty is unsatisfying and lonely. But what does this fullness consist of? For example, a life with love, peace, wisdom, courage and concern for other people could properly be called full. A common mistake is to take quantity of activity for fullness and the result is busy-ness. People fill up their lives with one activity after another without any rest between them. It is not that activity is bad in itself, but the lack of rest is the mistake and it inevitably results in a less effective response to the need of the moment. Ceaseless activity is ignoring the natural need for rest of the mind, as well as the body. It has been found to be one of the main causes of the severe stress and tension.

"To keep up with the fast-changing world, one has to come to stillness in oneself."
Hans Leewens

We mistake servitude for service

Service is natural and everyone loves to be of service. However, for many people in today's world bent on acquiring things for me and mine, service is often thought of as being the same as servitude, one step away from being a slave. The result is that many people shy away from service instead of accepting it as a natural part of life.

228

"Man finds happiness only in serving his neighbour. And he finds it there because rendering service to his neighbours, he is in communion with the divine spirit that lives in them."
Leo Tolstoy

We mistake an activity of 'giving to get' for generosity

Real generosity is giving without any desire or expectation of anything in return. It is not only being generous with money, time or anything else, but it is generosity of spirit that is needed. This means being open and available to serve, seeing the best in people and responding to that. It involves giving attention, time and love to other people without any motive for personal gain. Where one seeks to get something in return, true generosity is missing.

"We make a living by what we get, but we make a life by what we give."
Winston Churchill

We mistake detachment for not caring

Detachment is often confused with not caring. Detachment in its true sense is the key to caring. For example, a doctor may be a highly competent and disciplined person, working selflessly for his patients. If a patient is cured, he does not seek a certificate of success to show his greatness as a doctor. Equally, when a patient dies, he will be sorry, but will not give way to excessive grief or lamentation. Were he to do so, his ability to care for other patients would be impaired. In the same way, if we become bound up or identified with our desires or feelings, it can actually reduce our capacity to care for other people. It

229

easily leads to misery when those desires or feelings are frustrated or when they contradict each other.

"He who would be serene and pure needs
but one thing—detachment."
Meister Eckhart

We mistake money for wealth

Money is a part of wealth, but by no means is the only factor. Wealth also includes such things as an abundance of love, wisdom, goodwill and generosity of spirit. A man or woman with a great deal of money who is selfish and mean cannot truly be called wealthy, nor is such a person happy. In fact, if you have only enough money, you are truly wealthy. If you have more than enough money, but feel you need more, then you are poor.

"He who is content is rich."
Lao Tzu

We mistake speed for efficiency

Efficiency does not necessarily mean only getting everything done quickly. Sometimes it is necessary to make careful preparations so the action will be effective and have the desired result. Doing things too fast often leads to poor results in the long term. It usually turns out to be ineffective and often the action has to begin again. This involves more time and energy sorting out the mess caused by the hasty action.

"There can be economy only where there is efficiency."
Benjamin Disraeli

We mistake information for knowledge

Knowledge is used here in the sense of real understanding which arises from practice and experience. For example, there is a story about a group of philosophers who decided to learn to play tennis. They read all about the game and studied pictures and diagrams showing how the various strokes were played. They proceeded to the tennis court and began to play. Not surprisingly, they found they had no control over the ball which, when they did manage to hit it, either went into the net or out of court. After a short time, they concluded that the game of tennis was a foolish one and thoroughly unsatisfactory. They had the information about how to play, but not the knowledge, which can only be acquired by correctly putting the information into practice.

"An investment in knowledge pays the best interest."
Benjamin Franklin

We mistake the opinion of other people for self-respect

It is perfectly good and natural to have self-respect. This means that we are thinking, speaking and acting in a way that is being true to oneself. When a person has self-respect, the opinion of other people is not the dominating factor. We can in fact learn from the view of other people, while living based only on other peoples' opinions is a kind of tyranny. Many people today are forever fearful of what other people think. A tremendous effort is made to impress them. The slightest remark or comment, which may have been quite unintentional, can have devastating consequences on their confidence. Here is some very inciteful and practical guidance from Mother Teresa:

"*People are often unreasonable, illogical and self-centred;*
Forgive them anyway.
If you are kind, people may accuse you of selfish, ulterior motives;
Be kind anyway.
If you are successful, you will win some false friends and some
true enemies;
Succeed anyway.
If you are honest and frank, people may cheat you;
Be honest and frank anyway.
What you spend years building, someone may destroy overnight;
Build anyway.
If you find serenity and happiness, they may be jealous;
Be happy anyway.
The good you do today, people will often forget tomorrow;
Do good anyway.
Give the world the best you have, and it may never be enough;
Give the world the best you've got anyway.
You see, in the final analysis, it is all between you and God; it was
never between you and them anyway."

SUMMARY

The following is an assessment of what are considered our cultural accomplishments, along with what we actually have achieved.

How many of these points do you agree are valid?

- We spend more, but have less; we buy more, but enjoy less.

- We have bigger houses and smaller families; more conveniences, but less time to use and enjoy.
- We have more information, but less judgement; more medicine, but less wellness.
- We have multiplied our possessions, but reduced our values.
- We have learned how to make a living, but not a life.
- We have been all the way to the moon and back, but have trouble crossing the street to meet a new neighbour.
- We have conquered outer space, but not inner space.
- We have done larger things, but not better things.
- We have conquered the atom, but not our prejudice.
- We write more, but learn less.
- We plan more, but accomplish less.
- We have learned to rush, but not to wait.
- We build more computers to hold more information, but we communicate less and less.
- These are the times of fast foods and slow digestion, big people and small character, steep profits and shallow relationships.
- These are the days of two incomes, but more divorce, fancier houses, but broken homes.
- We drink too much, smoke too much, spend too recklessly, laugh too little, drive too fast, get too angry, stay up too late, get up too tired, read too little, watch television or work on a computer or smartphone too much, talk too much, hate too often, love not enough.

233

The conclusion drawn is that our Western society is currently going through a difficult and challenging period in which too much of our life is dominated by negative factors, meaning we are in a weakened state. This assessment does not point only to Europe and the United States, but also the other Western developed countries who are all slipping into a less influential economic state. There is greater recognition of this weakened state of our culture by many young people today, who represent a great hope that the current values and standards causing the decline can be altered. Given the ease of global communications, useful guidance can be drawn from Eastern cultures, as well as from our own rich Western tradition.

When a crisis occurs, the initial response may be one of fear and panic. The somewhat gloomy picture of society which we have highlighted is not meant to provoke that type of response. The word crisis comes from the Greek *krisis* meaning 'decisive moment'. When such a critical condition is recognised and acknowledged, there is an opportunity to pause, to reflect and respond. An important message espoused by all the major spiritual traditions is that there is a spiritual dimension to our being. It is in fact the essence of our being, which is the same for all humanity, totally pure and complete. Faith and trust in this principle gives us a greater sense of self-confidence needed to meet the severe challenges being presented.

The sun is always shining somewhere in the world. The rays of the sun are the manifest consciousness which lights the way forward. Our experience is that the light of the sun is often covered by clouds, so days can go by when there is no direct vision of the sun and, as such, our thoughts, words and actions are not fully conscious, but rather powered by the mechanical past.

These clouds are our ego-based ideas and assumptions, which have been reinforced over time such that they are seen to be without doubt the true view of the creation. These ideas have been formed by a mind which has not been properly controlled. For example, we see, smell, taste, hear something and we form an opinion of either 'I like that' or 'I don't like that.' This view is stored in our memory box and brought out whenever that object is experienced. Our view can change, but that also becomes a fixed item in memory. When we respond to an experience based on that view we are actually being guided by the past. We are not in the present moment giving our full attention to the situation at hand.

The same kind of misguided experience occurs when we have a sensory experience and we immediately begin to imagine what it will be like in the future. I like this and want to find a way to have more or I have my doubts and concerns about what will be the consequences in the future. A continual stream of; 'What If?' questions can arise to block a fully present experience. This collection of perspectives about the creation, based on the past and the fears and doubts about the future are repeated. They become the firm covers, the clouds that hide the sun of our true nature. The main pattern of the mind becomes to judge, compare and often criticise what we experience through the senses. This is what we need to eliminate.

3. ACKNOWLEDGE THE CULTURAL ISSUES THAT NEED TO BE ADDRESSED

This section offers a summary of the broader cultural issues which need to be acknowledged and addressed.

A recognition of the need for economic growth to be balanced against concerns for environmental sustainability.

There has been a growing concern about how the values of our consumer-oriented society and the subsequent habitual patterns of behaviour are causing dangers to the environment and to the state of the planet. Here some observations expressed by Gordon Brennan, a *Jyotisha* practitioner who has studied in-depth the cultural patterns over time for various cultures.

> *'Organisations that care for the Earth have started in the 20ᵗʰ century, many with apparently little chance of success at the outset, but they are resilient and are here. There are green movements, peace movements, conservation movements and environmental movements. Examples of these are, the Green Party, the Ban the Bomb movement, the Ecology Party, Greenpeace, Shelter, the United Nations, UNESCO and thousands of other such bodies devoted to caring for the Earth and its inhabitants. James Lovelock introduced the concept of* Gaia, a Living Earth, *to the public in the 1960s, and E F Schumacher brought economics down to earth with a book* Small is Beautiful, *as a counter to the dreamy macro-economic theories of the time.'*

Famous individuals have sprung into prominence in the 20th century to carry out specific tasks in this change of elements, defined by the movement of Saturn and Jupiter conjunctions from fire into earth signs. For example, Mahatma Gandhi and other proponents of non-violence, such as pacifist movements and lately animal rights movements.

Climate Change - A Crucial Problem

As has been noted Climate Change is an existential threat to not only the western culture, but to all of humanity. Global carbon emissions and the declining wildlife are part of the bleak picture. In a 2018 article in the Sunday Times it was pointed out by Jonathan Leake that in 2010 the world poured 46bn tons of greenhouse gases into the air. In 2018 it was 52bn, enough to warm the planet by 4C-5C by 2100. Many warnings have been sounded, but as yet major changes to our wasteful way of life have not been implemented. Time is running out so what is needed is a unified global effort to change our patterns of living.

Here are the key issues highlighted by Matthew Pye:

Artic Ice Melting

Arctic sea ice is retreating, shores are eroding, glaciers are shrinking, permafrost is thawing, and as a result insect outbreaks and wildfires are becoming more common. Alaska, among the fastest warming regions on the planet was 2.7°C hotter than average. In addition, the Boreal forests of Alaska are drier, hotter and more prone to lightning storms, which means that the number and intensity of forest fires are set to increase. This is a trend shared right across the planet's largest greenbelt.

237

In July 2019, the WMO reported that: *"Since the start of June, the Copernicus Atmosphere Monitoring Service (CAMS) has tracked over 100 intense and long-lived wildfires in the Arctic Circle. In June alone, these fires emitted 50 megatonnes of carbon dioxide into the atmosphere, which is equivalent to Sweden's total annual emissions. This is more than was released by Arctic fires in the same month between 2010 and 2018 combined."* The CAMS added that: *"A recent study found Earth's boreal forests are now burning at a rate unseen in at least 10,000 years."*

The Fate of the Forests

The fate of the forests is tied up with the rest of humanity. If forests collapse, human civilisation as we know it today will crash with them. Forests perform major functions, as central cogs in the global biosphere. If these forests flip from acting as major carbon sinks of the planet into acting as major carbon sources, this will be a catastrophic tipping point. From such a point, all human efforts to keep their fate in their own hands will become puny, futile gestures.

Global Heating

A rise of 2°C average global temperature might not sound like a big deal, but anyone who has had a fever for a few days at 39°C will know how lethargic and grumpy it can make human beings feel. Moreover, doctors inform us that if an elevated temperature is not treated for several weeks, then vital organs can start to break down. A 4°C rise for humans is a medical emergency; vital organ damage would occur and death follow if the temperature is not lowered. It is called hyperpyrexia.

Energy Sources

Our emissions are increasing due to the fact that we are still meeting the large majority of our energy demands with fossil fuels. 81% of global energy is produced by either coal, oil or gas. These statistics are taken from the latest data of the International Energy Agency. It shows that wind and solar power has dramatically increased from around 110 Twh to over 1,580 Twh since 2005, a major 1,450% increase. However, increasing the size of a such a small percentage does not change the overall problem very much. The whole energy system is in a state of paralysis where there has been no "transition". the growth in green energy has only been enough to take care of the extra consumption and population. Indeed, population and material consumption are still projected and are being stimulated to grow. so the flipping of our infrastructure has to be very radical and immediate to get ahead of the curve. and bring it down, not just get it flat.

Globally, wind, solar, hydro and all other renewable non-emittive energy sources still only account for 4% of humanity's energy supply. Nuclear Power, for all of its other complications, is at least carbon friendly, so we get to 9% with this included. Biomass (which is emittive and has great unsustainability issues) is about 10%

In fact, all of the recent policy commitments to new investments in green energy are not even sufficient to deal with the increased demand for energy that will come in the years ahead from factors such as consumption and population growth. Therefore, it is predicted that fossil fuel use and emissions will continue to increase until 2030 and beyond.

Greenhouse Gases

Science has known of the greenhouse gas effect since 1824, through the work of French physicist Joseph Fourier. In 1856, Eunice Foote provided the first key chemical details of this effect when she established that H_2O and CO_2 trap heat. Modern science can measure, in a remarkably precise manner, which particles make up the atmosphere above our heads. Since 1958, the Mauna Loa Observatory in Hawaii has been measuring the concentration of atmospheric molecules. The current level of CO_2 corresponds to an equilibrium climate last observed 3-5 million years ago, a climate that was 2-3°C warmer than today, and sea levels that were 10-20 m higher than those today. expressed as parts per million (ppm) or billion (ppb) (the number of molecules of a gas per million/billion molecules of dry air).

This data has been plotted onto a graph known as 'The Keeling Curve', so named after the scientist Charles David Keeling, who set it up. The Mauna Loa reading at the time of writing signalled that there were 414 particles of CO_2 in every million (414ppm). Nitrogen (N) makes up over three-quarters of the rest with 780,900ppm, alongside Oxygen (O) that occupies 209,500 ppm.

This is a concentration of CO_2 that is unprecedented in around 4 million years and when geologists look back in time to previous epochs that had the same levels of CO_2, they do not see a world which is compatible with human civilisation as it is now.

GDP

For all of the advances in our civilisation, we seem to lack so much imagination and wisdom when calculating our progress. The standard measure of economic development across the globe is GDP. GDP is a hopelessly reductive valuation of what we all get up to every year. It was first introduced as a key indicator by the Nobel Prize-winning statistician and economist Simon Kuznets during an address to the US Congress in 1934. GDP has been criticised ever since as a clumsy and narrow measure of economic growth. Indeed, Kuznets himself warned that the simplicity of GDP would make it prone to abuse by those who might benefit from oversimplifying matters. However, despite all of the criticism, we seem to be stuck with it.

It might just be a statistic, but the formative effect that this blunt measure of human progress has had on our policies and thinking must not be underestimated. The quarterly reporting of GDP is a key pivot around which so much government planning and media attention moves. It is a measure that is blind to countless stores of wealth that are held in the biosphere, in families and in communities.

Financial Growth

Our whole economic system is predicated on growth. It is the one fundamental axis that everything in the system turns on. This would not be a problem if we inhabited some infinite landscape. However, continual limitless economic growth is not possible in a closed mass system. Indeed, the excessive influence of wealth on the decision-making process deserves greater attention as it is a direct threat which can warp our civic thinking. The spectacular growth of these three aspects of modern civilisation: democracy, industrialisation and capitalism is well accepted. When applied in the right measure they can serve each other. However, we must continually ensure that our democratic institutions are safely insulated from the dangers that accompany the atomisation of people in industrial societies and which insulate them from the misuse of the power of money.

Money is a form of power, it is not just a method of transaction. This is an issue that requires real attention, given the vast size of some private pockets of wealth that exist in the modern economy. If these interests grow to form such a formidable strength that they pose a genuine threat to the authentic functioning of our democracies, then we should be willing and able to ask uncomfortable questions about their place in society of those individuals with that wealth.

Major corporations spend millions through lobbying, political campaigns and various traditional media and social media channels to influence the way in which citizens vote. The political parties that then form a government either protect existing legislation or change legislation (often simply by deregulation); this favours the interests of those corporations. The extra capital is then reinvested into reinforcing public opinion, which leads to votes and then legislation. This feedback loop continues to gather strength to the advantage of those in that jet-stream.

The fossil fuel industry has strategically invested their resources into undermining and suspending definitive climate action. They have pumped their money into all the pipes of our democratic thinking under the auspices of democratic virtues of 'freedom', 'tolerance' and 'individual rights'.

We are suffering from a serious case of **Truth Decay** at many levels of our democratic system and this corrosion of our ability to think and act in a public way is connected to the symbiotic relationship between democracy and capitalism. An honest and open discussion about the dangers of capitalism is needed, a real Dialogue.

The long-term problem is that we will run out of essential minerals and metals from the Earth's crust that we need. The short-term problem is that climate change is a direct consequence of the extraction of resources. Clearly then, if all of our government and private policies are geared towards achieving maximum material growth, then there is a fundamental problem. Pushing for this economic growth drives extractions, that drives energy use, that drives emissions, that drives global heating. We have had an economy that is fundamentally based on combustion since the Industrial Revolution, and we have motored ourselves into a dangerous spot Anybody who thinks that the solutions to climate change can be found by leveraging our growth to more advanced technologies has not understood some of the first principles of physics.

Have we asked ourselves the most basic questions about economics? How long will our limited resources last to deliver our current consumption habits? How do these figures play out when we have an expanding population? How many tonnes of greenhouse gases will be emitted, simply in the process of building all the new green infrastructure that is required to sustain our current lifestyles? Will such an overhaul of our energy and transport systems bring us too close to the limit of the remaining carbon budget for 1.5°C or 2°C?

The Need to Shift to Electrification Generated by Renewables—Wind and Solar Power

There is significant potential for electrification, as the global energy transition will concern the entire value chain, from production to distribution and usage of electricity. Electricity will replace petrol and diesel as fuel for road vehicles, replace the oil and gas we burn for heating and lighting and more. What is required is that renewables become the primary source of electricity. Generation is becoming more decentralised, with large-scale fossil-fuel plant being replaced by wind and solar farms. When it comes to electrification, which sectors will impact the climate change agenda the most? We cannot curb emissions without electrifying transport. Tomorrow's vehicles will need to be electric. Even in the short term, numbers are expected to rise rapidly with thirteen million zero and low-emission vehicles on the road by 2025, up from fewer than one million today.

Here is some information from the Raconteur Report on Climate Change which was released in October 2020. One section highlights five organisations who are making a positive contribution to the electrification solution.

Tesla is the largest provider of electric cars, tripling the number sold from 2017 to 2019. this conversion can make a big difference in helping to also curb pollution. While this area is growing it also means there is a need for more electricity which thus requires an increase in the amount of energy generated through wind and solar power, The combination of both these developments, shifts in power source and power consumption, will make a big difference

Vestas Wind Systems has more than 117 gigawatts (GW) of wind turbines in 81 countries, nearly 20 per cent of the world's 650GW of installed wind capacity, Vestas claims to have installed more wind power than any other provider. Not only does it consider "spear- heading the renewable energy transition" as central to its positioning, a key goal is to become "the safest, most inclusive and socially responsible workplace in the energy industry". This includes its human rights due diligence framework, which it claims is unique to the renewables.

Siemens Gamesa is a big player in the wind turbine business, present in 90 countries. Most recently and notably it has helped ease power shortages in Pakistan by rolling out eight wind farms in one year, along- side launching its Forests of Siemens Gamesa initiative to plant 50,000 trees to extract more than one million kilo- grams of CO_2 from the atmosphere. The initiative forms part of the company's new social commitment strategy to reduce poverty and promote STEM (science, technology, engineering and maths) education, while improving the environment

RusHydro is the leading producer of renewable energy in Russia, with the country's government recently boosting its stake as primary share- holder from 60.56 to 61.73 per cent. Its main goal is to be the dominant provider of hydroelectricity in the Far East and its 2025 strategy establishes the company's responsibility to support the socio-economic development of these regions.

Verbund operates 131 hydropower plants in Austria and Germany, and also have partnered with steelmakers Voestalpine and Siemens to run the world's largest pilot plant for carbon neutral production of hydrogen to be used in steel production.

The pilot will show whether technology can be used to replace fossil fuels on an industrial scale.

There is still a long way to go in this area, especially in the US, China and India. This is a complex area. China has been the largest investor in green energy for about a decade. It also suffers from the fact that it makes all the products that the Western world consumes. China thus needs to acknowledge that it has a responsibility to produce the goods in a more energy efficient manner. A more true picture is that the West has outsourced its emissions.

Correct the wrong assumption—that science and technology can solve all problems.

The rise of the importance of science and technology in this current cycle has been quite dramatic. It has been especially influential in the Western culture because it reached the peak of its ascending cycle in the 19th century. There are indications that this power of this idea is waning and there needs to be a reassessment of such fixed and rigid dogmas. An excellent book on this subject, *The Science Delusion*, written by a scientist Rupert Sheldrake, suggests that what is needed is further open and honesty enquiry. He lists some fixed core beliefs of modern science which need exploring:

"All matter is unconscious
Nature is purposeless
Everything is essentially mechanical
Minds are nothing but activities of brains
Unexplained phenomena like telepathy are illusory."

Contemporary science is based on the claim that all reality is material or physical. This is the theory that supports the materialistic-based culture that has arisen, whose fundamental proposition is that matter is the only reality. According to Sheldrake, until the 17th century university scholars and Christian theologians taught that the universe was alive, pervaded by the Spirit of God. All plants, animals and people had souls. The stars, planets and the Earth were living beings. Mechanistic science rejected these doctrines and expelled all soul from nature. This materialist philosophy was closely linked to the rise of atheism in Europe in the late-19th century which has continued to grow, using the mantra that we don't need God to explain the world, science can do it all.

A major effort is needed to re-establish the stability of family life which is dependent on women AND at the same time enable women to also have a greater influence role in the decision-making process of business and politics.

There has been a decrease in the recognition of the value, importance and need for a strong family, the most fundamental relationship in society and also an unwillingness to work to help sustain families in bad times, as well as good times. Greater recognition is needed about the strength and power of a stable family and less attention be given to making divorces as simple and easy as possible. Support programs to enhance the quality of the work environment and experience are also needed that can help women manage both important aspects of life. It must be said that it is the emotional power of the woman that is crucial for strengthening and binding a family, so she must be supported for the good of the family.

We need to reduce our extensive dependence on technology.

One aspect being access to an excessive amount of information available on a global basis. The challenge is for the individual to decide clearly; *'What is actually needed?' 'What is valid?' 'What is important now?'* Most people do not have confidence in their ability to decide and therefore, become dependent on the media for clarity in interpretation. Google seems to be the preferred way to learn anything these days. Mobile phone technology has resulted in the appearance of many smartphone zombies, who, with phone in hand, head bowed looking at the screen, walk through the streets oblivious to what is happening around them. This excessive attachment to the telephone is also seen in people driving cars while chatting on the phone and by young women pushing baby carriages, giving more attention to the phone than to their children. Advances in Artificial Intelligence (AI) will pose further challenges in the 21st century.

Efforts need to be made to find ways to re-establish the importance and influence of spirituality on daily life.

The lack of a regular spiritual impulse has resulted in a reduction or loss of a sense of community, good company, and reminders about living natural values. In the past, it was the local church that was the source of spiritual guidance, as well as the main organiser of charitable activities and services for the community. For a variety of reasons attendance at regular church services has declined dramatically. The majority of young people, 25 years old and younger, have not had a reasonable spiritual education.

An interesting assessment of world religions appears in the book, *The Clash of Civilisations-and the Remaking of World Order* by Samuel P Huntington. It shows a sharp decline in any religious tradition in China, the decrease in the followers of Orthodox Christianity, the sharp increase in Muslim adherents and the most dramatic rise in the nonreligious and atheists to more than 20% of the world's population.

The author uses the term modernisation to explain the significant changes. Modernisation involves industrialisation, urbanisation, increasing levels of literacy, education, wealth, and social mobilisation. It is a product of the vast expansion of scientific and intellectual development which began in the eighteenth century. The West was the first culture to embrace this approach to life and others are following, so that increasingly traditional aspects of all cultures are being set aside in favour of a more universally accepted standards of modernisation.

Will this continue when the next outward cycle emerges for the Indian, Chinese and Islamic cultures? Judging from the historical patterns we have examined, these cultures are in the process of renewing their spiritual and cultural traditions as they achieve greater freedom from the undue influence of other cultures. This is very obvious today in India where significant efforts are now being made to resuscitate the Hindu tradition after centuries under the control of Islamic and Christian based powers. It is also happening in the Chinese and Islamic cultures, but it is not so obvious. It will take time, but that is the nature of the final Earth period, slowly but surely.

As noted, the ability to communicate globally has increased the links that the West to the spiritual traditions of the India. An excellent quote by Dale Riepe a modern American philosopher, was found in *The Journey of the Upanishads to the West* by Swami Tathagatananda. It summarises quite nicely the situation that Western European Culture, current led by America, finds itself.

"If the American Empire meets with the fate of the British Empire, if Americans cannot resolve their life-and-death struggle with the intelligent use of technology, if the alienation in American society cannot be alleviated, then a new attitude may gradually replace the 300-year reign of optimism. Such eventualities may lead to more philosophers turning to contemplation, meditation and increased poring over the Hindu and Buddhist scriptures."

11

THE NINE STEPS
THE 2ND THREE:
MORE QUIET TIME—
BE STILL

MORE QUIET TIME

The brief but relevant assessments of the human condition in the current world have shown that the universal search for happiness is all too often focused externally, be it on wealth, relationships, work and/or worldly pursuits. Sometimes, we find a morsel of happiness in these, but given the rapidly changing world, very soon it is gone, leaving a vestige of pain at our loss.

The issue as to what brings long-lasting happiness to human life is the real question. The direction we need to explore is an inward journey of discovery, into the heart of our being. One has to learn to withdraw one's senses from the outward material world. The senses are outgoing and can never see the power that lies behind them. The next logical question is; 'How do we get there?' The nature of this journey has been described in various ways by the spiritual traditions of all cultures. It has been explained by myths, for example, *The Iliad and The Odyssey*, by spiritual stories such as *The Bhagavad Gita* and *In Search of the Holy Grail*, as well as scriptural teaching and sacred practices. Here is a useful direction offered by Richard Rohr, a Franciscan priest and author of *Everything Belongs:*

"Be still and know that I am God;
Be still and know that I am;
Be still and know;
Be still;
Be."

"To be or not to be?", is an important question. The clear answer offered here is simply to be, to be our natural self. This requires that we learn to live in the now, the present moment.

Given the greater global communication between the cultures of the East and West, the common wisdom accessed by different cultural traditions has been revealed. What has been useful about this open exploration of global spirituality is the fact that the ways to reach within are being shared. The problem is common, as is the solution.

The essence of this new direction is turning the attention inwards by: quieting the moving mind; surrendering the excess baggage of ego-based ideas and feelings; and simply connecting with our true 'inner being'.

Spirituality

Common to these practices recommended is that they help give access to the spiritual dimension of our human existence. It is useful to try and clarify what is meant by spirituality. The word spirit comes from the Latin word *spiritus*, whose primary meaning is 'breath'. It also has a secondary meaning, 'inspiration', which literally means breathing in or inner breath. The word spirit comes to denote those invisible, but real qualities which shape the life of a person or community such as: love, courage, peace, and truth. Our spirit is our inner identity or soul, the essence of those invisible, real forces that are elements of our true nature. The Vedic system calls these elements *shakti* or 'power'. The key is that the spiritual dimension of our being cannot be accessed by the senses, or by a moving mind or by agitated emotions. The spiritual dimension is beyond time and space, but is can be experienced.

This is where the conflict with scientific thinking arises. In scientific terms every element needs to be identified and measured. A quantitative measure is necessary. If it cannot be identified and measured, according to the scientific community, it does not exist. Rupert Sheldrake, in his work, *The Science Delusion*, expresses it this way:

"Contemporary science is based on the claim that all reality is material or physical. God exists only as an idea in human minds and hence in human heads. Minds are inside heads and are nothing but the activities of brains". By denying the existence of a spiritual dimension to our being, we will be unable to relieve ourselves of the tensions and stresses that have arisen due to mental and emotional conflicts. This is why the practices designed to quiet the moving

mind in order to make a deeper connection within are so important.

Bishop Richard Harries—in his book *Is There a Gospel for the Rich?*—addresses the issue of spirituality in the following way:

"Spirituality can help us realise our true humanity, can help us find our true centre, our soul's soul, in which to rest and from which to act. I would suggest that a genuine spirituality, by whatever religion it is formed, would be characterised by two things. First, a sensitivity to human suffering. This can be a great burden, so great is the load of suffering, but bear it in some way, so far as we can without ourselves being broken, is essential to our own humanity. The opposite, to let oneself become indifferent, unfeeling, uncaring is to become less than human.

Secondly, solidarity. We need to ask questions about my own society and its political policies and the ways they help or hinder those who lose out in the world as it is now. This is the way we can act in solidarity with them. Once I wrote a prayer in which I tried to express what this meant for me.

Grant that I may be in such solidarity with those who lose out now,

That I too may be one of the poor whom you pronounce blessed;

And grant that I may so stand against the forces that crush the powerless,

Looking and working for your new order of love,

Trusting in you, That even now I may be filled with the richness of your presence

And know the glory of your kingdom."

THE NEXT THREE STEPS

4. Mindfulness; a practice to help bring us to stillness, to be in the present moment **AND Quiet Reflection / Contemplation;** with a quiet mind and heart consider important questions so that right and good decisions are better able to be made.
5. Meditation; to take us all the way to a state of unity.
6. Silence; to enable us to withstand the onslaught of noisy desires and distractions and to connect with our inner being.

4. MINDFULNESS

What has also caught on quite dramatically with individuals, schools, and businesses is the practice of mindfulness. This Buddhist-based practice is simple, easily learned but, like meditation, needs to be practised regularly to fully experience the benefits of inner stillness and peace.

The essence of mindfulness can be gleaned from the name. We need to have access to a full mind, the full potential of the mind. As discussed, this can only happen in the present moment when all distractions of the past or the future are put aside and our attention is concentrated on whatever task is at hand. Being in the present moment is the key to rectifying the conditions created by the wrong actions of the past. The present is stronger than the past and the future, so we need to use this power in the right way.

Here is some useful guidance from Jon Kabat-Zinn, which appeared in the Foreword of the book *Mindfulness—A Practical Guide to Finding Peace in a Frantic World* by Mark Williams and Danny Penman.

"As mindfulness is a practice rather than merely a good idea, its cultivation is a process, one that of necessity unfolds and deepens over time. It is most beneficial if you take it on as a strong commitment to yourself. One that requires a degree of stick-to-it-ness and discipline, while at the same time, being playful and bringing to each moment, as best you can, a certain ease and lightness of touch."

His advice is good. In addition to strong resolve and determination, combined with the lightness of touch, we need to diligently practise the exercises designed to refine our attention and maintain that mindful awareness in carrying out the various tasks of our everyday life. Another excellent book, *Mindfulness for Life* written by recognised mindfulness experts, Dr Craig Hassed and Dr Stephen McKenzie, sets out clear guidelines on how we can live a more mindful life. Their research confirmed that when mindfulness is regularly practised, there will be:

- a reduction in stress and anxiety;
- greater ability to relax;
- improvement of health; and
- most importantly, increased clarity of mind to be able to deal with the inevitable challenges of life.

Berenice Boxler from the organisation, *Brussels Mindfulness,* wrote an interesting article *Inner Peace,* in 2018 showing how mindfulness can enhance the performance of one of the key values we are recommending, equanimity. The practice of mindfulness is a crucial element in the process of moving from talking about values to actually living them.

"An equanimous mind is balanced and peaceful inside, while also being right in the middle of the experience. It is feeling sad without feeling overwhelmed. It is being happy without wanting to hold on to the pleasant

experience. It is being at peace with everything, exactly as it is." 'Being at peace' does not mean that we must like everything. It means that we accept what is presented with detachment, which can be tremendously liberating. It frees us from the endless web of opinions and preferences and allows a more conscious response.

A Mindfulness Exercise

There are many Mindfulness exercises available all with the sim of quieting and then focusing the mind. Here is an example of one.

Connect with the sense of touch. Feel the weight of the feet on the floor...the weight of your body on the chair...the touch of your clothes against your skin. If the mind wanders away, just simply return to the sense of touch.

A Pause

In our society today, there is a belief that we need to fill our day with constant activity and not waste a moment. All too often it is the speed of an activity that counts as opposed to the quality.

Robert Poynton, author of *Do Pause*, points out clearly that the use of time today is in a way imitating machines who are able to operate continually without a pause. We constantly push on from one task to the next, ticking them off our To Do list as we go.

An interesting historical reference is that in 1880 Nietzsche was complaining of; *"a growing culture of indecent and perspiring haste".* Actually in 1815 Nietzsche said in a letter to Goethe:

"Young people are swept along in the whirlpool of time; wealth and speed are what the world admires and what everyone strives for".

The race had already begun more than 200 years ago. What is actually needed are regular pauses between activities, to give the mind moments of quiet time that allow rest and the recharge of fine energy. Pausing can have an impact on all our decisions be they practical, intellectual, emotional or moral. The pause is an active presence, not just an absence of thought or action. A pause creates a fine sense of space and freedom, which gives a greater dimension to an experience. In that space creativity is born, true and effective communications manifest, and mental and physical rest are availed.

The Present Moment

This simple but powerful quote from Marsilio Ficino is a good guide. It is important to recognise that the present moment is the only one that counts when confronted with difficult situations. In response we need to avoid slipping into autopilot mode. To be mindful, we need to remember to pause before responding. The space that is created by the pause brings finer attention, enabling knowledge to arise that advises us not to mechanically react, but to maintain a balanced state. No energy is lost and there is a better chance that a creative idea will arise in the moment.

Using a Mindfulness exercise to come into the present, the next stage is to quietly Reflect on important questions. Here is some guidance on that process.

Quiet Reflection/Contemplation

As noted in the examination of the final stage of the Roman Empire, the West's response to the excess prevalent at the time was to revert to a more inward direction in search of peace and happiness. One of the primary guides was the practice of contemplation and prayer, which was recommended by several spiritual guides of the day, including Plotinus from the Platonic tradition and the Christian monk, John Cassian.

The Oxford Dictionary definition of contemplation gives us several dimensions; 'deep consideration, reflection, meditation, profound thinking'. The word comes from the Latin word, 'contemplatio', which in essence means, 'a clear space'. It is the clear, balanced, state of mind that is sought by contemplation, which can also be spoken of as quiet reflection.

We need to find a way to lessen the negative influences of the mental delusions and ego-based ideas about; 'Who I am and how I am reacting to the world?' We need to find ways to retrain the mind to enable it to assume more frequently and in greater depth, a balanced and poised state. Being fully present, we will be better able to effectively respond to the many challenges of our over-active society.

What is a good example of quiet reflection or contemplation?

All spiritual traditions have substantial bodies of scripture designed to guide us to a full realisation of our true nature. These texts make up the main aspect of religious worship and are repeated time and again in holy services. What is needed is that people give their full attention to the words so that the meaning is better understood and a strong resolve to follow the prescribed direction will emerge. Being together in a group gives support to this process. As we all know, if our attention is not fully on the words as they are spoken, the true meaning will not be fully grasped. It may be that a certain idea about the meaning arises and that might be readily accepted as the answer and therefore intense listening is no longer required. Is that familiar?

Practising contemplation or quiet reflection is a system that combines the ability to focus and concentrate with the need to let go of the stream of thoughts that cloud the show. Contemplation also comes from the Greek word *temvo*, meaning cut off, a letting go. As we know, when the water is still, the reflection is clear, and the detail can be seen. Contemplation is only possible when we can surrender our mental and emotional attachments and curb the stream of our personal desires that prompt us into action. This process requires a degree of self-control and discipline and a strong resolve to make it happen. The attainment of a still and balanced mind, given the external clamour and demands of all the senses, is not easy.

This is where good company is important. Exactly as the monasteries offered the support of a group of like-minded people working together according to an agreed program, so we need to find groups of well-motivated individuals to work with in the refinement process.

Charji, the present spiritual teacher of the Sahaj Marg spiritual community of India, explains the need for both material and spiritual practices.

"As a bird needs two wings to fly, so a human being
needs the two wings of existence, the spiritual, and the material,
to lead a natural and harmonious life. If either is neglected for the
other, such a life becomes unnatural and the result cannot be what
we desire it to be."

All spiritual traditions encourage reflection on the teaching put forth by their teacher. A common direction is to internally repeat the statements, giving full attention to the words. When contemplating or reflecting with the attention remaining focused, the meaning simply arises from within, an intuitive experience. This also has been described as a mystical experience and in all religions there are mystics who have confirmed that knowledge and experience of unity is beyond the mind. Words or thoughts cannot go there. What is needed is a total surrender of all ideas, feelings, desires so there can be a direct connection with the single unchanging 'being'. As Plato described it; *"we move from becoming to being"*.

On a more practical note, here are some Mindfulness exercises and then questions for you to quietly reflect on which will help discover the best way forward. Such an approach helps shift your attention away from excessive concern for 'me and mine' towards that of 'the common good'.

Mindfulness Exercise

Look at the palm of your right hand as if you have never seen it before. Notice the small and bigger lines, the space between your palm and the top of your hand. Observe the different colours, tones and texture. Simply Observe

Question:

What are those situations that I meet, where I am more naturally inclined to focus on the needs of others and not my own ?

Mindfulness Exercise

Connect with the listening. Hear the sounds as they arise from silence and return to silence. Let the hearing go right out to the most distant sounds. Do not mentally comment about the sounds. . . Just simply Listen.

Question:

What are those situations I have avoided because the way ahead was unknown to me—like a step into the dark?

Reflection and Dialogue (R&D)

If change is going to be brought about on a group level, whether that be a family, a business organisation, a political party or a nation, what is needed in our democratic society is open and effective dialogue. It is important that we make a clear distinction between discussion and dialogue. The common term is discussion, but all too often this amounts to a dueling match regarding individual opinions as opposed to a joint conversation to discover the truth of the subject.

Hans Leewens has not only written on the subject of

dialogue, but has put it into practice for many years in his consulting organisation called Van Ede and Partners. Here are some of his thoughts on the subject and a prescribed way to carry out an open dialogue with a group.

'Discussion stems from *'dis'* 'apart' and *'quatere'* 'to shake'. Dialogue from the Greek *dia,* 'between' *legein,* 'to speak'. The dialogue process is one of adressing a specific question with the common aim of all to discover the true answer.

These guidelines are to be handled with care and discrimination, and much importance is to be laid on the role of a coordinator or guide.

1) Wait till there is a real question.

2) If there is no question spontaneously arising, or the guide has a specific question prepared, then the guide takes the lead in evoking the first question. Everyone is invited to listen carefully and fully without any distracting mental activity in order to fully grasp what is being said.

3) All participants are invited to reflect for some minutes on the question.

4) Then one by one give the result of their reflection—at this stage without ever relating to what has been said by somebody else.

5) In a second round, after some minutes of quiet reflection, everybody can refine his/her statement or put one or more open questions relating to the statements of others.

6) In a third and following rounds answers and new considerations may be given. No discussion.

What regularly happens in well-run dialogue-groups is an emerging of the truth about the subject. In many cases what is experienced is an opening of the heart. and a common understanding is reached. Then each participant is more willing to take it upon her/himself to abide by the conclusions.'

This is not an easy discipline to follow, especially when one is convinced that my view is correct and that I need to be free to keep arguing , to make my case to show that *'I am right'* and *'You are wrong.'* Political debates are a good example of this.

5. MEDITATION

Meditation has been practised for thousands of years in the various spiritual traditions, versions of which are consistent with their teaching. While there are different systems of meditation, the practice itself is universal. It helps create a real sense of unity, which is crucial in our world today.

Some useful guidance on the system of meditation and its benefits comes from Sri Shantananda Saraswati:

The system of meditation is simple and easy, is not religious and can be practised while remaining in the world of normal life. It is designed for the spirit of a person which is not bound to any religion. Meditation brings us to the bedrock of our being, a place of light, confidence and peace.

The essence of the practice is about attention, one-pointed attention, be it on a mantra or on a flame. There will be the inevitable distracting thoughts which consume vast amounts of our energy. In mantra meditation by continually returning our attention to sounding the mantra and listening to it, we avoid losing the energy. If the attention is maintained, the sounding and listening becomes finer and finer, until a point is reached where there is no sound, no listening, only a profound silence. It is in these moments that great peace is experienced.

It is said that the process of surrendering the mental and emotional activity that block the meditation process results in a recharging of energy, fine energy which naturally becomes available. While you cannot quantifiably measure the increase in energy, it is self-evident to those people who meditate regularly, myself included, that positive energy has been received.

My initiation into meditation came via The School of Meditation based in London which has taught meditation to thousands of people. The mantra meditation system came to the School in the 1960s via the Advaita Vedanta sage, Shri Shantananda Saraswati.

Here is some basic guidance about the process of mantra meditation. It begins in the physical realm, with the body and the senses. Having the right posture of the body is the starting point, a position that is balanced, upright and relaxed, without tension. Meditators do not have to sit cross-legged on the floor. Sitting on a chair of the right height is fine. When you look carefully at your posture, you may discover that habitual slouching might be viewed as normal. This is the first phase of surrender. It will take time, but gradually we become aware of the comfort and ease of an upright and balanced body. When this balance is obtained the next stage in the physical realm is stillness of the body.

When there is no physical movement, you find that the breath naturally becomes quieter and slower. You need to resist the temptations to scratch an itch, wiggle your toes or move your hands or head about. This is practising self-control, control of the senses, which prepares the way for the sounding process to begin.

The next stage is more difficult because it requires control of the subtle realm, the mind and the emotions. The process begins by repeatedly sounding a mantra, not verbally, but in the mind. The aim is to give our full attention to the sound from the beginning to the end of each repetition. Many meditation guides suggest that the initial sounding be loud and rapid, which gradually slows down. This sounds like an easy ask, but in reality the habitual workings of the mind with its concern for our plans, dreams, hopes, worries, some of which are powered by strong emotional involvement, creates a great attraction for the mind. The usual result is that our mind leaves the mantra and dwells on these thoughts relating to the past and the future. It requires a calm discipline to draw the attention away from these thoughts and bring the mind gently back to concentrate on the mantra. The process is simple but due to our habitual ways, it does take continual practice and gradual refinement to achieve the full benefits.

What is required is a strong resolve to not give in to the habitual mental processes, but rather let them go. "Not now!" is a useful command. The more often this clear discrimination is exercised, the more energy is available to attend to the mantra. As the resolve strengthens, the letting go of thoughts becomes a more gentle and effective process and the attention become finer.

The sounding of the mantra continues and we find the process of sounding the mantra gradually shifts to one of listening to the sound of the repeating mantra. At this stage, we need to trust the mantra and follow it and not feel that we need to be in control of this process. If we stay with it, we find the sound of the mantra becomes more full, fine and expansive. Confidence grows, personal effort reduces and when the inevitable distracting thoughts appear, it becomes easier to let them go. This is an example of the effect of a quiet mind, which enables the process to refine. The power of discrimination becomes stronger, greater clarity is experienced, thus enabling the process of meditation to refine even further.

If we can continue the process unimpeded, the final stage may be reached. In this stage, there is total silence and stillness of the mind and emotions and an experience of something beyond the subtle realm, which is said to be a connection with our true unchanging self. The Sanskrit word *samadhi*, meaning 'bliss', is used in the Indian tradition to indicate this state of being where there is full peace and happiness. *Nirvana* is the term used in the Buddhist tradition. When this state is experienced, even for a few moments, we become convinced that real happiness can be found within. This state is not dependent on anything or anyone else. It is natural and the degree of happiness experienced makes the happiness of the external world puny by comparison.

This has simply been an outline of the fine process. There are several schools of meditation that teach the techniques and provide ongoing support for people practising. A wonderful example of where meditation has helped to merge the spiritual traditions of the East and West cultures is the fine work of the World Community of Christian Meditation (WCCM). The founder of the organisation was Father John Main, a Benedictine monk, who had through the practice of meditation, prayer and contemplation, experienced a true sense of unity in the centre of his being, which he described as becoming one with the spirit of God. Here is a quote from him that appears in one of the many WCCM books, *The Business of Spirit:*

"We live in a world that makes great demands on us and is
continually threatening our ability to stay rooted
in the centre of our being. Meditation is the way to rootedness
in ourselves. If we live on the surface of activities, our lives
will degenerate into a search for security or
ways of self-protection."

Father Main went to India where he discovered the practice of mantra meditation. He returned and established a Christian oriented mantra, *Maranatha*, which is in Aramaic, the language of Christ. It means; 'Come, Lord'. Since the passing of Fr Main the WCCM, has been led for many years by a Benedictine monk Father Laurence Freeman They are now active in more than a hundred countries, with more than a thousand small groups of people who meet regularly to meditate. They have also helped set up meditation classes in more than 100 schools worldwide, which is a major contribution in helping the next generation to avoid the materialistic value trap and to have the confidence and courage to work for a real change.

Father Laurence is a person of immense energy and intelligence. He is a prolific author, speaker, teacher and retreat leader. He is active in inter-religious dialogues, peace initiatives and does not hesitate to use relevant material from Eastern spiritual traditions in his presentations and conversations. This is an important step in making Christianity a more inclusive spiritual tradition and not one that is mired in the; 'I am right and you are wrong' mentality.

He also strongly recommends that Christianity embrace more fully contemplation practices and place less emphasis on rigid ritualist practices, i.e. those which no longer truly communicate the message of Christ. Here is a statement from Fr Laurence's book, *Good Work*:

"Meditation is a very simple practice of universal wisdom found throughout humanity for about 4000 years. In recent years, meditation has become more mainstream because its benefits have been well proven. Over fifty years of research show that it has significant psychological and physical benefits. Examples are that it can reduce stress, improve blood pressure and reduce cholesterol. When these physical elements are under control, a person is more able to look at their life in terms of deeper and more subtle qualities."

The fruits of daily meditation

- The mind becomes calmer and attention can be sustained for longer periods, both within and outside the times of meditation.

- When we continue to practise taking the attention off our thoughts during meditation it is helping to give us the strength and confidence, we need to let go of the ego-based thoughts that dominate most of our waking hours. When we are free of ego domination, we are more naturally selfless, more other-centred, more **we** than **me**.

- Meditation is the work of controlling and transcending the ego, which is the cause of our fears, desires and illusions.

Here is statement about the ego from Sigmund Freud: *"The ego is the source of all suffering. The Buddha saw egotistical attachment as the cause of the cycle of suffering and harmful consequences. Jesus said to leave the little self, the ego behind, so the true self could rise."*

- Meditation teaches us how to deal with failure and imperfection, which is important in our society that worships success and condemns failure. When we meditate by repeating a mantra and we become distracted which is inevitable, we learn not to judge, not to criticise and most importantly, not to give up. We need to faithfully continue, trusting that the process of one-pointed attention will prevail. I have come to realise, through constant practice that every single time I let go of the distracting thoughts and return to the mantra, my ability to meditate improves. I can't measure it, but I do know it to be so.

- The spiritual fruits of meditation were described by Saint Paul as: love; joy; peace; patience; kindness; goodness; faithfulness; gentleness; and self-control.

A most productive initiative to introduce meditation in the West, is the Transcendental Meditation (TM) movement launched in the 1960s. Maharishi Mahesh Yogi, who was sent by his Guru to introduce meditation to the West, taught thousands of people during a series of world tours from 1958 to 1965, including celebrities like the Beatles, to help promote the practice. In the 1970s, the Maharishi shifted to a more technical presentation and he began training TM teachers and created specialised organisations to present TM to specific segments like business people and students. By the early 2000s, TM had been taught to millions of people worldwide.

The TM organisation carried out significant research on the effectiveness of meditation in the support of education, They produced a report which summarised more than 650 studies conducted at over 250 universities and research institutions in 33 countries which verified the benefits of meditation. The four main benefits are:

- Improved brain functioning, increased intelligence and improved academic performance
- Increased integration of personality
- Improved school-related behaviour
- Improved health

Meditation in schools is also becoming more prevalent. St James School in London offers students from 10 years old and above the option to be introduced to meditation as well as guidance and practice of Mindfulness. All the classes have one to two periods of quiet time each day to help enable the students to experience the inner peace and clarity we have been speaking about. More than a thousand children have been introduced to meditation at St James.

6. Silence

What I have observed over the years has been a strong aversion in our society to silence. This is best exemplified by the response of Justin Timberlake to a question about the value of silence. He said, *"Silence, that is so boring".*

It was my positive experience of silence and the many wise

words about the subject expressed by all cultures that prompted me to write a book on the subject, *In Praise of Silence*. Much of the material that follows comes from that work.

What is silence?

Silence is always present. It is the source, the substance from which all sounds arise; sounds in the form of thoughts and verbal sounds in the form of speech. Sounds are vibrations, movements. When there is silence, there is stillness. Both silence and stillness are characterised by no movement. We will confirm the points made about silence with of quotes from various traditions.

"In silence there are no thoughts, just being.
In total silence the mind comes upon the eternal."
Krishnamurti

Through silence we connect with the unseen; the unmanifest. To experience deep silence is to come into contact with the beginnings of things. Silence brings us in touch with our inner self; it is the source of real joy. It awakens us to the present moment from which inner knowledge can arise.

"The equivalent of external noise is the inner noise of thinking.
The equivalent of external silence is inner stillness."
Eckhart Tolle

Connecting with the silence within:
- has a calming effect on the body, mind and heart;
- gives rest to the body, stillness to the mind and
- openness to the heart; and

- produces fine energy, clarity of mind and a loving,
- generous heart.

> *"Silence is a true friend that never betrays."*
> **Confucius**

To still the body, mind, and heart requires quiet contemplation, a refining and quieting of the senses and the mind, so we are able to experience fully the soundless silence. We can actually learn through silence.

> *"Silence is the great teacher, and to learn its lessons you must pay attention to it. There is no substitute for the creative inspiration, knowledge, and stability that come from knowing how to contact your core of inner silence."*
> **Deepak Chopra**

These two quotations outline the importance of a pause between activities, a silence between the sounds, and the benefits of quieting the chattering of our mind.

> *"The practice of mental silence refreshes our mind and quickens our inner faculties. It is why many philosophic and spiritual traditions recommend a pause, a moment's silence, before any task. It is usually recommended that there also be a pause at the end of any action which sets the best basis for the beginning of the next task."*
> **Swami Paramananda**

> *"It is when we silence the chattering of our mind that we can truly hear what is in our heart and find the still, clear purity that lies within the soul. Spiritual love carries us into the silence of*

our original state of being. This silence contains the power to create harmony in all relationships and the sweetness to sustain them. It is when I am silent within that I can let God into my heart and mind, filling me with peace, love and power."
Dadi Janki

The enemies of silence; noise and desire

Today, the practise of silence and stillness are not given an honoured and essential place in our lives. They have at various times in the history of our culture been greatly valued, but today our age is hostile to them. We are addicted to noise and movement and cannot accept their absence. We belong to a restless culture with life that is firmly attached to a steady stream of activities, sensory experiences and material possessions. We are often uncomfortable in silence and stillness.

"Silence and solitude have never been more important.
They preserve us from the world of continual stimulation
which results in exhaustion, fanaticism and restlessness.
They liberate us from agitation and preserve us from excess."
John Lane

We have been speaking about how the internal agitations of the mind distract us and waste precious energy and as they build momentum great stress and tension are experienced. What is the main cause of these agitations? They all come from desires, wanting something that we believe we do not have. All action follows desire; desire to have; or to avoid. When there is desire, we are not in the present moment. We are either in the future, imagining what it will be like to have our desire satisfied or frustrated, or we are dwelling in the past, remembering the experience of the past, which was the basis for the desire.

"A quiet mind is all you need. All else will happen rightly, once your mind is quiet. In the calm and steady self-awareness inner energies wake up and work miracles on your part."
Nisargadatta

Communicating

We have also been speaking about the importance of communications, within families, communities, our own culture, and with other cultures. Key to effective communications is fine listening. When we give our full attention to listening, we will be able to connect with something greater, a silence that is beyond sound that cannot be understood through thought. When there is silence there is communication at a different level, which is deeper. This is an important point for a teacher. It acknowledges the fact that the teaching process is two way. If it is to be effective there needs to be both learning and teaching. Silence is golden.

"Silence is a better communicator than the spoken or written word. In silence prejudices and pre-conceptions fade away."
Mahatma Gandhi

"Without some degree of silence, we are never living, never tasting, as there is not much capacity to enjoy, appreciate or taste the moment as it purely is."
Richard Rohr, Franciscan monk

Decisions made in such a quiet state enable us to rightly

discriminate and choose. Coming into the present moment where silence rules opens up the possibilities for a unique creative response to be made; one that satisfies the need of the moment in the best way possible.

"The precious gift is not something that someone gives you. It is a gift that you give yourself."
Samuel Johnson

A statement of guidance from the Indian sage *Sri Shantananda Sarasvati* sums up nicely where we are and the way forward:

"Life on earth moves in cycles and all cycles work according to a system held by cause and effect in general. Nature works out these cycles automatically but human beings have consciousness which has come to realise the possibility to break away from cycles so as to gain and retain bliss through choice."

THE REST IS SILENCE

12

THE NINE STEPS
THE FINAL THREE:
VALUES AND SERVICE—
SERVE

7. VALUES

We have explored the nature of values and some of the mistakes we make about them. This step is about the benefits of living natural human values as an integral part of our life.

"Our values are important because they help us to grow and develop. They help us to create the future we want to experience."
Barrett Values Centre

What is a natural value?

It is a value which is inherent in the nature of a human being. For example, when you ask anyone what it feels like if they consciously tell a lie, the overwhelming response is that it is not comfortable, physically, mentally or emotionally. This is valid and it is the reason that lie detector machines can work, because there is a natural reaction within when we do not speak the truth. To speak the truth is natural, to lie is unnatural.

In 1999, when the World Parliament of Religions, consisting of senior religious leaders from all faiths, met one of the questions they addressed was; *'What values would do we recommend to the global business community so they might better serve the needs of society?'* They were unanimous is agreeing that love, truth, justice and freedom as the most important. These are examples of natural values.

This direction was an inspiration for me and a fellow businessman, Chris Rees, and in 2006 we jointly authored a book on values and principles in business, highlighting these four as the foundation stones. The book, *From Principles to Profit-The Art of Moral Management* attempted to show how the spiritual and the material worlds can be integrated. Business can be: *principled & profitable; ethical & effective; conscious & commercial.* This message was reinforced in my recently released E-Book and E-Learning course, *Ethical Entrepreneur.*

Recommended values coming from various traditions
- **Christianity**; St Paul–Galatians
  Love; joy; peace, gentleness; goodness; faith; humility;
- **Confucius**
  Honesty; justice; modesty; courage; respect; forgiveness; kindness; benevolence; integrity; loyalty and wisdom.

- **Plato – Divine Values**
  Wisdom; justice; courage; and temperance.
  Bhagavad Gita; Divine Values Fearlessness; generosity;
  self-control; harmlessness; truth; renunciation; modesty
  compassion; gentleness;
- **Islam; Quran**
  Freedom; accountability; justice; kindness; mercy; love;
  equality; honesty; compassion; fairness; and devotion.

In all traditions opposite qualities are also noted, called by such names as sins, gates to hell, ego- based deceptions. Well known in western culture are the Seven Deadly Sins: *Gluttony, Lust, Greed, Anger, Sloth, Envy, and Pride*

8. Apply Natural Values in How We Think; Relate to Others; and Act in Life.

In our daily activities there are three material aspects of our being which are continually engaged; our mind, our emotions and our physical body. How we use these faculties will influence the quality of our access to the fourth dimension, our spiritual being. It is my strong belief that if we live natural human values in the performance of daily activities, we will achieve a high degree of peace, happiness and love, which will manifest naturally in guiding us to serve the common good. This is the universal Golden Rule in practice.

The material offered in this step comes primarily from the If I Can...and Ethical Entrepreneur online apps provided by my Community Interest Company If I can...CIC, which was founded in order to communicate this important message about values. In addition to some text, videos, stories and quotes about the values from a wide range of sources; Eastern and Western, spiritual and secular, a mindfulness exercise and question for reflection is asked in each section regarding how the particular value under consideration can be better applied in your life. What follows are some examples of how the guidance is offered.

HOW WE THINK

We should establish a stable and balanced state of mind when making decisions.

There are many decisions that need to be made every day, usually with several options. These involve significant external pressures, for example, to meet expectations of other people, or internal pressures, I want to win and gain personal recognition. What is needed is a decision-making process based on a mindful awareness that enables you to remain calm and still within. To concentrate so you are clear about your motives and the guiding principle that should be used as the basis for the decision. Key values in this realm are: **stillness/inner silence; self-control and calmness.**

"There is no substitute for the creative inspiration,
knowledge and stability that comes from
knowing how to contact your core of inner silence."
Deepak Chopra

"Self-control means having the ability to
channel thoughts in the right direction."
Dadi Janki

280

"A calm mind brings inner strength and self-confidence, so that's very important to good health."
Dalai Lama

Practice a Mindfulness exercise and then Reflect on this question:

What are the situations that cause my mind to be agitated and difficult to control?

HOW WE THINK

We need to be clear about the vision, values and long-term, sustainable objectives of our work.

One of the defining traits of a full productive life is a dedication to the service of other people through the proper fulfilment of our duties. To best serve we need to see clearly a real need that can be met by our capabilities and resolve to carry forth and complete the chosen task. The direction chosen needs to be sustainable during an extended period, which will happen if the vison is followed faithfully, without being diverted due to a fear of failure. The values that can help here are: **service, duty/responsibility and perseverance.**

"All Power comes from the Spirit and that Power should be used to Serve Humanity."
Hari Prasad Kanoria

"The best way to find yourself is to lose yourself in the service of others."
Mahatma Gandhi

281

"Never, never, never, never give up!"
Winston Churchill

Practice a Mindfulness exercise then Reflect on this question:
Why is it natural and so fulfilling to serve?

HOW WE THINK

We need to be free from excessive desires, habitual reactions and claims for success or failure.

The guiding values should encourage a more balanced and consistent approach, free from personal, ego-driven motives, and mechanical reactions. One statement often heard is 'We have always done it that way.' Quite common are also excessive claims for success or blaming other people for failure. We all have acquired certain habits and fixed expectations, which if mechanically followed can limit our response to the real needs of the moment. Useful values here include: **consistency, temperance/moderation, detachment.**

"Consistency is the foundation of virtue."
Francis Bacon

Plato spoke of temperance as one of the four divine virtues which was echoed by a follower:

"Temperance is the greatest of the virtues."
Plutarch

Here is a statement about attachment:
> *"If you can make one heap of all your winnings*
> *And risk it all on one pitch and toss;*
> *And lose, and start again at your beginnings*
> *And never breathe a word about your loss."*
>
> **Rudyard Kipling**

Practice a Mindfulness exercise and then Reflect on this question:
Why do people today, myself included, find it so difficult to know when to stop, to know what is enough?

HOW WE RELATE TO OTHERS

We should establish and maintain a harmonious environment for all activities with other people.

When a high level of voluntary co-operation is in place, the results are greater than the sum of the individual parts. Crucial to the personal efficiency, motivation and satisfaction is a positive atmosphere, where mutual respect and an active concern for the needs of other people prevails. Such an environment puts more emphasis on 'we' than on 'me'. **Co-operation; respect; and compassion** are values that help create fine harmony.

> *"Alone we can do so little; together we can do so much."*
>
> **Helen Keller**

> *"A wise mother knows: It is her state of consciousness that matters.*
> *Her gentleness and clarity command respect. Her love creates security."*
>
> **Vimala McClure**

"If you want others to be happy,
practise compassion.
If you want to be happy,
practise compassion."
Dalai Lama

Practice a Mindfulness exercise and then Reflect on this question:

How often do I think about the less fortunate people in the world and consider how I might help them?

HOW WE RELATE TO OTHERS

Be truthful and transparent in all your dealings with yourself and other people.

To speak the truth is natural. Truth binds. The binding is called trust, which is essential to every kind of relationship. Trust involves a confidence in the goodness, strength, reliability of another, which is only possible when people are open, transparent and consistently speaks and acts truthfully. It results in firm long-term relationships which last through good times and bad. The vital values here are: **truth/honesty, integrity; and trust.**

Confucius spoke about **honesty:**
"Be honest in thought, word and deed."

and **integrity:**
Let your words correspond to your actions and your actions with your words."

284

"Trust is a treasured item and relationship. Once it is tarnished,
it is hard to restore it to its original glow."
William Ward

Practice a Mindfulness exercise then Reflect on this question:
When I say that will do something, is it important to me that I
fulfil my promise?

HOW WE RELATE TO OTHERS

We need to demonstrate real concern for other people by
helping them fully recognise and develop their talents.

It is important to firstly acknowledge the talents and
capabilities of other people, without making comparisons with
our own, and where necessary to assist in their full development.
It is a great blessing to have the freedom to enable the discovery
of our natural talents and to be inspired to fulfil our true
potential with natural enthusiasm. By generously assisting other
people in this quest, we are benefiting as well. The related values
here are: **empathy; patience; generosity.**

"When you stretch your arms upward in parallel, this is like
Sympathy. In Empathy they gradually bend towards
each other and become one."
Els Leewens

"Be patient with everyone, but above all with yourself. Do not be
disturbed because of your imperfections and always rise up
bravely after a fall."
St Francis de Sales

*"A gift is pure when it is given from the heart to the right person
at the right time, and in the right place, and when we expect
nothing in return."*
Bhagavad Gita

Practice a Mindfulness exercise and then Reflect on this question:

When I give a gift, do I usually have an expectation of something in return?

HOW WE ACT

We need to think about how we act and focus our energies on the right priorities and in the right way.

Important here is to act correctly following a decision; to find effective ways of making the idea practical. This happens when there is fine discernment concerning the conditions existing in the moment, memory of the guiding principles and a determination to do what is right. It is not an easy process. I like the approach voiced by Matthew Taylor the Chief Executive of the RSA whose model is *'thinking like a system and acting like an entrepreneur.'* The important values here are: **discrimination, justice/fairness; and courage.**

*"The finest discrimination is between the real and the unreal,
but it is also between the right and the wrong,
the important and the unimportant,
the useful and the useless, the true and the false,
and the unselfish and the selfish."*
Krishnamurti

286

"Courage is the most important of all the virtues because without courage, you can't practice any other virtue consistently."
Maya Angelou

Practice a Mindfulness exercise and then Reflect on this question:

What are those situations that I have avoided because the way forward was unknown to me?

How we act

We must learn to deal effectively with challenges, mistakes and uncontrollable external factors.

Life is full of uncertainties and the best way to respond to the inevitable challenges, be they self-imposed or from an external source, is to maintain a balanced and unattached state so that our full faculties are available to discern the best response. The related values here are: **equanimity, steadfastness, and determination.**

"Those souls who overcome the desire for sensual pleasure and maintain a state of equanimity,conquer the pains of mundane existence."
Mahavira

"Be like the cliff against which the waves continually break; but it stands firm and tames the fury of the water around it."
Marcus Aurelius

"Do all the good you can, By all the means you can,
In all the ways you can, In all the places you can,
At all the times you can, To all the people you can,
As long as ever you can."
John Wesley

Practice a Mindfulness exercise and then Reflect on this question:

What fine value am I determined to make an integral part of my life?

HOW WE ACT

We need to inspire other people by actions based on the natural human values, thus setting a fine example.

Inspiration comes naturally and is most powerful when someone sets a fine example. It arises in full measure when actions are performed with love and care for other people, when actions are selflessly and humbly performed and when there is true integrity; as we think; so we speak; and thus we act. Such a fine example establishes a high standard for other people to follow, which is crucial for any society, at any time. The important values here are: **selflessness, humility and loving care.**

"There is nothing more worthy than the virtue of selflessness.
Selflessness unites people."
Buddha

"We come nearest to the great when we are great in humility."
Rabindranath Tagore

"When the power of love overcomes the love of power,
the world will have peace."
Jimi Hendrix

Practice a Mindfulness exercise and then Reflect on this question:

How can I begin to reduce my ego-driven demands for praise and attention?

THE RESULTS

By putting into practice, by living the natural human values, great benefits accrue for all; family, friends, neighbours, work colleagues, the community, nation, society at large, and you. While certain material resources are required for life, they need to be achieved without violating basic moral principles and great care must be taken to avoid excess. What is really sought by everyone is happiness, a sense of contentment and peace, all of which naturally arise when you think, speak and act consistently, in the right way. This is real success. The natural results here are: **happiness; peace/contentment; and unity.**

"He who is virtuous is wise; and he who is wise is good
and he who is good is happy."
Boethius

"Peace begins with a smile."
Mother Teresa

289

"Unity in diversity is the order of the universe. A man is different from a woman, but in being all humans, we are one."
Swami Vivekananda

Practice a Mindfulness exercise and then Reflect on this question:

What have I found to be the best ways to bring myself to a state of quiet peace and contentment?

9. Service

The Nature of Service

The prolific author of spiritual books embracing all traditions, Andrew Harvey, offers an excellent view on the need for and the power of fine service. In his book *The Direct Path* he explores the mystical traditions of all religions. He says:

"In all the serious mystical traditions, the final aim of the Path is not ecstasy or revelation, or the possession of amazing powers, or any kind of personal fulfillment, however inspired or exalted, but rather to become humble, supple, selfless and tireless instrument of God and servant of divine love."

A comment from the *I Ching* of Taoism offers this advice to leaders:

"He who wants to rule must first learn how to serve." In the Bhagavad Gita, Krishna the Divine lord tells his devotee Arjuna that those who love him most perfectly live *"simple, self-reliant lives based on meditation and use speech, body, mind to serve the Lord of Love."*

Andrew Harvey states that an important message from Jesus was that divine illumination was not real unless it was put into direct and passionate action. The world is a real kingdom of God-inspired love and justice which needs to be experienced, to be lived. We need to bring the whole of our human existence; social, economic and political, into living dynamic harmony with the will and love of the Divine. In considering the fundamental nature of service there are three vital elements that influence the quality:

- Intention
- Attention
- Retention

Intention is the motive behind the service, that is, for whose benefit is the service. We may perform an action that on the surface is for the benefit of another, but if the real motivation is for the sake of one's self, the quality of the action will suffer.

Attention, which relates to the execution of the service, is at its finest when done attentively with love and care. We have shown that such actions are helped by mindfulness, being in the present moment. Here is a quote about intention and attention working together from Leon MacLaren, the founder of the School of Philosophy and Economic Science.

"Love removes all personal obstacles in service, devotion establishes direct relationship, all the steps leading to a proper completion of an action fall into place. Sometimes people respond to service according to the sense of duty, but when the emotional import goes into it then it works much better and leads to fullness. It creates happiness for the person who serves and procures most benefit to the recipient of the service."

Retention refers to the degree to which an individual claims credit for their actions. Actions performed to satisfy the need without any personal claim on the results has a finer quality than the same action performed for the sake of a result that is claimed by 'me'.

We have addressed the importance of attending to an action in the present moment and also the need not to claim the results, be they positive or negative. Here is a brief expansion of the various levels of intention i.e. to whom the service is dedicated. The following diagram will help our exploration:

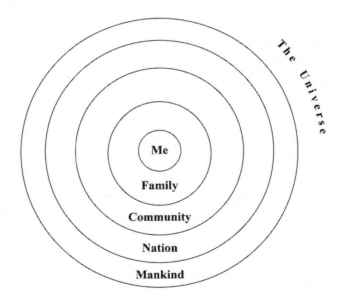

It begins with the small circle in the middle, **Me**. This represents the situation where we act solely for our own benefit; one serves 'Me'. I am the main beneficiary; my advancement; my enhancement; my pleasure are the main motivators. It is rather small and limited perspective.

Some people might say, "Isn't that true all the time for everyone?" I would suggest that while this picture does describe our intentions a great deal of the time, there are occasions when the view widens to embrace others.

Let's look at the next stage of opening out to another circle which is 'Family'. This represents that state when our thoughts, speech and actions are devoted to the service of the family; our wife, husband, children, parents, grandparents etc. I am sure we have all experienced this expansion. What happens is that the boundary, that limited attention to 'Me' dissolves and we take in quite naturally, something larger. When we are in this state, what does it feel like? Isn't it a most natural response to a need to 'sacrifice' your own concerns for that of your mother, father, brother, sister, child? Me is part of the whole, called family, so 'Me' continues to be looked after.

The next stage is what we will call 'Community'. It can be the town/housing estate where you live, the company you work for, the club in which you are a member, the charity that you serve etc. Here again we see the same principle; there is an apparent sacrifice of my own time, energy, even money. There may be less time with the family all for the sake of what is seen as a greater good. Now remember we are looking at intention. This stage is only valid if our true motivation is for the good of the 'Community'. Some people participate actively at this level, but often the inner intention and motivation continues to be 'Me'. It is the mark of a great team or an excellent company when team or company 'spirit' is strong and consistent. This spirit, which with effort can be maintained over a long period, sustains an enterprise and enhances its reputation. It also makes the activity attractive and many people desire to be associated with it.

Going further, we can act for the sake of the 'Nation'. Times of disaster, crisis and war are examples of people realising higher human potential inspired by this wider view. Competing in the Olympics for your country can generate great energy and enthusiasm on the part of the performer and the audience of supporters. Performance is enhanced because of the high degree of support being offered by other people. There are men and women in all aspects of everyday life who have a strong sense of devotion to the service of the 'Nation'.

There are those great teachers and leaders in all civilisations who have worked tirelessly for the benefit of 'Mankind', and there have been a few people whose life has been devoted to the betterment of the entire 'Universe'. With intention at this level one is certainly working towards the common good.

"A human being is part of the whole, called by us "Universe", a part limited in time and space. He experiences himself, his thoughts and feelings as something separated from the rest—a kind of optical delusion of his consciousness. (our normal life) This delusion is a kind of prison for us, restricting us to our personal desires and to affection for a few persons nearest to us. Our task must be to free ourselves from this prison by widening our circle of compassion to embrace all living creatures and the whole of nature in its beauty."

Albert Einstein

The idea put forward by many people is that real happiness comes from caring for and serving other people.

"Man finds happiness only in serving his neighbour. He finds it here because in rendering service to his neighbour, he is in communion with the divine spirit within them."

Leo Tolstoy

The final and most potent motive for action is when we serve from a real sense of love. The ego-based ideas and desires have been put aside and our whole energy and emotional power is channelled into providing a needed service. The needs of other people become the paramount concern and there are no claims for anything in return. Providing service based on love is most satisfying.

" Being happy in other people's happiness melts the heart. The heart having melted a new relationship arises and the quality of responses changes. A different spirit of devotion comes about and the activity gets the flavour of love. If one could be made to understand that caring for oneself is bondage, while feeding others is freedom, then life would be easy for all."

Sri Shantananda Saraswati

Service—Make a Positive Contribution to Climate Change
Key Elements of the Solution

Climate change needs a positive story line at the end. This is not because we optimistically assume that there will be a happy ending for us: this is the real world. The positive narrative that needs to be asserted is simply based on the fact that it is still possible to avert the collapse of our societies. We are still in control of our own destiny. As far as the mainstream scientific models show, we have not yet pushed nature over a tipping point.

Rational Laws

In any society, the only way to get a systemic handle on a situation is through legislation. Climate change cannot be managed by piecemeal initiatives; instead, it needs one singular core legislation that sets the speed for a nation's overall emissions. A law that is based on science and fair per capita responsibility. The various protest movements are indications that there is a real demand for change.

A national law for the climate could be an equivalent to the US Civil Rights Act of 1964. The law would stipulate the annual percentage emission reductions required for that nation, starting from the year in which the legislation was passed. A full table of the national reductions required, along with a full explanation of how those figures are calculated, can be found at the website www.Cut11Percent.org. Indeed, there are some simple practical ways out of the crisis. The trees of the Boreal and Amazon forests indicate two lines in our tragic plot where the story could be reversed: the trees that we are currently slashing down are a part of the solution to climate change. Trees offer us a resource to divert or postpone the tragedy we have created.

Trees

Planting trees is one of the obvious and beautiful ways to mobilise ourselves in the climate crisis. The power of forests to capture our emissions is extraordinary, and the chemical reaction which enables them to do this also provides so much of the oxygen we breathe. Trees also act as keystones for small ecosystems and provide habitats, food and shelter. Any investment in trees is, therefore, also a significant addition to the planet's biodiversity. This aspect of the natural world is often overlooked, but without the breadth of biodiversity, the towering stack of agricultural necessities that we have can easily get tipped over (with or without the help of climate change). Just as trees need wide roots to remain stable, so it is with the biosphere.

Of all the flanks of our assault on the climate emergency, greening our environment poses the fewest political problems and offers attractive rewards. If we were in any way serious about the threat of climate change, this would be the first sign of dramatic action. Our inner cities, suburbia and our countryside would have their green volume turned up to the maximum. It would be the most rewarding type of warfare we've ever engaged in.

Engaging the Power of the Young & Politicians

Indeed, Greta Thunberg has provided a jolt to the usual media currents. Her directness and depth have provided a vast democratic space for millions of others to occupy. There is an impetus and energy that has enabled the crisis to break important ground in our thinking, most notably through the strong female voices of Anuna De Wever and Adélaïde Charlier (Belgium), Hilda Flavia Nakabuye (Uganda), Marie-Claire Graf (Switzerland), Louisa Neubauer (Germany) Alexandria Villasenor (US) and many others.

Rebellion

Demonstrations have helped bring together a beautifully wide range of people who are committed to deep change to the surface of the media. The millions of people who hit the streets in protest across the globe in 2019 demonstrate that once people start to envisage change it can become highly contagious. Indeed, there does seem to be an awakening in recent months of just how irrational we have been in our actions. Although we have only ever increased our greenhouse gas emissions, there is still a window of opportunity to turn our ship to the opposite direction. This could be the moment, just on time, when these essential virtues of democracy enable us to shift course. It seemed utterly implausible a short time ago, but this could be the moment at which we could regain our common sense.

Politicians, those who are responsible for establishing laws and monitoring compliance, need to be convinced of the seriousness of the problem and the need to act now. They also need confirmation that the citizens, the voters, agree and are ready for change.

Your Spiritual Compass

Here is an interesting perspective regarding a recommended way forward so that we can avoid the terrible consequences of Climate Change. The insights come from a book written by Satish Kumar, entitled *Spiritual Compass*. Satish is the Editor Emeritus of the magazine Resurgence & Ecologist and a long-term peace and environment activist. The section chosen is called *The Eleven Point Programme for Sattvic Action*. Sattva in the Indian

Vedic tradition represents the quality of energy which results in clarity, stillness, peace which in essence is a higher state of consciousness. It becomes more dominant when a person meditates, reflects on fine scripture or even just comes fully into the present moment i.e. the result of more quiet time.   Here is a brief summary of the points made along with some commentary linking it to our approach.

1. Change our Attitude — out highly industrialised, urbanised culture looks upon nature for its usefulness in helping maintain our current way of life and as a result we have abused nature and are beginning to pay the price. We need to shift our attitude about the natural world to one which embraces it as an integral part of life

2. Live Simply — Do not follow the current scheme of acquiring money and material possessions, doing lots of different activities i.e. living a life based on quantity. Rather live an eco-friendly quality life.

3. Consume Less — On the physical side, eat less, especially meat, drink, drugs. On the mental realm, spend less time watching TV, on social media using your phone or computer, sometimes consuming trash like pornography. Again, greater emphasis needs to be on quality.

4. Waste Not — This includes excess food which gets thrown away, objects like phones, computers, appliances and most seriously plastic. We must address the excessive use of plastic which is non—recyclable.

5. Use No Harmful Products — When performing cleaning and maintaining objects use environmentally friendly products. In agriculture avoid pesticides; in building projects use locally sourced materials whenever available, even if they cost a bit more. Quality vs Quantity again.

6. Walk – In addition to walking, cycling is another option we need to embrace more fully. We need to lose our dependency on pollution generating motorised vehicles. Additional walking is also a good way to get more needed exercise and to counter the strong trend towards obesity.

7. Bake Bread – What is recommended here is reconnecting with older traditions, consuming less fast-food and doing something that requires careful attention. When someone makes a meal with care and attention, the quality of the food is enhanced and the people eating it benefit greatly.

8. Meditate – More quiet time, as we have recommended, which will restore a greater sense of balance, peace and self-confidence so that the right motivation will arise and quality actions result.

9. Work Less – Reduce the excess, provide for important needs like time with family and friends, practicing and performing actions that are expression of your talents. It could be such activities as writing, artistic work like painting or drawing, photography or simply reading books which you purchased, but which have rested on a shelf untouched for some time.

10. Be Informed – Take time to study subjects including those designed to feed and help develop your spiritual realm.

11. Organise – Become part of groups who share your finest ideals and work together. The power of a group will benefit you and all members.

An even more specific set of practical suggestions on how we can reduce our individual Carbon Footprint has been offered by Meditatio, the publishing arm of the World Community of Christian Meditation in a book, *Meditation & Earth* written by Deborah Guess.

- Reduce or opt out of patterns of extreme consumption by simply buying less, by asking, 'Do I really need this?'
- Buy goods which involve the least amount of processing and packaging possible.
- Consume food that has been locally and organically grown, and produce some of your own food if possible.
- Consider second-hand and recycled options for clothes and household items.
- Adopt the minimalist principle of de-cluttering and of owning fewer things.
- Support renewable energy either by installing solar energy or using a power company that has good credentials.
- Make public transport, walking or cycling your usual method of transport. Before booking a flight, ask yourself if you really need to make the trip.
- Find ways in the home and at work of having a lighter footprint by using less energy and fewer resources; for instance, switch from disposable plates, cutlery and cups to washable ones; from tissues to washable handkerchiefs; prepare food at home rather than getting a take-away; put on an extra jumper instead of turning up the heating; insulate your home or redesign it to reduce your need for cooling in the summer.

THE WAY FORWARD

Go in peace to love and serve the Lord

EPILOGUE

SUMMARY OF
THE NINE STEPS

THE ESSENTIAL MESSAGE OF THE RECOMMENDED WAY
FORWARD IS TO SERVE THE COMMON GOOD

- See It – Acknowledge The Problems
- Be Still – More Quiet Time
- Serve – Live Fine Values, Serve

THREE ACKNOWLEDGEMENTS

A good part of this book has tried to make clear, using historical evidence over 2500 years from the four main cultures of the period, that many of the prevalent conditions in Western society today are negative in that they oppose the natural law; that which is natural for the human being. One of the reasons this negative state of our society continues is that too many people will not admit that we have a problem. Therefore, the first step in improving conditions is to acknowledge the main mistakes we are making.

I. Acknowledge the State of Western Culture Today

The key items of concern about our culture that we offered are:

- Major values of the day are wealth, power, fame and pleasure. Excess has become the norm.
- A predominantly materialistic society dominated by scientific dogma, which says if something cannot be quantifiably measured, it is illusion; it is not real.
- Increasing atheism with no spiritual education offered to many young people and little practised by adults.
- The collapse of the family as a cohesive unit causing increased stress and tension in young people raised with- out the love and discipline offered by both parents.
- Highly advanced technologically, resulting in increasing dependence on the Internet and social media, with little control resulting excessive use and damaging material available to young children.
- Economically powerful, due to the continual emphasis on consumerism which needs to grow if the economy is to grow. The result is greater excess.
- Over-emphasis on my freedom and equality; my rights - not duties - and my idea is as good as yours, leading to a fragmentation of society.

- Continually growing disparity between rich and poor.
- Climate Change, which is a global problem. The West, being the current dominant economic power, needs to make significant changes to its policies and actions that damage nature for the sake of economic gain.

2. Acknowledge the Mistakes We Make About Values
- We mistake continual activity for fullness of life
- We mistake servitude for service
- We mistake an attitude of 'giving to get' for generosity
- We mistake not caring for detachment
- We mistake money for wealth
- We mistake speed for efficiency
- We mistake information for knowledge
- We mistake the opinion of other people for self-respect

3. Acknowledge the Cultural Issues that Need to be Addressed
- A recognition of the need for economic growth to be balanced against concerns for environmental sustainability.
- We need to correct the wrong assumption that science and technology can solve all problems.
- A major effort is needed to re-establish the stability of family life which is dependent on women and at the same time enable women to also have a greater influence role in the decision-making process of business and politics
- We need to reduce our extensive dependence on technology.

THREE WAYS TO CREATE MORE QUIET TIME

All human beings have the power, as well as the mental and emotional faculties, to not only see and acknowledge the problems, but also to make the needed changes. To do so we must resolve to act in such a way as to eliminate the obstacles that are blocking the way towards living a happy, peaceful and productive life. That way is attained through creating **More Quiet Time.**

4. Mindfulness; which is a daily practice to help bring us fully into the present moment. Being in the present moment is the key to rectifying the conditions created by the wrong actions of the past. The present is stronger than the past and the future, so we need to use this power in the right way.

AND

Quiet Reflection or Contemplation

Practising contemplation or quiet reflection is a system that combines the ability to focus and concentrate with the need to let go of the stream of thoughts that cloud the show. The attainment of a still and balanced mind will enable us to make right and good decisions.

What is recommended is that we practice a Mindfulness exercise then quietly Reflect on some of the key issues facing us.

5. Meditation; which has the potential to take us all the way to a state of unity. It is said that the process of surrendering the mental and emotional activity that block the meditation process results in a recharging of energy, fine energy which naturally becomes available. It is this energy that enables us to look afresh at the situations before us and act appropriately.

6. Silence; which needs to be resorted to at times on our journey in order to withstand the onslaught of noisy desires and distractions which continue to emerge. Connecting with the silence within has a calming effect on the body, mind and heart; gives rest to the body, stillness to the mind and openness to the heart; and produces fine energy, clarity of mind and a loving, generous heart.

THREE WAYS TO BEST SERVE THE COMMON GOOD

7. Natural Values

Carefully examine our motives for actions and resolve to live our life guided by the natural human values, ones that are part of human nature and manifest like rays of the sun. Values such as truth, justice, and love are universally recognised by all cultural traditions. We looked briefly at some of the values which appear in the holy scriptures of different spiritual traditions.

- **Christianity; St Paul–Galatians**
  Love; joy; peace, gentleness; goodness; faith; humility; and temperance.
- **Confucius**
  Honesty; justice; modesty; courage; respect; loyalty; forgiveness; kindness; benevolence; integrity; wisdom; and righteousness.
- **Plato – Divine Values**
  Wisdom; justice; courage; and temperance.

- **Bhagavad Gita; Divine Values**
  Fearlessness; generosity; self-control; harmlessness;
  truth; absence of anger; renunciation; serenity; modesty
  compassion; absence of envy; gentleness; constancy;
  forgiveness; fortitude; purity; absence of pride.
- **Islam; Quran**
  Freedom; accountability; justice; kindness; mercy; love;
  equality; honesty; compassion; fairness; and devotion.

8. Apply Natural Values in How We Think; Relate to Others; and Act in Life.

HOW WE THINK

We should establish a stable and balanced state of mind when making decisions.

Key values in this realm are: *stillness / inner silence; self-control and calmness.*

We need to be clear about the vision, values and long-term, sustainable objectives of our work.

The values that can help here are: *service, duty / responsibility and perseverance.*

We need to be free from excessive desires, habitual reactions and claims for success or failure.

Useful values here include: *consistency, temperance / moderation, detachment.*

HOW WE RELATE TO OTHERS

We should establish and maintain a harmonious environment for all activities with other people.

The values that help create fine harmony are *Co-operation; respect; and compassion.*

Be truthful and transparent in all your dealings with yourself and other people.

The vital values here are: *truth/honesty, integrity; and trust.*

We need to demonstrate real concern for other people by helping them fully recognise and develop their talents.

The related values here are: *empathy; patience; generosity.*

HOW WE ACT

We need to think **about how we act and focus our energies on the right priorities and in the right way.**

The important values here are: *discrimination, justice/fairness; and courage.*

We must learn to deal effectively with challenges, mistakes and uncontrollable external factors.

The related values here are: *equanimity, steadfastness, and determination.*

We need to inspire other people by actions based on the natural human values, thus setting a fine example.

The important values here are: *selflessness; loving care; and humility.*

THE RESULTS

By putting into practice, by living the natural human values, great benefits accrue for all; family, friends, neighbours, work colleagues, the community, nation, society at large, and you.

The natural results are: *happiness; peace / contentment; and unity.*

9. Service

CLIMATE CHANGE—
THE KEY ELEMENTS TO A SOLUTION

Rational Laws

In any society, the only way to get a systemic handle on a situation is through legislation. Climate change cannot be managed by piecemeal initiatives; instead, it needs one singular core legislation that sets the speed for a nation's overall emissions.

Care for Trees and Forests

Planting trees is one of the obvious and most beautiful ways to mobilise ourselves in the climate crisis. The power of forests to capture our emissions is extraordinary, and the chemical reaction which enables them to do this also provides so much of the oxygen we breathe. Trees act as keystones for small eco-systems to provide habitats, food and shelter.

Engaging the Power of the Young

There is an impetus and energy that has enabled the crisis to break important ground in our thinking. The millions of people who hit the streets in protest across the globe in 2019 demonstrate that once people start to envisage change, it can become highly contagious.

This could be the moment, just on time, when these essential virtues of democracy enable us to shift course. It seemed utterly implausible a short time ago, yet this could be the moment at which we could regain our common sense.

Reducing our Personal Carbon Footprint
- Reduce or opt out of patterns of extreme consumption by simply buying less, by asking, 'Do I really need this?'
- Buy goods which involve the least amount of processing and packaging possible.
- Consume food that has been locally and organically grown, and produce some of your own food if possible.
- Consider second-hand and recycled options for clothes and household items.
- Adopt the minimalist principle of de-cluttering and of owning fewer things.
- Support renewable energy either by installing solar energy or using a power company that has good credentials.
- Make public transport, walking or cycling your usual method of transport. Before booking a flight, ask yourself if you really need to make the trip.
- Find ways in the home and at work of having a lighter footprint by using less energy and fewer resources; for instance, switch from disposable plates, cutlery and cups to washable ones; from tissues to washable handkerchiefs; prepare food at home rather than getting a take-away; put on an extra jumper instead of turning up the heating; insulate your home or redesign it to reduce your need for cooling in the summer.

Serving the Common Good

Let us resolve to fulfil one of the important purposes of our life, which is to serve the needs of others. This begins by seeing the need and opening the heart and mind to find the way to best satisfy that need. In this way life becomes more 'we' then 'me'.

The three vital elements that influence the quality of service are:

- **Intention**

- **Attention**

- **Retention**

Intention is the motive behind the service, that is, for whose benefit is the service.

Attention, which relates to the execution of the service, is at its finest when done attentively with love and care.

Retention refers to the degree to which an individual claims credit for their actions.

And finally, **love, love, love**, that is all we need. Give love fully to all. This we can do because pure love is part of our true nature. Give unselfishly, without seeking anything in return. Widen the circle of compassion to embrace all living beings and nature in its beauty.

IF WE TAKE THESE NINE STEPS AS PRESCRIBED, WE WILL
BE MAKING A MAJOR CONTRIBUTION TO THE
FULFILMENT OF THIS UNIVERSAL VEDIC PRAYER:

*"May all beings everywhere be happy and free, and may the
thoughts, words, and actions of my own life contribute in some
way to that happiness and to that freedom for all."*

The Practical Journey

Paul has published four books:

• *In Praise of Silence*; a compilation of what has been said by spiritual and secular guides on the value of silence and the need for more silence in society today.

• *From Principles to Profit-The Art of Moral Management*; co-author with Chris Rees; on the application of moral values in business.

• *If I can...Timeless Values for Today*; documenting the material offered in the *If I can.App* about the application of universal human values in life.

• *Ethical Entrepreneur*; an E-book showing why a values-based approach to business management is needed to restore trust in business.

He has been a contributing author in two other books:
• *Managing by the Bhagavad Gita, Timeless Lessons for Today's Managers*
• *The Return of Ethics and Spirituality in Global Development*

His personal website is: www.timelessvalues.co.uk

Current Roles

Founder and Director of If I Can...CIC, a Community Interest Company, which offers Mindfulness-based Values Apps for individuals, schools and businesses, including If I can..., a free daily app (www.ificanapp.com) and Ethical Entrepreneur, a values-based business management E-Learning Company, **Intellexis**, course and E-Book. (www.ethicalentrepreneur.org) A free E-mail version is also available via the website.

He is currently a Guest Lecturer at *Regents University* London, contributing to their business entrepreneurship program.

Board Director for Waterperry Gardens Ltd, a Charity based organisation committed to providing as environmentally-friendly garden and careful devoted service.

Education/Business Career

Paul has an Engineering degree, BScEE, and an MBA which helped prepare him for a number of entrepreneurial activities in the computer industry where he began employment in 1964 with an American company, Control Data. He moved to Brussels in 1972, to become the European Sales and Marketing Manager and in 1977, started up the first European Computer-based Training (CBT) business. After a sabbatical year at Oxford

University studying Education, he set up as a self-employed E-learning consultant in London. In 1987, he founded and was the CEO of an E-learning company, Intellexis which grew and became a listed company on the London Stock Exchange (AIM) in 2001. He retired in 2011. The core values of the organisation were Integrity and Service

The Spiritual Journey - A Personal Perspective

I have a great feeling of gratitude for the spiritual guidance received from some very fine teachers and for the real experience of a deeper state of awareness, which has enabled me to gradually put the knowledge into practice. It is this experience that I am seeking to share.

When I arrived in Brussels in 1972 from the United States, good fortune greeted me in the form of the School of Practical Philosophy, which I joined three months after my arrival. The school is associated with the School of Philosophy and Economic Science (SPES), a London-based educational charity, founded in 1937. Our Brussels study group included people from several European countries and my awareness of the world began to expand.

Most importantly, the teaching provided was a beautiful mix of Western and Eastern philosophy. The teachings of Plato were featured along with Christian teachings and the Indian Vedic Advaita tradition. References were also made to the teachings of Buddha, Lao Tzu, Islamic mystics, such as Rumi, and a wealth of other spiritual guides. The common elements of these spiritual traditions were a real eye-opener for me. What was most important about this school's approach was the strong emphasis

316

on the practical application of the teaching, not just merely reading and discussing.

The mindful awareness practice, which was introduced in Session One of the first course, was a huge wake-up call. I knew in the first moments of practising it that giving my full attention in the present moment was a key to living a better life at all levels. The awareness came to me like a flash of light. Subsequent classes over many years keep returning to the key practice of giving one's full attention in the present moment to the work at hand, be it listening, touching or the use of any of the senses. This is true Mindful Awareness.

After two years attending weekly classes our group was offered meditation. This was another great gift. I remember vividly the first session, when I was introduced to the mantra that was the basis for our meditation. I had no expectations, only an offering of full attention to the sound, which brought a real sense of inner peace and expansion. This practice of meditation made a significant initial impression, but I learned quickly that one needs to be consistent in meditation practice for the benefits to continue and grow. I have continued meditating on a daily basis for more than 45 years. As noted, while the practice is simple, it is not easy to perform without the many well-established, ego-based ideas drawing my attention away from the mantra. I can confirm that when my full attention is given to the sound of the mantra, with full trust and no expectations, there is at times an experience of peace, contentment and happiness that goes well beyond anything attainable in the material world.

Another great benefit I received from the study of philosophy came after attending classes for three years, when I was asked to be one of the tutors. This was another major step ahead because I had held in my heart - since I was a young boy - an unfulfilled desire to be a teacher. The opportunity had not presented itself until that moment. I have carried on teaching classes in philosophy and other related subjects ever since.

I experienced the positive power of silence when I was only 18 years old. My uncle Henry asked me if I would accompany him on a weekend Silent Retreat to be held at a local Jesuit Monastery. It was the first time he had attended such an event and he was looking for company. He probably also thought it would do me good. How right he was.

The retreat was attended by about 100 men who, except for a meeting on Saturday evening when questions could be asked and observations given, maintained total silence for the weekend. I was surprised how easily we were able to communicate without words. What I discovered as the weekend progressed was how my mind gradually became quieter and at the same time clearer. I decided the best use of my time was to undertake self-examination. This took the form of a reflection on my life, considering what had transpired so far, the main lessons learned and what might be the best direction for the future. The silence and good company created the ideal conditions for such a reflective activity. I wrote down the findings in the form of notes to refer to in the future, as a reminder. It was a beautiful experience with the thoughts and the written words flowing naturally without any effort. There was natural honesty and humility present in the observations made.

It was as a result of that initial experience I became a convert to the power of silence and for the next 12 years while living in the United States, I continued to accompany my uncle on a weekend Silent Retreat. After moving to Europe, I continued with such reflective activities and for many years now I have been attending a week-long Silent Retreat.

After a sabbatical year studying the principles of Education at Oxford University, I moved to London and was able to join the school there. Part of the its programmes are weekend and week-long retreats, where opportunities are offered for quiet reflection, mindful activities, meditation, and silence. I also attended courses in Calligraphy, Plato, Vedic Mathematics, and Vedic Astrology, called Jyotisha. Many of us were also motivated to learn the Sanskrit , the language of the Indian spiritual classics.

I was involved for 35 years as a volunteer in an art festival organised by the school, Art in Action, which was held yearly from 1975 until 2016. For more than 10 years I fulfilled the role of the Assistant Organiser of the event which in the final years attracted an audience of around 25,000 people over 4 days. It was a wonderful example of true service as more than 600 volunteers per day worked to service the needs of the visitors, artists, teachers and suppliers.

The Journey continues.

ACKNOWLEDGEMENTS

This work has developed over a period of more than 30 years. While I have not been fully engaged in the work all that time, elements appeared along the way, which finally resulted in a more dedicated effort starting two years ago. I would like to acknowledge the contributions provided by a number of knowledgeable people including my teachers; those people whose work has inspired me to undertake the task; those people who helped in the production by providing content; and those patient souls who have reviewed, edited and commented on the content.

Ms Sheila Rosenberg, now deceased, who studied history and in the early1980s wrote a paper describing the existence of a 900 year cultural cycle. We had several conversations on the subject. This was the start.

My interest at the time in Vedic Astrology (*Jyotisha*) caused me to consult fellow Astrologers, Geoffrey Pearce, Jan Willem van Doorn and later Gordon Brennan regarding the planetary pattern that could explain such a cycle. It was through our collective efforts that the proposed 854-year cycle was discovered, which is a primary element of this book. Jan Willem also reviewed and commented on the final text.

Brian Hodgkinson, a fine historian and fellow philosopher, has been a major contributor to my understanding of Western history of the last 2,500 years.

Arthur Farndell, in addition to making a major contribution regarding the influence of Marsilio Ficino in the period of the Western Renaissance, has been extremely helpful in his meticulous proof-reading of the versions along the way.

Professor Jonathan Liu, Regents University London, a Council member of the Universities China Committee in London and a trustee and Chairman of the Board of the Directors of Ming-Ai (London) Institute, who reviewed the chapter on the Chinese culture.

Professor Brikha Nasoraia, Arabic, Semitics and History of Religions at the University of Sydney, who reviewed and verified the validity the Islamic material presented.

For contributions to and reviews of the Indian cultural history there are several people who need to be acknowledged. As noted in the text Kamalesh Sharma, former Indian High Commissioner to the United Kingdom and later Secretary General of the Commonwealth, was and continues to be a useful contact.

Two people who have inspired me to learn more about the Indian tradition are Dr Hari Prasad Kanoria and his close associate Dr Rahul Varma. I first met them when I was invited to give a presentation at the yearly conference run by their charitable SREI Foundation, on the subject of *Humanity, Power & Spirituality*, which is part of their many activities designed to rejuvenate the Indian culture and to serve humanity. Recently, the SREI Foundation was appointed as a member of the Economic and Social Council of the United Nations.

The third close link with India is with Mr Rajendra Jain, one of the Jain family who runs one of India's oldest publishing companies, Motilal Barnasidass which have existed for 116 years. He kindly helped me to better understand the Jain tradition as expounded by Mahavira, one of the main avatars of the Axial Age. Through his introduction, I met Dr Ashvini Agarwal, an Indology scholar who reviewed the chapter on Indian culture and made useful suggestions which have been included in the book.

Regarding Climate Change I am very grateful for the full cooperation with Matthew Pye who has given us free access to his extensive research on the subject, much of which is included in *Plato Tackles Climate Change* and his other work on the subject, *No Common Sense.*

One of my great supporters over a long period of time is Hans Leewens who also fully supports Matthew. Hans is fellow philosopher who has contributed to my understanding of the system of Reflection and Dialogue (R & D) in helping to resolve the serious, complex issues facing us. He is also engaged in writing a book entitled *The Twenty-First Century Renaissance.*

Those people who have contributed to both my personal understanding and the content of the final three chapters are; the Founder of the School of Philosophy and Economic Science, Leon MacLaren, now deceased; and the current leader, Donald Lambie; as well as two Indian sages, Sri Shantananda Saraswati, now deceased; and Sri Vasudevananda Saraswati. These

Indian sages have since 1965 answered questions of the School regarding the practical application of the Advaita teaching on the Way to Realisation. The teaching gleaned from attending weekly classes in the school along with being initiated into the practice of mediation, tutoring groups, plus most importantly attempts at living the teaching in daily life, has helped me to develop a more expansive and inclusive spiritual perspective.

Father Laurence Freeman, Director, World Community of Christian Meditation (WCCM) who helped me integrate my understanding of the common links between the fundamental principles of the Christian tradition and the spiritual teachings of other cultures, to which I have since been exposed.

On the subject of silence, I acknowledge my deceased Uncle Henry. I also thank Rudyard Kipling, whose poem *If* has been a major influence in helping me to understand the importance of living our life according to natural human values. Three of the four books I have written are aimed at communicating this important message about the value of values.

There are several authors and friends I would like to thank for reviewing the book and offering useful guidance.

Lord Stephen Green, whose book *The Human Odyssey*, covers similar periods of time and cultures. We have had very useful conversations on the subject.

Robert Arnett and Smita Turakhia, who also offered the use of images from Robert's book, *India Unveiled.*

John Adago, author of two books on the subject of spiritual awakening; *Ancient Wisdom* and *East Meets West.*

Karen Armstrong, as previously noted, has made a major contribution via her fine work, *The Lost Art of Scripture.*

Andrew Marr's masterly work *A History of the World*, has been a useful source of information. Andrew personally agreed that I could use some of it, which I have.

Satish Kumar who also agreed that we could use material from his beautiful work, *Spiritual Compass*, which combines nicely spiritual guidance with the practical steps needed to help address the Climate Change challenge.

Bishop Richard Harries made several useful contributions regarding the Christian perspective. Two of his books were referenced directly, *Is There a Gospel for the Rich?* and *God Outside the Box: why spiritual people object to Christianity*

Another fine author, Andrew Harvey, whose book *The Direct Path* has provided us some useful material about the inclusive view of spirtualty and the nature of Service.

Professors Satinder Dhiman and A D Amar, on the guidance offered by the *Bhagavad Gita* and the role of values in business.

Authoring guidance at a seminar run by Richard McMunn, and follow up support from Joshua Brown and Jordan Cooke

Ian McLellan, the MD of Arcturus Publishing, who published *From Principles to Profit* and who gave some useful guidance.

Thanks for the design and editing services provided by Wendy Yorke, Jessica Palmarozza, and Janet Lee. I am also very grateful for the highly professional cover design and formatting performed by Ranchor Prime.

Finally, my sincere thank you to Susan Mears for her tireless work in getting the book published by both UK and the US publishers.

Thank you all.

Quotation References by Chapter

Chapter 1: Introduction; History; Time
History
Conversations with Shantananda Saraswati, School of Economic Science, 2018
The Fate of Empires and Search for Survival, Sir John Glubb, Windmill Press, 2002
World History, Philip Parker, Dorling Kindersley Ltd, 2010
The Death of the Past, J H Plumb, The History Book Club, 1970
The Cycle of Time, Simone Boger, Self-Published, 2014
Time
Richard II, William Shakespeare, Folio Society, 1960
The Dialogues of Plato, Jowett Trans. Random House, 1937
St Augustine, Westminster Collection of Christian Quotations, Westminster John Knox Press, 2001
Ecclesiastes, The Holy Bible–King James Version, Oxford University Press,1980
How the World thinks: A Global History of Philosophy, Julian Baggini, Granta Publishers, 2018
Do Pause, Robert Poynton, The Do Book Company, 2019
The Origin and Goal of History, Karl Jaspers, Yale Publishing, 1953
The Great Transformation, Karen Armstrong, Atlantic Books, 2006

Chapter 2: Cycles; Astronomy/Astrology
Cycles
Cycles, The Mysterious Forces That Triggers Events Edward R Dewey,

Hawthorn Books Inc, 1971

The Long Waves in the World Economy, Leo & Simone Nefiodow, 2014

Business Cycles, Joseph A Schumpeter, Porcupine Press,1939

The Fate of Empires and Search for Survival, Sir John Glubb, Windmill Press, 2000

Nature by Number, Article in The Times, 2011

Asclepius, Trans: Clement Salaman, Duckworth Publishers, 2007

The Holy Science, Jnanavatar Swami Sri Yukteswar Giri, Self-Realization Fellowship, 1990

The Dialogues of Plato, Jowett Trans. Random House, 1937

The Advancement of Civilisation in the Western World (3 Vols), Brian Hodgkinson, Shepheard Walwyn Pub, 2018

Astronomy / Astrology

Dialogues of Plato, Jowett Trans. Random House, 1937

Julius Caesar, William Shakespeare, Folio Society, 1960

Planetary Influence on Human Affairs, B V Raman, Raman Publications, 1992

Conversations with Shantananda Saraswati, School of Economic Science, 2018

A Little Book of Coincidence in the Solar System, John Martineau, Wooden Books, 2002

Fibonacci Series-As easy as 1,2,3... Jonathan Jones, Guardian Newspaper, 2005

Nature by Numbers, Ian Stewart, Times Newspaper, 2011

Jupiter-Saturn-2020-the-tipping-point, Edith Hathaway, www.edithhathaway.com

The Mood-altering Power of the Moon, Linda Geddes, www.psiencequest.net

Chapter 3: Western European/American Culture; Cycle I

Process and Reality, Alfred North Whitehead, Free Press, 1929

The Greek Philosophers, Rex Warner, Mentor Books, 1958

The Golden Verses of Pythagoras, Theosophical Publishing Society,1912

The Dialogues of Plato, Jowett Trans. Random House, 1937

Plato Tackles Climate Change, Matthew Pye, Pub. By Matthew Pye, 2020

The Spiritual Teachings of Marcus Aurelius, Mark Forstater, Hodder &

Stoughton, 2000

The History of the Decline & Fall of the Roman Empire Vol 1, Ed Betty Radice, Folio Society, 1983

The Consolation of Philosophy, Boethius, Original Classic Book, 2016

The Enneads, Plotinus, Cambridge University Press, 2017

Chapter 4: Western European/American Culture; Cycle II

John Cassian Conferences, Translated by Colm Luibheid, Paulist Press, 1985

The Holy Rule of St Benedict, Anthony Clarke Books, 1975

The Holy Rule of St Benedict, Benedictine Nuns of Holy Trinity Monastery, Herefordshire www.benedictinenuns.org.uk

The Re-Enchantment of Morality, Richard Harries, SPCK, 2008

The Carolingians, Stephen Stewart, Philosophy Now, March/April 2005

Chapter 5: Western European/American Culture; Cycle III

Industrial Revolution, Paul Goodman, www.owlcation.com

The Letters of Marsilio Ficino, School of Philosophy and Economic Science, Shepheard-Walwyn, 2012

The Human Odyssey, Stephen Green, Society for Promoting Christian Knowledge, 2019

A History of the World, Andrew Marr, Macmillan, 2012

American Century, wikipedia.org/wiki/American_Century

Chapter 6: Chinese Culture

Tao Te Ching, Trans: John H McDonald, Arcturus Pub, 2010

Chinese Philosophy, Wen Haiming, Cambridge Univ Press, 2010

The History of Chinese Civilisation, Jacques Gernet, The Folio Society, 2002

The Human Odyssey, Stephen Green, Society for Promoting Christian Knowledge, 2019

China Global Impact, The 48 Group Club, www.chinaglobalimpact.com/2019/06/11/china-and-the-world-2/

A History of the World, Andrew Marr, Macmillan, 2012

Journey to the East and Records of Knowledge About the East, Marco Polo, www.cosmolearning.org/documentaries/marco-polo-journey-to-the-

east/1/
Lao Tzu- www.TheQuotes.net

Chapter 7: Indian Culture
Sanskrit Quote by David Frawley(sent to the author upon reading the text of this book) www.wikipedia.org/wiki/David_Frawley
The Bhagavad Gita, Sri Sankaracharya Commentary, Trans: A.M. Sastry, Samata Books, 1977
Ralph Waldo Emerson, Henry David Thoreau, Albert Einstein, www.spiritualdom.blogspot.com/2011/04/quotes-on-bhagavad-gita-by-famous.html
Aldous Huxley, www.quotabulary.com/noteworthy-quotes-from-bhagavad-gita
Rebuild India, Swami Vivekananda, Advaita Ashrama Pub, 2009
The Holy Science, Jnanavatar Swami Sri Yukteswar Giri, Self-Realization Fellowship, 1990

Chapter 8: Arab Culture
Selected Verses from the Qur'an, Islam International Publications, 1988
A History of the Arab Peoples, Albert Hourani, Faber & Faber, 1991
Peace and Humanitarianism, Moulavi SH Athambawa. Islam International Publications, 2016
Peace and World Crisis, Mirza Masroor Ahmad, Islam International Pub, 2013
The Holy Qur'an, Islam International Pub, 2016
Dr Muhammed Tahir-ul-Quadri interview with Brian Appleyard, Times article, 2019

Chapter 9: Lessons learned & the Way Forward
The Lost Art of Scripture, Karen Armstrong, Penguin Random House, 2019
Plato Tackles Climate Change, Matthew Pye, Pub.by Mathew Pye, 2020
https://www.healthline.com/health/left-brain-vs-right-brain
https://quotes.thefamouspeople.com/origen
https://quotecatalog.com/quote/XpG9Zg1- Rumi

Chapter 10: Nine Steps; Acknowledge the Problem
Robert Lowell, www.brainyquote.com/quotes/robert_lowell

Pankar Mishra, and Matthew Taylor, RSA Journal, 2019

Plato Tackles Climate Change, Matthew Pye, Pub by Mathew Pye, 2020

Conversations with Shantananda Saraswati, School of Economic Science, 2018

John F Kennedy, www.ushistory.org

Divine Harmony, Dr Mary Doak, Paulist Press, 2017

Confucius www.brainyquote.com

www.wikiquote.org/wiki/Memorabilia_(Xenophon)

A Useful Person, Hans Leewens, Van Ede & Partners, 2010

Eternal Wisdom, Leo Tolstoy, Sri Aurobindo Ashram,1993

www.goodreads.com/author/quotes/14033.Winston_S_Churchill

Dangerous Mystic-Meister Eckhart, Joel F Harrington, Penguin Press, 2018

Tao Te Ching, Lao Tzu, Arcturus Publishing, 2010

www.goodreads.com/author/quotes/47030.Benjamin_Disraeli

Eternal Wisdom, Sri Aurobindo Ashram, 1993

Benjamin Franklin www.brainyquote.com/authors/benjamin-franklin-quotes

Christian Quotations-Mother Teresa, Westminster John Knox Press, 1992

www.goodreads.com/author/quotes/838305.Mother_Teresa

The Science Delusion, Rupert Sheldrake, Coronet Pub, 2013

The Clash of Civilisations, Samuel P Huntington, Simon & Schuster, 1997

Journey of the Upanishads to the West, Swami Tathagatananda, Advaita Ashrama, 2002

Chapter 11: Nine Steps; More Quiet Time
Spirituality, Reflection, Contemplation

Everything Belongs, Richard Rohr, Crossroad Publishing, 2003

The Science Delusion, Rupert Sheldrake, Coronet Pub, 2013

Charji www.sahajmarg.org/web/guest/sm/what-is-spirituality

The Holy Bible-King James Version, Oxford University Press,1980

The Holy Qur'an, Islam International Publications Ltd, 2016

Life of the Buddha, Ashva Ghosha, New York University Press, 2008

Mindfulness

Mindfulness - a practical guide to finding peace in a frantic world, Mark Williams & Danny Penman, Jooser, 2016

Mindfulness for Life, Craig Hassed & Stephen McKenzie, Exisle Publishing, 2012

Inner Peace, Berenice Boxler, 2018 www.brusselsmindfulness.be/free-

resources/gaining-inner-peace-with-equanimity
Do Pause, Robert Poynton, The Do Book Co.,2019
Meditation
Business of Spirit, Meditatio Publications, 2012
Good Work, Laurence Freeman, Meditatio Publications, 2019
Silence
In Praise of Silence, Paul Palmarozza, Paul Palmarozza, 2015
Education and the Significance of Life, Krishnamurti, Harper & Row, 1981
Stillness Speaks, Eckhart Tolle, Hodder & Stoughton, 2003
Confucian Analects, Confucius, Dover Publications, 1971
The Seven Spiritual Laws of Success, Deepak Chopra, Amber-Allan
Concentration and Meditation, Swami Paramananda, Sri Ramakrishna Math, 1997
Stepping into Happiness, Dadi Janki, BK Pub, 2015
The Spirit of Silence, John Lane, Green Books, 2006
I am That, Sri Nisargadatta Maharaj, Chetana Pub, 1973
Thus Spoke Gandhi-Quotes of Mahatma Gandhi, *Gandhi Sahitya Bhander*, 2011
Falling Upward, Richard Rohr, John Wiley, 2012
The Precious Present, Samuel Johnson, Penguin Random House, 1984

Chapter 12: Nine Steps; Values and Service
Richard Barrett, Barrett Values Centre, www.valuescentre.com
From Principles to Profit-The Art of Moral Management, Paul Palmarozza & Chris Rees, Arcturus Pub, 2006
The Holy Bible-King James Version, Oxford Univ Press,1980
Confucius, Confucian Analects, Dover Publications, 1971
The Dialogues of Plato, Jowett Trans. Random House, 1937
The Bhagavad Gita, Sri Sankaracharya Comm, Trans: A.M. Sastry, Samata Books, 1977
The Holy Qur'an, Islam International Publications Ltd, 2016
Deepak Chopra, The Seven Spiritual Laws of Success, Deepak Chopra, Amber-Allan Publishing, 1993
Dadi Janki, Stepping into Happiness, Dadi Janki, BK Publications, 2015
Hari Prasad Kanoria, Enlightenment, Business Economics Publications. 2017
Mahatma Gandhi, Thus Spoke Gandhi- Quotes of Mahatma Gandhi, *Gandhi Sahitya Bhander, 2011*

www.goodreads.com/author/quotes/14033.Winston_S_Churchill

Plato, The Dialogues of Plato, Jowett, Random House, 1937

Plutarch, Eternal Wisdom, Sri Aurobindo Ashram,1993

Francis Bacon, Eternal Wisdom, Sri Aurobindo Ashram,1993

If Rudyard Kipling, www.kiplingsociety.co.uk/poems_if.htm

https://www.goodreads.com/author/quotes/7275.Helen_Keller

www.azquotes.com/author/78563-Vimala_McClure

*Dalai Lama's Book of Transformation,*Element,2000

Confucius, Confucian Analects, Dover Publications, 1971

Els Leewens, www.inspiremykids.com/2016/great-empathy-quotes-kids-students-children/

St Francis de Sales, The Saints Little Book of Wisdom, Harper Collins Pub, 2016

The Bhagavad Gita, Sri Sankaracharya Comm, Trans: A.M. Sastry, Samata Books, 1977

Krishnamurti, Education and the Significance of Life, Harper & Row, 1981

Maya Angelu, www.brainyquote.com/authors/maya-angelou-quotes

The Spiritual Teachings of Marcus Aurelius, Mark Forstater, Hodder & Stoughton, 2000

www.goodreads.com/author/quotes/151350.John_Wesley

Buddha Eternal Wisdom, Sri Aurobindo Ashram,1993

Jimi Hendrix, www.PassItOn.com

Rabindranath Tagore, India Calling, Anand Giridharadas, St Martin's Griffin, 2011

Boethius, The Consolation of Philosophy, Boethius, Original Classic Book, 2016

Christian Quotations-Mother Teresa, Westminster John Knox Press, 1992

www.goodreads.com/author/quotes/9810.Albert_Einstein

Leo Tolstoy, Eternal Wisdom, Sri Aurobindo Ashram,1993

Conversations with Shantananda Saraswati, School of Economic Science, 2018

Matthew Taylor, RSA Journal, Issue 3 2019

https://www.gaia.com/article/what-is-the-meaning-of-lokah-samastah-sukhino-bhavantu

Spiritual Compass, Satish Kumar, Green Books, 2007

Meditation & Earth, Deborah Guess, Meditatio, 2020

BIBLIOGRAPHY

Chapter 1 History, Time
History
The History of the World, J M Roberts, Penguin Books, 1976
World History, Philip Parker, Dorling Kindersley Ltd, 2010
The Timetables of History, Bernard Grun, Simon & Schuster, 1975
A History of the World, Jeremy Black, Arcturus Pub, 2018
A Little History of the World, E H Gombrich, Yale University Press, 2008
Complete History of the World, Ed. Geoffrey Barraclough & Richard Overy, Harper Collins, 2004
The Pelican History of the World, U M Roberts, Penguin Books, 1988
A Soaring Spirit 600-400BC, The Editors of Time-Life Books, Time-Life Books, 1988
The History of the World, Alex Woolf, Arcturus Pub, 2017
How the World thinks: A Global History of Philosophy, Julian Baggini, Granta Publishers, 2018
The Death of the Past, J H Plumb, The History Book Club, 1970
World History, Ed. Jeremy Black, Dorling Kindersley, 2005
A Little History of Religion, Richard Holloway, Yale University Press, 2017
The Medieval Economy & Society, M M Postan, Penguin Books, 1975
Millennium, Tom Holland, Little Brown Publishers, 2008
Megachange-The World in 2050, Ed. Daniel Franklim & John Andrews, Profile Books, 2012
Conversations with Shantananda Saraswati, School of Economic Science, 2018

The Fate of Empires and Search for Survival, Sir John Glubb, Windmill Press, 2002

Time
Richard II, William Shakespeare, Folio Society, 1960
The Dialogues of Plato, Jowett Trans. Random House, 1937
St Augustine, Westminster Collection of Christian Quotations, Westminster John Knox Press, 2001
Ecclesiastes, The Holy Bible-King James Version, Oxford University Press,1980
The Cycle of Time, Simone Boger, Self-Published, 2014
How the World thinks: A Global History of Philosophy, Julian Baggini, Granta Publishers, 2018 *Do Pause*, Robert Poynton, The Do Book Company, 2019 *The Origin and Goal of History*, Karl Jaspers, Yale Publishing, 1953
The Great Transformation, Karen Armstrong, Atlantic Books, 2006

Chapter 2 Cycles, Astrology
Cycles
900 Years — The Cycle of a Culture, Sheila Rosenberg, Self-published article, 1984
Cycles, The Mysterious Forces That Triggers Events Edward R Dewey, Hawthorn Books Inc, 1971
The Long Waves in the World Economy, Leo & Simone Nefiodow, 2014
Business Cycles, Joseph A Schumpeter, Porcupine Press,1939
The Fate of Empires and Search for Survival, Sir John Glubb, Windmill Press, 200
Asclepius, Trans:Clement Salaman, Duckworth Publishers, 2007
The Holy Science, Jnanavatar Swami Sri Yukteswar Giri, Self-Realization Fellowship, 1990
The Dialogues of Plato, Jowett Trans. Random House, 1937
The Advancement of Civilisation in the Western World (3 Vols), Brian Hodgkinson, Shepheard Walwyn Pub, 2018

Astrology
Planetary Influence on Human Affairs, B V Raman, Raman Publications, 1992
Opening the Way of Hermes, Clem Salaman, School of Economic Science, 2018

Story of Mathematics, Anne Rooney, Arcturus Pub, 2015
Conversations with Shantananda Saraswati, School of Economic Science, 2018
The Dialogues of Plato, Jowett Trans. Random House, 1937
A Little Book of Coincidence in the Solar System, John Martineau, Wooden Books Gift Book, 2002
Fibonacci Series-As easy as 1,2,3... Jonathan Jones, Guardian Newspaper, 2005
Search of Destiny, Edith Hathaway, Vintage Vedic Press, 2012

Chapters 3, 4, 5 Western European/American Culture
Process and Reality, Alfred North Whitehead, Free Press, 1929
The Greek Philosophers, Rex Warner, Mentor Books, 1958
The Golden Verses of Pythagoras, Theosophical Publishing Society, 1912
The Letters of Marsilio Ficino, Shepheard Walwyn, 1975
The Medieval Economy and Society, M M Postan, Penguin Books, 1975
From the Dark Ages to the Renaissance, Mitchell Beazley, Octopus Publishing, 2006
The Dialogues of Plato, Jowett Trans. Random House, 1937
The Shortest History of Europe, John Hirst, Old Street Publishing, 2009
The End of Europe, James Kirchick, Yale Univ Press, 2017
John Cassian Conferences, Translated by Colm Luibheid, Paulist Press, 1985
The Consolation of Philosophy, Boethius, Original Classic Book, 2016
The Holy Rule of St Benedict, Anthony Clarke Books, 1975
The Holy Rule of St Benedict, Benedictine Nuns of Holy Trinity Monastery, Herefordshire, 2010
The Re-Enchantment of Morality, Richard Harries, SPCK, 2008
Barbarians-Secrets of the Dark Ages, Richard Rudgley, Channel 4 Books, 2002
Byzantine Art and Civilisation, Steven Runciman, The Folio Society, 1975
The Strange Death of Europe, Douglas Murray, Bloomsbury, 2017
The Panorama of the Renaissance, Edited by Margaret Aston, Thames & Hudson, 2000
Medieval Panorama, Edited by Robert Bartlett, Thames & Hudson, 2001
Plotinus, Margaret Miles, Blackwell Publishers, 1999
Marcus Aurelius — The Dialogues, Alan Stedall, Shepheard — Walwyn, 2005
The Spiritual Teachings of Marcus Aurelius, Mark Forstater, Hodder &

Stoughton, 2000

The Crisis of the Modern World, Rene Guenon, Indica Books, 1999

The Advancement of Civilisation in the Western World (3 Vols), Brian Hodgkinson, Shepheard Walwyn Pub, 2018

Asclepius Trans:Clement Salaman, Duckworth Publishers, 2007

From Atheism to Zoroastrianism, Employers Forum on Belief, 2004

Empire, Niall Ferguson, Penguin Books, 2004

Why the West Rules—For Now, Ian Morris, Profile Books, 2010

Messages for the New Millennium, Dr Bruce Lloyd, London South Bank Univ, 2009

A Prophet of Doom, William Rees-Mogg, The Times of London, September 20, 1999

The Science Delusion, Rupert Sheldrake, Coronet Pub, 2013

The Renaissance, Jerry Brotton, Oxford University Press, 2006

Christian Spirituality, Ed. Gordon Mursell, Lion Pub, 2000

The History of the Decline & Fall of the Roman Empire Vol I, Ed Betty Radice, Folio Society, 1983

In God's Holy Light -Wisdom from the Desert Monastics, Joan Chittister, Franciscan Media, 2015

The Human Odyssey; East, West and the Search for Universal Values, Stephen Green, SPCK, 2019

Plato Tackles Climate Change, Matthew Pye, Pub by Mathew Pye, 2020

A History of the World, Andrew Marr, Macmillan, 2012

Chapter 6 Chinese Culture

The History and Civilization of China, Tientsinstudio, 2006

The Silk Roads, Peter Frankopan, Bloomsbury, 2015

The Subterranean Army of Emperor Qin Shi Huang, China Travel & Tourism Press, 2004

Encyclopedia of China, Dorothy Perkins, Checkmark Books, 2000

Eastern Philosophy, Kevin Burns, Arcturus Pub, 2004

Tao Te Ching, Trans: John H McDonald, Arcturus Pub, 2010

When China Rules the World, Martin Jaques, Penquin Books, 2012

On the Grand Trunk Road, Steve Coll, Penguin Books, 2009

1434, Gavin Menzies, Harper Collins, 2008

Kublai Khan, John Man, Bantam Books, 2007

The Three Religions of China, W E Soothill, Oxford University Press, 1923
Chinese Philosophy, Wen Haiming, Cambridge University Press, 2010

Chapter 7 Indian Culture
India Unveiled, Robert Arnett, Atman Press, 2014
India in World Wisdom, Capexil Book Division, 2006
India Through the Ages, Bharat Bhushan, Niyogi Books, 2006
The Wonder That Was India, A L Basham, Sidgwick & Jackson, 1954
The Bhagavad Gita, Sri Sankaracharya Comm, Trans: A.M. Sastry, Samata Books, 1977
Adi Sankara-Finite to Infinite, Prema Nandakumar, Chinmaya International Found, 2013
A Concise History of India, Frances Watson, Thames & Hudson, 1974
Indian Wisdom 365 Days, Danielle & Olivier Follmi, Thames & Hudson, 2005
Gandhi & Jainism, Shugan C Jain, International School of Jain Studies, 2017
Thus spoke Gandhi, Compiled by Dr Ramesh Bhardwaj, Gandhi Sahitya Bhander, 2011
Six images of India, Dr Oscar Pujol, India International Centre Publications, 2009
The History of India 1, Romila Thapar, Penguin Books, 1966
The Great Moguls, Bamber Gascoigne, Constable & Robinson, 2002
A Concise History of Classical Sanskrit Literature, Gaurinath Sastri, Motilal Banarsidass, 1998
Rebuild India, Swami Vivekananda, Advaita Ashrama Pub, 2009
India Calling, Anand Giriharadas, St Martin's Griffins, 2011
Conversations with Shantananda Saraswati, School of Economic Science, 2018
The Holy Science, Jnanavatar Swami Sri Yukteswar Giri, Self-Realization Fellowship, 1990

Chapter 8 Arab Culture
Islam A Short History, Karen Armstrong, Phoenix, 2000
A History of the Arab Peoples, Albert Hourani, Faber & Faber, 1991
Doctrina Arabum, Colin Wakefield, Bodleian Library, 1981

The Philosophy of the Teachings of Islam, Mirza Ghulam Ahmad, Islam International Publications, 2010

Selected Verses from the Qur'an, Islam International Publications, 1988

Women in Islam, Discover Islam, 1999

Peace and Humanitarianism in Islam, Moulavi S H Athambawa, Kalmush-Sharq Publication. 2013

World Crisis — Peace, Mirza Masroor Ahmad, Islam International Publications, 2013

The Philosophy of the Teachings of Islam, Mirza Ghulam Ahmad, Islam International Publications, 2010

Tales from Arabia, Sharifah AlOboudi, Sharifah AlOboudi, 2004

The Prophet, Kahlil Gibran, Alfred A Knoff Pub, 1926

The Holy Qur'an, Islam International Publications Ltd, 2016

Chapters 9, 10, 11, 12: Lessons Learned; Nine Steps; The Problem; Quiet Time; Values and Service

The Lost Art of Scripture, Karen Armstrong, Penguin Random House, 2019

Plato Tackles Climate Change, Matthew Pye, Pub by Mathew Pye, 2020

A New Earth, Eckhart Tolle, A Plume Book, 2006

The Seven Spiritual Laws of Success, Deepak Chopra, Amber-Allan Publishing, 1993

First Sight, Laurence Freeman, Continuum International Publishing Group, 2011

21 Lessons for the 21st Century, Yuval Noah Harari, Jonathan Cape, 2018

Pankar Mishra, and Matthew Taylor Interview, RSA Journal, 2019

Divine Harmony, Dr Mary Doak, Paulist Press, 2017

Times Newspaper-Obituary, Jean Vanier, 2019

Wisdom is One, Compiled by B W Huntsman, Stuart & Watkins, 1969

Learn to Meditate, Sahaj Marg, Shri Ram Chandra Mission, 2014

Business of Spirit, Meditatio Publications, 2012

Good Work, Laurence Freeman, Meditatio Publication, 2019

Contemplative Leadership, Peter Ng Kok Song, Meditatio Publication, 2014

In Praise of Silence, Paul Palmarozza, Paul Palmarozza, 2015

East meets West, John Adago, Shepheard-Walwyn Pub, 2014

The Ideal in the West, David A Beardsley, Ideograph Media, 2012

Arriving at your Own Door, 108 Lessons in Mindfulness, Jon Kabat-Zinn,

Piatkus Books, 2005

A Useful Person, Hans Leewens, Van Ede & Partners, 2010

Eternal Wisdom, Sri Aurobindo Ashram,1993

Life of the Buddha, Ashva Ghosha, New York University Press, 2008

Divine Harmony, Dr Mary Doak, Paulist Press, 2017

Dangerous Mystic-Meister Eckhart, Joel F Harrington, Penguin Press, 2018

Lao Tzu *Tao Te Ching,* Lao Tzu, Arcturus Publishing, 2010

Transcendence, Abdul Kalam, Harper Element Books, 2015

The Science Delusion, Rupert Sheldrake, Coronet Pub, 2013

The Clash of Civilisations, Samuel P Huntington, Simon & Schuster, 1997

Everything Belongs, Richard Rohr, Crossroad Publishing, 2003

Dancing Standing Still, Richard Rohr, Paulist Press, 2014

From Principles to Profit, Chris Rees & Paul Palmarozza, Arcturus Pub, 2006

Ancient Wisdom, John Adago, Program Publishing, 2018

If I can. . . Timeless Values for Today, Paul Palmarozza, SREI Foundation, 2012

Word into Silence, John Main, Darton-Longman & Todd, 1980

The Re-Enchantment of Morality, Richard Harries, SPCK, 2008

In Praise of Silence, Paul Palmarozza, Paul Palmarozza, 2015

Mindfulness for Life, Craig Hassed & Stephen McKenzie, Exisle Publishing, 2012

My Journey Through Time, Dens Merrian, Sitaram Press, 2017

Silence and Stillness in Every Season, John Main, Medio Media, 2010

The Precious Present, Samuel Johnson, Penguin Random House, 1984

Do Pause, Robert Poynton, The Do Book Co.,2019

Paths between Head and Heart, Oliver Robinson, O Books, 2017

Silence, Diarmaid MacCulloch, Penguin Books, 2014

The Great Transformation, Karen Armstrong, Atlantic Books, 2006

Concentration and Meditation, Swami Paramananda, Sri Ramakrishna Math, 1997

The Spirit of Silence, John Lane, Green Books, 2006

I am That, Sri Nisargadatta Maharaj, Chetana Pub, 1973

Confucius - Confucian Analects, Dover Publications, 1971

Enlightenment, Business Economics Publications, 2017

The Dalai Lama's Book of Transformation, Dalai Lama, Element, 2000

Education and the Significance of Life, Harper & Row, 1981

Stillness Speaks, Eckhart Tolle, Hodder & Stoughton, 2003

Plotinus, Margaret R Miles, Blackwell Publishers, 1999
Ethical Entrepreneur, Paul Palmarozza, If I can …CIC, 2019
Enlightenment, Hari Prasad Kanoria, Business Economics Publications, 2017
Education and the Significance of Life, Krishnamurti, Harper & Row, 1981
Stepping into Happiness, Dadi Janki, BK Pub, 2015
The Consolation of Philosophy, Boethius, Original Classic Book, 2016
…isms Understanding Religions, Theodore Gabriel & Ronald Geaves, Herbert Press, 2007
Beyond Religion, Dalai Lama, Houghton Mifflin Harcourt Pub, 2011
Mindfulness, Mark Williams & Danny Penman, Piatkus Pub, 2011
Rule Makers-Rule Breakers, Michella Gelfaud, Robinson Pub, 2018
Teachings of His Holiness, Shantananda Saraswati, Study Society, 2010
Into the Silent Land, Martin Laird, Darton, Longman & Todd, 2006
Inner Beauty- A Book of Virtues, Brahma Kumariis Pub. 2009
https://www.gaia.com/article/what-is-the-meaning-of-lokah-samastah-sukhino-bhavantu
Spiritual Compass, Satish Kumar, Green Books, 2007
Meditation & Earth, Deborah Guess, Meditatio, 2020

Images
Online Sources
www.kondratieff.net/kondratieffcycles
www.astropro.com/features/tables/geo/ju-sa/ju000sa.html
www.scarboromissions.ca/Golden_rule/
bing.com/images; Revolving speed cycles
bing.com/images; Air, Fire, Water, Earth
bing.com/images; Pythagorian triangle
bing.com/images; Timeline of crusades
All others-www.shutterstock.com/explore/royalty-free-images
Photographers:
Photographer: Paul Palmarozza-Fibonacci Flowers,
Special Design
Cycles and Astrological diagrams; Jasper Cooper, Paul Palmarozza
Rejoice in the Present Calligraphy; Frederick Marnes
Astrological Clockfaces; Martin Lubikowski, MLDesign
Sanskrit Lettering - Shanti, Alan Young